INTO THE SAME IMAGE

Expository Studies of the Christian Ideal

by

REGINALD E. O. WHITE M.A., B.D.

London
MARSHALL, MORGAN & SCOTT
Edinburgh

LONDON
MARSHALL, MORGAN AND SCOTT, LTD.
33 LUDGATE HILL, E.C.4

AUSTRALIA
317 COLLINS STREET
MELBOURNE

NEW ZEALAND
23 MONTGOMERY ROAD
ROTHESAY BAY
AUCKLAND

SOUTH AFRICA
P.O. BOX 1720, STURK'S BUILDINGS
CAPE TOWN

U.S.A. AND CANADA
BROADMAN PRESS
127 NINTH AVENUE NORTH
NASHVILLE 3
TENNESSEE

First published 1957

MADE AND PRINTED IN GREAT BRITAIN BY PURNELL AND SONS, LTD.
PAULTON (SOMERSET) AND LONDON

To
G. M. W.

FOREWORD

THIS IS a book of expository studies, designed for devotional use. The reader is asked to bear in mind both parts of that description. The chapters are *studies*, intended (as the numerous scriptural references show) to help the reader understand his New Testament. No attempt has been made to provide a bedside book of restful reading packed with apt illustration and happy anecdote, for the writer is convinced that the true diet for evangelical Christians is neither spiritual excitement nor religious entertainment, but solid and searching exposition of the Word of God. On the other hand the purpose is *devotional*. This is no textbook; the theme is a somewhat neglected but supremely important aspect of Scripture's practical guidance for everyday life.

In his first hesitating steps on the Christian way, the writer possessed two great advantages for which he has never ceased to be grateful. One was a personal friend, whose sympathetic and thorough teaching opened up page after page of Scripture. The other consisted of one or two small booklets on several Bible themes, now long out of print, expounding the New Testament doctrine of life in Christ in a way that nourished his young faith, fed his mind and deepened his experience as few larger books have done. If these Bible studies do just that for any standing in similar need, the writer —and the reader—will be well rewarded.

SYNOPSIS

THE PURPOSE

   God's purpose in salvation: the new creation and the old: the
   controlling pattern of the new creation, the image of God in
   Christ: recovered knowledge, restored glory.

   The divine family: Jesus on resemblance and relationship: John
   on likeness as evidence of life: Paul and Hebrews on similarity
   and sonship: the family likeness in Christ.

   Conversion as re-choosing the way: defining the Way as following Christ's example: treading the way—Jesus on the meaning
   of his example and the motive implied.

   "Dead"—either in sin or to sin: faith and "quickening": our
   recapitulation of Christ's death-resurrection-ascension: clothing
   the risen soul with "Christ".

THE PROCESS

   The fivefold price of immaturity: puffed up or built up? the
   things that edify: the goal of spiritual development, the fullness
   of the stature of Christ.

   The Christian's environment: "as his Master": Hebrews on the
   discipline inseparable from sonship: Paul on the key to the
   providence of God—conformed to his image.

THE PORTRAIT

CONCLUSION

THE PURPOSE

CHAPTER 1

CREATION'S PATTERN

THE FUNDAMENTAL truths of Scripture are easily distinguished by two simple characteristics, repetition and variety. Less essential themes may be referred to only once or twice, perhaps by a single writer: the central truths recur again and again, in different contexts of thought, in varied modes of expression, first one writer and then another contributing to their exposition. They are too profound and many-sided to be caught in a single definition: varied repetition is the sign of their richness and importance.

This is certainly true of the theme before us. The idea of Christlikeness is so fundamental, so near to the heart of the Gospel, that we come upon it in unexpected places, expressed oftentimes in surprising ways, reflected in every great doctrine of the faith, implied in every great spiritual experience. Just because it is so central we catch glimpses of it from every point on the circumference of Christian truth; because it is implied in almost everything we find it almost everywhere. Of course it is a common temptation to imagine we see some favourite truth in every chapter of the Bible, and we must beware lest we make texts yield a meaning their authors never intended. But there is no need: we shall find more than enough unmistakable references to our theme to convince us that the imitation of Christ had a primary place in apostolic doctrine and ethics.

Our first task must be to gather together the New Testament passages in which the idea of conformity to Christ is set forth as *God's purpose in salvation*. We begin at the beginning, with the New Testament descriptions of the first steps in Christian life. What has been said of the varied repetition of important truths is well illustrated in the Bible doctrine of conversion, for "coming to Christ" is described not only as "conversion" but as new creation, as new birth, or regeneration, and as resurrection from the dead.

15

Each of these expressions stresses the utter newness of the life in Christ; each suggests that it begins in something done to man rather than in something done by him; each hints at something miraculous in the experience, something only to be explained by divine power and grace. Yet each expression puts these things in a different way, and each adds something of its own; while each, as we shall see, definitely looks forward towards the goal of likeness to Christ.

I. THE NEW CREATION

Every Christian's story begins with a new first chapter of Genesis. "If any man be in Christ, there is a new creation: old things are passed away; behold, all things are become new. And all things are of God . . ."[1] That is to say, when any man begins to live "in Christ" what happens in him is nothing less than a repetition, on the smaller scale of individual experience, of that original creative act of God by which at the beginning of time all things came to be. The soul itself, with its thoughts, motives, aims, tastes and desires, is wholly transformed—"he is a new creature". But so also is his world: former things no longer exist for him, and what remains is changed. Life has now a new centre of gravity; all things tend no longer towards self, but towards God—"he does not any longer live unto himself, but unto him which died for him". And all things are seen to be of God—all things that are, that are received, that come to pass, derive from the God who has reconciled us to himself by Jesus Christ. Christ—the Alpha, the Beginning, the Dayspring from on high, the Morning Star—has indeed made all things new.

Paul described his own conversion in this way. Into the darkness, barrenness and chaos of his life without Christ there had sounded again that majestic Voice whose mere word achieves what it commands, saying "Let there be light !"—and once more the darkness had fled, chaos gave place to order, barrenness to beauty: "For God, who commanded the light to shine out of darkness, hath shined in our hearts, to give the light of the knowledge of the glory of God in the face of Jesus Christ."[2] The same parallel sprang to Peter's mind when, also thinking of the mercy of God, he spoke

[1] 2 Cor. 5: 17, 18 R.V. margin.
[2] 2 Cor. 4: 6.

of "him who hath *called* you out of *darkness* into his marvellous *light*".[1]

Nothing less than this total re-creation of the soul and of its world will pass for Christian conversion. To have confidence in aught else, however sanctioned by ancient custom or prized by conventional religion, is to delude oneself: "For in Christ Jesus neither circumcision availeth anything, nor uncircumcision, but a new creation."[2] Nothing less could satisfy God. He who in the beginning of time "saw everything that he had made, and behold it was very good" could not be content until once again his handiwork merits the same approval, and "we are his workmanship, created in Christ Jesus unto good works, which God hath before ordained that we should walk in them".[3]

But the most profound use of this great parallel drawn between the original creation story and the inward experience of every believer, is that which sees in Christ another Adam, the Origin, and Representative and Head of a new humanity. Jesus stands to the new creation in every relation in which Adam stood to the old.[4] Adam thus becomes a symbol, a prophetic "type" of Christ, "the figure of him that was to come". Just as sin, ruin, death passed, through Adam's disobedience, to all who are united with him in the solidarity of the human race—so grace, righteousness, and life pass, through Christ's sublime obedience, to all who are one with him in that new humanity of which he is Founder and Head. "As in Adam all die, even so in Christ shall all be made alive; the first man, Adam, was made a living soul, the last Adam was made a quickening Spirit; the first man is of the earth, earthy: the second man is the Lord from heaven." In verses like these the doctrine of the new creation in Christ is much more than a vivid metaphor to describe what it feels like to be converted; it implies also that on the broader plane of his purposes in history, the divine Creator has, with infinite patience, *begun his work again*. By a new creative act of the divine will there has come into being a new humanity, possessing a new nature, and deriving its new life from a Second Adam: and in them, this time, the original pattern of Creation will be fulfilled.

[1] 1 Pet. 2: 9.
[2] Gal. 6: 15.
[3] Eph. 2: 10.
[4] Rom 5: 12–19; 1 Cor. 15: 21, 22, 45–9.

B

O loving wisdom of our God !
When all was sin and shame,
A second Adam to the fight,
And to the rescue came.
O wisest love ! that flesh and blood,
Which did in Adam fail,
Should strive afresh against the foe—
Should strive, and should prevail.

II. THE PATTERN OF THE NEW CREATION

God, who sees the end from the beginning, and works all things after the counsel of his own will, follows faithfully his own divine design, in creation as in providence and redemption. With significant insistence the writer of Genesis declares that the first creation reached its goal only when God made man in his own image, and after his likeness. "And God said, Let us make man in our image, after our likeness . . . So God created man in his own image, in the image of God created he him . . ."[1] Five times we read that God saw what he had made, and it was good: but when the work of the sixth day was accomplished, and man stood amidst the Garden, bearing his Maker's likeness, "God saw everything that he had made, and, behold, it was *very* good. Thus the heavens and the earth were finished . . . and he rested." Familiarity dulls the splendour of this great truth. All true craftsmanship, the ancient writer knew, enshrines something of the mind and heart and character of the craftsman: even so, he dared to say, with God. The work was not finished until there was reflected back from the creation some part at least of the likeness of the Creator. Beyond that even divine craftsmanship could not go. The pattern was complete.

Equally insistent is the New Testament, concerning the controlling pattern of the new creation. "As we have borne the image of the earthy, we shall also bear the image of the heavenly," the image of the Second Adam, "the Lord from heaven".[2] The new creation is directed towards the same original purpose at which the first creation aimed: in Christ God seeks again to make men in his own image. As Christ himself is "the brightness of his Father's glory and the express image of his person", "the image of the invisible God",[3] so the new humanity which derives from him shall bear his image. The pattern of the *new* creation is the likeness of God.

[1] Gen. 1: 26, 27.   [2] 1 Cor. 15: 47, 49.   [3] Heb. 1: 3; Col. 1: 15.

Repeatedly these two thoughts are linked together, our new creation in Christ, and our bearing the divine likeness. The "new man" is "created in righteousness and true holiness" (there is the first thought) but it is also "after God", that is, after the divine image as a pattern.[1] Again, the light which the Creator's voice has commanded to shine into the darkened soul is "the light of the glorious Gospel of Christ", who is (Paul at once reminds us) "the image of God".[2] Putting the point beyond all doubt the Apostle explicitly declared "the new man is renewed . . . after the image of him that created him".[3] Peter also had the same twin thoughts in mind, when he wrote of our *showing forth the virtues of him* that hath called us out of darkness into his marvellous light".[4]

It is to be regretted that the great Scripture doctrine of the new creation has not always been presented together with its ethical safeguard in the truth of the divine pattern. Conversion is often a highly emotional experience, but becoming a new creature in Christ means much more than being endowed with a new set of feelings. The new life is not simply one of violent reaction from the old, a merely negative attitude; it is not left prey to various untested religious impulses; nor certainly is it enough to remain for long dependent just on the example and instructions of the one who led the way to Christ. In the very experience of being new-made a stupendous programme is set before us, a wonderful possibility opened to our view: the pattern of our new nature and life is set already, in the constant imitation of him who has made us new.

III. THE PRIVILEGES OF THE NEW CREATION

We cannot here follow all the paths along which this great New Testament thought might lead us, but two related ideas should be mentioned, to show how thoroughly the doctrine is developed in apostolic teaching. These are "knowledge" and "glory". Three times in the passages already quoted the thought of new creation in the divine image is joined to that of renewed knowledge. The new light that breaks into the converted soul is the "light of the *knowledge* of the glory of God"; putting on the new man, created "after God" is closely linked to "being renewed in the spirit of your

[1] Eph. 4: 23, 24.   [2] 2 Cor. 4: 4.   [3] Col. 3: 10.   [4] 1 Pet. 2: 9.

mind";[1] and again, the new man "is renewed unto knowledge after the image of him that created him",[2] where "unto knowledge" (not "in knowledge") defines the purpose, rather than the sphere, of the new creation.

The connection with knowledge may seem strange, until we notice that Paul (and the rabbis) held that since Adam in losing Eden had lost also the vision of God, man had fallen into ever darker ignorance of him. All that man might have known, from the creation itself, of the eternal power and Godhead, was rejected; God was conceived "after the likeness of beasts and four-footed things", until men become wholly estranged, "alienated from the life of God through the ignorance that is in them".[3] With the new beginning comes the opportunity of knowing God again, as he is in truth. The recovery of the marred image goes hand in hand with the recovery of the lost vision and understanding. And this is no accidental linking of ideas: always in Scripture the way to know God is to be like him—"The pure in heart see God", "when we shall see him we shall be like him".[4]

The other idea related to bearing God's image, in New Testament teaching, is "glory". Ideally, man is "the image and the glory of God",[5] and to Paul the two belong together. According to Rabbinic teaching, the glory was forfeited when Adam sinned. It was explained as the reflection, lingering upon his own person, of the glory of God in whose presence he walked "in the cool of the day". It is possible that such an idea underlies the story of the transfiguration of Moses, when "the skin of his face shone while he talked with God".[6] Perhaps also the story of the Transfiguration of Jesus enshrines the same idea.

Certainly, for Paul, the recovery of the lost glory was an essential part of salvation. It is Paul's telling definition of human sinfulness that "all have come short of the glory of God".[7] But, for the new creation, Christ is himself "the hope of glory"[8] and the re-created soul not only has peace with God but rejoices "in hope of the glory of God".[9] Human nature as we have known it, in separation from God, is but the pale and impoverished shadow of what God intended: not till the body is "raised in glory", "fashioned like unto

[1] Eph. 4: 23, 24.   [6] Exod. 34: 29–35.
[2] Col. 3: 10.   [7] Rom. 3: 23.
[3] Rom. 1: 23; Eph. 4: 18. [8] Col. 1: 27.
[4] Matt. 5: 8; 1 John 3: 2. [9] Rom. 5: 2.
[5] 1 Cor. 11: 7.

His glorious body", wearing the "crown of glory" will redemption
be complete, all the work of Adam be undone, and human nature
reflect again undimmed the glory of its Creator. Nor is this promise
for man alone. Paul's thought reached out in majestic poetry to
embrace the earth, as he recalled that the material creation shared
through the curse in the ruin of Adam, and fell under the thraldom
of decay and death. But now that Christ has come, the second
Adam, to "bear the curse for us", creation itself shares "the earnest
expectation" that the curse shall be removed and the "sufferings
of this present time" give place to "the glory that shall be revealed
in us" when "the creation itself shall be delivered from the bondage
of corruption into the liberty of the glory of the children of God".[1]

Knowledge and glory: these are the two marks of that image of
God which is to be reproduced in the new creation. It is after all
just what we should expect. The image of God, in which man was
made, must never be thought of as something physical, to do with
man's shape or uprightness. The whole of the Old Testament's
protest against graven images, against every attempt to portray God
after human or animal forms, opposes the idea that man's physical
frame in any way reflects the likeness of God. God's likeness and
image are in man's reasoning soul and his conscience of right.
God made another creature on the sixth day: but this he endowed
with mind and heart and conscience and will, involving freedom
and responsibility—a living spirit, as God is Spirit. There lies the
image that distinguishes man from the brutes: the intellectual grasp
of truth and the moral glory of goodness and love of right. But the
image was marred: the mind of man was darkened, the glory of
innocence exchanged for the stain of sin. The pattern was unfulfilled,
the purpose defeated, for the time. *But God began again* in Christ,
and his new creatures are to reflect the image anew—in restored
knowledge of God and of truth, in restored *glory* of purity and holiness. Once again the Creator's work shall merit his approval
and he shall be able to say "Behold, it is very good".

Thus at the threshold of Christian life a far-reaching goal is set
before the young Christian. Obviously the ideal of Christlikeness
is much more than a sentimental or external appeal to Christ's
example; it is not an optional or partial "aspect" of the Gospel:
it is the original divine purpose in creating us, resumed in the new
creation in Christ. It is not accomplished in the hour of conversion

[1] Rom. 8: 21.

nor suddenly achieved at some later crisis of consecration: but the pattern is set at the outset, and the intention clear from the start. From then onwards "the new man is *being renewed*"[1] continuously, day by day, after the image of the Creator. As in the first creation, so in the second, the initiative, purpose and power are God's: were it not for these assurances we might be discouraged from the commencement. But the Second Adam "shall prevail".

[1] Col. 3: 10 R.V.; 2 Cor. 4: 16.

CHAPTER 2

THE NEW BIRTH

RICH AND suggestive though it is, the truth of new creation does not convey all that happens to the soul that comes to be "in Christ". The whole circle of new relationships into which the converted man enters, and the new nature bestowed upon him by the creative spirit, are better described in the second great New Testament term for Christian conversion, regeneration or the new birth. This expression, often impatiently dismissed as incomprehensible, mystical, emotional, preserves much of the truth already noticed in the doctrine of the re-creation of the believer in Christ, but it adds also some fuller meanings of its own, and relates them to some of the most important Christian ideas.

This is best seen when the conception of new birth, or birth from above, is understood as one item in a whole series of ideas which together make up what might be called the one, distinctive and all inclusive conception in Christianity, the truth of the Divine Family. All the great Christian truths can be, and in the New Testament are, expressed in this way: God is the Kingly Father, Christ the beloved and only begotten Son, the Holy Spirit is the Spirit of sonship, the Spirit of adoption. Prayer is family conversation, addressed to "Our Father", and offered in the confidence of sons who know that if they ask bread they will not be given a stone; the family is entered by birth, and its members are both "children of God" as to nature and relationship, and "sons of God" as to status, assurance, freedom and inheritance. Fellow-Christians are brethren, and must be so treated, while the non-christian is a wayward son whose enjoyment of sonship has been forfeited by rebellious departure to a far country where he is "lost" and "dead" to the Father's love. The rule of the Christian's life is the Father's will, the process of training is the Father's chastening of his sons, the confidence relied upon is the Father's knowledge of our need, the hope and final reward of the Christian life is a welcome in the Father's house. Less familiar than these thoughts, but not one whit less important, is the application of this family idea to Christian character and behaviour: the members of the divine family share a family likeness, and resemblance is the proof of relationship.

I. RESEMBLANCE AND RELATIONSHIP

It was the Master himself who first insisted that the children of God must resemble their Father in heaven. The thought holds a most important place in his teaching. "Love your enemies, bless them that curse you, do good to them that hate you, and pray for them which despitefully use you and persecute you *that ye may be the children of your Father* which is in heaven: for he maketh his sun to rise on the evil and on the good, and sendeth rain on the just and on the unjust . . . Be ye therefore perfect, *even as your Father* which is in heaven is perfect."[1] "Love your enemies, and do good and lend, hoping for nothing again; and your reward shall be great, and *ye shall be the children of the Highest*: for he is kind to the unthankful and to the evil. Be ye therefore merciful *as your Father* also is merciful."[2] So, in the family prayer, the Father's forgiveness of his children is made the motive and pattern of the children's forgiveness of each other, while in the Beatitudes the peacemakers are specially described as "blessed" in resembling the Father: "they shall be called the children of God".[3]

It is probable that beneath Christ's words lies a mode of speech common in his mother-tongue, by which one could speak of someone as a "child of" wrath, rebellion, hell,[4] using the phrase for general description. Thus John could speak of men as "children of the devil, himself the father of lies".[5] But the meaning of our Lord's words must not be reduced to a mere idiom, or cliché; a firm idea underlies the language. A sharp debate with the Jews about descent from Abraham illustrates the same use of words. "Jesus saith unto them, If ye were Abraham's children, ye would do the works of Abraham. But now ye seek to kill me . . . this did not Abraham. Ye do the deeds of your father . . . If God were your Father ye would love me . . . Ye are of your father the devil, and the lusts of your father ye will do."[6] Here the connection between relationship and

---

[1] Matt. 5: 44–8.
[2] Luke 6: 35–6.
[3] Matt. 5: 9.

[4] Eph. 2: 3; Matt. 23: 15.
[5] John 8: 44; Matt. 13: 38.
[6] John 8: 39–44.

resemblance is plainly assumed, and the appeal (as in so many utterances of our Lord) is from the *fact* of the Father-child relationship to the *duty* of the Father-child resemblance. It is very probable that Paul had in mind an echo of such sayings when he also appealed to the principle of family likeness, and to the characteristic aptitude of children for learning by imitation of their parents, in exhorting the Ephesians to be "imitators of God, as beloved children".[1]

II. LIKENESS AND LIFE

It is within this setting that the new birth is to be understood. Resemblance may indicate relationship, but it takes more than resemblance to *constitute* relationship. Behind the outward similarity, the members of one family share a common nature; however scattered the family may become, one origin and inheritance links them together, and it is the possession of the common life that makes the group one family. The New Testament does not avoid this daring implication of the family metaphor. We "become partakers of the divine nature",[2] "begotten, not of corruptible seed but of incorruptible",[3] while "whosoever is begotten of God doeth no sin, because his seed abideth in him".[4] The ultimate truth which seeks expression in such words is probably set forth most clearly in the great saying of Jesus, "As the living Father hath sent me, and I live by the Father: so he that eateth me, even he shall live by me".[5] Here the implication of being one in God's family is carried to its furthest limit. Through Christ, by means of new birth, the believer comes to share in the life of God himself. The outward resemblance in conduct and character is the result of an inward resemblance of nature and life. Once again likeness to Christ is shown to be something much deeper than at first might appear.

It is however to the mystic John that we must turn to find this aspect of our theme fully expounded, in the doctrine and ethics of the new birth. In his Gospel we learn that the Kingdom is not to be entered, or even glimpsed, "except a man be born again"— except he start life afresh, upon new assumptions, for new aims, on new principles, in a new world, upon new resources, and in possession of a new, divinely imparted, life. The new cannot be

[1] Eph. 5: 1.   [3] 1 Pet. 1: 23.
[2] 2 Pet. 1: 4.   [4] 1 John 3: 9 R.V.
[5] John 6: 57.

started upon the old level, but "from above", something super-human breaking into experience from on high, lifting the soul above anything previously known. It is a birth "of water" in so far as it involves a change of attitude towards the old way of life that might be fittingly confessed in John's baptism of repentance. It is a birth "of the Spirit" because it is the Spirit of God who imparts the very life of God to be the centre, strength and energy of the new life of the believer. The former life, centred in the flesh, lived for its aims and upon its resources, befitted those born only "of the flesh", and possessing only common human nature. "That which is born of the flesh is flesh" and cannot rise above its own level. But the new life of the reborn soul is totally different: it is the life of the divine Spirit within the Christian, a new and Spirit-born selfhood, raised to the level of the life of the Kingdom—"that which is born of the Spirit is spirit".[1]

And all this is true, not only of the mystic, the "saint", the religious "specialist", but of all who believe: "as many as received him, to them gave he power to become the children of God, even to them that believe on his name, which were born, not of blood, nor of the will of the flesh, nor of the will of man, but of God".[2] "Ye are all the children of God by faith in Christ Jesus".[3]

The very practical conclusions which John draws from this high doctrine show how relevant it is to our main subject. When, in his First Epistle, John distinguishes the counterfeit Christian from the true, the heretic from the genuine believer, he offers three clear tests by which to know those who are really born again, three clear and simple definitions of the new birth. "Whosoever *believeth* that Jesus is the Christ is begotten of God"; "everyone that *doeth righteousness* is begotten of him"; "everyone that *loveth* is begotten of God".[4] It is significant that John's tests have nothing to do with depth of emotional experience, nor with readiness of spoken testimony, nor even with willingness to be persecuted, all of which can be counterfeited. Rather they have to do with the Master's own test of resemblance. For *faith* in us answers to the faithfulness of God in the witness he has borne concerning his Son: "He that believeth not, hath made God a liar."[5] *Righteousness* in us is the reflection of the divine righteousness: "If ye know that he is righteous,

[1] John 3: 1–8.   [3] Gal. 3: 26.
[2] John 1: 12, 13.   [4] 1 John 5: 1; 2: 29; 4: 7.
                    [5] 1 John 5: 10 R.V.

ye know that everyone that doeth righteousness is begotten of him."[1] And so with *love*: "Love is of God, and everyone that loveth is begotten of God, and knoweth God. He that loveth not knoweth not God, for God is love."[2] The rule is simple: "like father, like son."

Here is true Gospel teaching concerning the new birth, deeper, more ethical, more realistic it must be confessed, than some which passes for evangelical doctrine. The believing soul, born into the divine family by faith and sharing in the divine life, is stamped with the likeness of the Father himself, especially in his faithfulness (or truth), his righteousness, and his love. Through all the members of his family, scattered, various and numerous though they are, one family resemblance repeats itself, in varying degrees, increasing with the growth of spiritual life in each, and always witnessing unmistakably to that community of inner life which binds the children to one another and to God.

III. SIMILARITY AND SONSHIP

The features of the divine image to which Jesus and John draw attention—forgiveness, peacemaking, impartial kindness, mercy, faithfulness, righteousness and love—are gathered up and underlined, according to a third line of New Testament teaching about the divine family, in the portrait of Jesus himself. He is the "firstborn" Son, the Eldest in a vast family of brothers.[3] It is in Christ that the Father's likeness is portrayed in human colours: he perfectly "features" the Father. "He that hath seen me hath seen the Father."[4] The whole truth of the children's resemblance to the heavenly Father becomes more arresting and easier to grasp when related in this way to the person of our Lord in all the tender humanness of his perfect life. It is linked at the same time to the deepest and most fundamental article of our faith, that God was in Christ, the Word made flesh, the only-begotten Son, which is in the bosom of the Father, appearing in the likeness of men in order to "expound" God.[5]

The epistle to the Hebrews sets this forth most movingly. Christ the Son, the "outshining of his Father's glory and the express

---

[1] 1 John 2: 29.   [3] Rom. 8: 29 (Weymouth).
[2] 1 John 4: 7, 8.   [4] John 14: 9.
                [5] John 1: 18.

image of his person" is yet "not ashamed to call us brethren".[1] This is the first step of redeeming grace. We recall another elder brother, who with contemptuous sneer disowned all responsibility for a wayward boy—"This thy son . . ." receiving and deserving the father's reminder and rebuke—"This *thy brother* . . ."[2] In this admission by the eternal Son of responsibility towards a prodigal race, in this willingness to acknowledge us his brethren, the writer of Hebrews sees the first decisive step that led towards Bethlehem, Calvary and the priestly intercession at the mercy seat on high. But he did more than own us brethren: he consented "to be made like unto his brethren".[3] The epistle develops this point fully: Christ is made like unto his brethren

(*a*) In the limitations of human nature: "Forasmuch then as the children are partakers of flesh and blood, he also himself likewise took part of the same";[4] where "flesh and blood" means all the natural and innocent frailty and transitoriness of human powers;

(*b*) In the tribulations of human experience: "Though he were a Son, yet learned he obedience by the things which he suffered"; "It became him . . . in bringing many sons unto glory, to make the captain of their salvation perfect through suffering . . . Who in the days of his flesh, when he had offered up prayers and supplications with strong crying and tears unto him that was able to save him from death, and was heard in that he feared."[5]

(*c*) In all the temptations of human discipline: "We have not a high priest which cannot be touched with the feeling of our infirmities; but was in all points tempted like as we are, yet without sin"; "In that he himself hath suffered being tempted, he is able to succour them that are tempted."[6]

(*d*) In all the simple piety of human faith: He too lived by the energy of prayer and the inner resource of trust, so as to deserve to be placed last and highest in the roll of examples of the life of faith—"the pioneer and finisher of faith, who for the joy that was set before him, endured . . .". He too could say in life and in death "I will put my trust in him".[7]

This insistence upon the complete identification of Jesus with his brethren cannot be accidental. The eternal Son comes among his brethren to set forth, amid all the weakness, mortality, temptation,

[1] Heb. 1: 3; 2: 11.   [3] Heb. 2: 17.   [5] Heb. 5: 8; 2: 10; 5: 7.
[2] Luke 15: 30, 32.   [4] Heb. 2: 14.   [6] Heb. 4: 15; 2: 18.
[7] Heb. 11; 12: 1–3; 2: 13.

suffering and simple piety of human experience, the likeness of the divine nature. Why? To what end? Simply, convincingly, the answer is given: "That he might bring many *sons* to glory"[1]—sons, that is, of the same family, though not of the same status, as himself; brothers, and bearers of the family likeness. He consents to bear our image that we might bear his: "He became what we are, that he might make us what he is."[2] Christ, in Hebrews, is the Elder Brother who did *not* stay home, but left the Father's house and came into the far country, to bring his prodigal brethren back "to glory".

Lest this appear a strained interpretation, peculiar to one epistle, we must set beside it another passage, to which we shall return in a later chapter. Precisely the same connection of thought—that Christ is the Elder Brother of the divine family, concerned to bring to God a vast company of brethren all bearing his likeness—is found in Paul's famous review of the saving purposes of God: "Whom he did foreknow, he also did predestinate to be conformed to the image of his Son, that he might be the firstborn among many brethren."[3] In the essential glory of his eternal Sonship, Christ is and must remain unique, incomparable, "the only-begotten Son"; but in the moral beauty and spiritual grace of his incarnate life he is the "First-begotten", pre-eminent but not alone, "declaring God's name unto his brethren in the midst of the church"[4] "the children which God hath given"[5] to him.

By three different roads, then, the New Testament leads us to the same truth: the likeness of Christ, the Elder Brother, is to be reflected in all who by faith have been reborn into the family of God. Resemblance proves relationship, says Jesus. The life of God within implies the likeness of God without, says John. Christ became like us that we might become like him, our Kinsman-Redeemer, says Hebrews. And the family likeness, the image of the divine Father, is made visible, intelligible, unforgettable, in the human life of the divine Son. As with the doctrine of the new creation, so with the truth of new birth into the divine family, the very form of its expression offers encouragement to the faint-hearted. The ideal of Christlikeness seems so remote, even impossible: it is comforting to remember (a) that we are not alone, for the whole vast family

---

[1] Heb. 2: 10, cf. 13.   [3] Rom. 8: 29.
[2] Irenaeus.   [4] Heb. 2: 12, 13.
[5] Heb. 2: 13.

of God share with us in the glorious purpose that shall yet bring many sons to glory; (b) that the most difficult task has been already accomplished: we are reborn, we have the divine life; "Beloved, *now are we* the children of God . . ." The rest cannot be impossible if that be already true; (c) that Christlikeness is no mere external conformity laboriously achieved by external discipline and rigorous endeavour: it springs from within, as the natural and (if we do not hinder it) inevitable expression of the life of God within the soul.

CHAPTER 3

CONVERSION

To MODERN Christians the term "conversion" is much more familiar as a description of the beginning of Christian life than either "new creation" or "new birth". The word has no prominent place in the New Testament, and it must be confessed that as it is commonly used it does not suggest very great depth of thought or richness of meaning. It is much less theological than ethical, and perhaps it is the simpler, more practical flavour of the word that explains its popularity. For all that, the term belongs to yet another great circle of New Testament ideas in which the thought of the Christian's likeness to Christ emerges once more as the purpose of salvation.

I. CHOOSING THE WAY

Although the Scripture itself nowhere describes the experience of Paul on the road to Damascus as his "conversion", that event is probably the best Bible illustration of the meaning of the word. With mind, heart and will intent upon a deliberate course of action, in pursuance of a chosen career, Paul was journeying towards the Syrian capital when, without warning, he was apprehended—arrested[1] —the whole course of his life was changed, the immediate plan was at once abandoned, the assumptions and convictions upon which it was based were totally rejected, the career of which it formed a part was completely renounced, and Paul's mind, heart and will were suddenly diverted into a wholly new path, facing a new direction, and headed for altogether different goals. This "halt, about turn" on the journey of life, the turning around from previous paths to set one's face in new directions, is the precise meaning of "conversion". It is instructive to compare the experience of Paul with that of Nicodemus[2] and Zaccheus.[3] To Nicodemus the "about turn" was primarily intellectual, the *rethinking* of his whole con-

[1] Phil. 3: 12.   [2] John 3: 1f.   [3] Luke 19: 1f.

ception of God, himself and religious truth, and it is evident that the process took some time. To Zaccheus the "about turn" was primarily moral, the *reform* of his whole character, behaviour and principles of action, and the process in his case appears to have been instantaneous. To Paul[1] the "about turn" may be said to have been, broadly speaking, primarily religious, the *re-adjustment* not only of ideas and character but of personal faith, allegiance and career. These distinctions must not be pressed, but they suggest the elements which must be present in every true conversion.

This analysis is supported by our Lord's few references to " conversion". "Except ye be converted, and become as little children, ye shall not enter the kingdom of heaven"[2] well illustrates a radical transformation of the whole attitude to life, a complete new start, such as came to Paul. Christ's quotation from Isaiah : "This people's heart is waxed gross and their ears are dull of hearing, and their eyes have they closed; lest at any time they should see with their eyes, and hear with their ears, and should understand with their heart, and should be converted, and I should heal them"[3] suggests the kind of revolution in understanding which conversion meant for Nicodemus. And the word spoken in anticipation of Peter's denial and recovery: "When thou art converted, strengthen thy brethren"[4] suggests a new realisation of his own frailty and a humbler dependence upon the grace of Christ such as would produce in Peter just such transformation of character as came to Zaccheus. The prominence given to one or other of these aspects of conversion will of course vary with each individual: but no conversion is complete until mind, character, attitude to God have been wholly changed by the encounter with Christ on the road of life.

In the light of such sayings and illustrations in the ministry of Jesus we can understand the fuller meaning which was later attached to the term "conversion", as when Peter called upon Jerusalem to "repent . . . and be converted, that your sins may be blotted out . . ."[5] and Luke used the same word to describe the salvation of the Gentiles.[6] The negative and positive implications of conversion are well stated in Paul's reminder to the Thessalonian Christians that they had "turned" to God *from* idols—conversion is always a matter of "to" as well as "from".[7] And finally James

---

[1] Acts 9: 3f., cf. 22: 3f., 26: 12f.   [3] Matt. 13: 15.   [5] Acts 3: 19.
[2] Matt. 18: 3.   [4] Luke 22: 32.   [6] Acts 15: 3.
[7] 1 Thess. 1: 9.

gave the expression its full depth of significance when he said, "Brethren, if any of you do err from the truth, and one convert him; let him know, that he which converteth a sinner from the error of his way shall save a soul from death, and shall hide a multitude of sins."[1] This, the last of the New Testament occurrences of the term, provides the clue to that whole circle of ideas to which this one belongs, for James completed the thought—"converteth . . . from the error of his *ways*". Conversion is only the initial *step*; being *turned* we *walk*, in the *way* of the Lord. In these simple and familiar metaphors another field of New Testament thought about the Christian life is opened up, one in which the idea of likeness to Christ arises most naturally, and inescapably, and with most practical significance.

The "doctrine of the Two Ways" is beloved of religious teachers and moralists in all ages and in many lands. It was familiar in Jewish thought before Christ, and reappears in his famous saying "Enter ye in at the strait gate: for wide is the gate, and broad is the way, that leadeth to destruction, and many there be which go in thereat: because strait is the gate, and narrow is the way, which leadeth unto life, and few there be that find it."[2] From an ancient Christian manual of instruction known as the "Didache" and a devotional writer named Hermas, both of near-apostolic times, down to Bunyan's superb allegory of the spiritual journey from the city of destruction to the celestial city, the symbol of the Christian road and the godly pilgrimage reappears in Christian thought. It is possible that the very earliest name for Christianity was "The Way"[3] while the letters of the apostles are full of exhortations to "walk worthy of the Lord . . . walk in love . . . walk in the light . . . walk in truth".[4] The converted soul is set upon a pathway entirely new, and henceforth his life consists in the careful—and joyful—treading of that path at the command and in the company of his new-found Leader. We shall see that the new path cannot be described, and its goal cannot be defined, without introducing the ideal of Christlikeness.

II. DEFINING THE WAY

There can be no finer description of the Christian Way than is implied in the original, authentic call of Christ in far-off days in

---

[1] Jas. 5: 19, 20. [3] See Acts 9: 2; 19: 9; 22: 4.
[2] Matt. 7: 13, 14. [4] See Col. 1: 10; Eph. 5: 2; 1 John 1: 7; 3 John 4.

C

Galilee—"Follow me!" This is the first, and final, Gospel invitation, from the lips of him who is the only Evangelist in his own right. In some form or another the phrase occurs over sixty times in the New Testament. We are a little startled to hear Paul plead "Be ye followers of me"[1] even though he adds "even as I also am of Christ". But when we recall the situation of the early Christians, without a New Testament, tradition or experience to guide their untried feet, we realise how vital was the example of leading Christians. Inevitably the Christian life became a solemn version of the children's game of "Follow-my-leader", each copying the one or two who went ahead, and the leaders copying Christ. To stop choosing your own way, to cease from following your own devices, and join that lengthening column of followers of Jesus, was to be converted.

Such an idea must certainly not be dismissed as too simple, or too shallow, a description of Christian beginnings. For the later Christians, as for the first disciples, to follow Christ implied *faith*, faith in his utter trustworthiness, faith in his leadership; without that confidence such following must be perilous. It implied, too, *fellowship*: for John and Andrew and Peter and the rest it meant sharing Christ's nights and days, his words, thoughts, conversation, meals, sleep, prayers, emotions; it meant bringing their lives every day for three years alongside his, their hearts, their reactions, always beneath his scrutiny, their hopes and fears and ambitions under his judgement. It meant walking, working and worshipping with Christ there at all times to instruct, rebuke, inspire. And for later Christians, after his ascension, following still meant fellowship, through the Spirit, with the same risen Lord. In consequence, it was impossible to follow him, however simply one conceived it, without being *fashioned* anew: following thus involved, thirdly, *imitation*, for the Leader was the Pattern, the Exemplar, the Ideal. To follow Jesus meant the gradual modelling of life on his example, the readjustment of life to his design, keeping in step and "doing the actions" as the children say. So Peter understood it, to whom the simple call came not once but twice, at the opening of Christ's ministry and again beside the lake at its close: for Peter defines the following in terms of imitating Christ's example. "He left us an example, that ye should follow his steps."[2]

[1] 1 Cor. 4: 16; Phil. 3: 17; 2 Thess. 3: 9; 1 Cor. 11: 1.
[2] 1 Pet. 2: 21.

This is the earliest manner of describing the Christian Way, but it is not the only one. Yet the underlying thought is constant: the Way we enter at conversion is the Way of Christlikeness. Jesus declared to Thomas, "I am the way",[1] and in the Temple courtyard cried, "I am the light of the world: he that followeth me shall not walk in darkness, but shall have the light of life":[2] in both sayings the "way" in which the Christian is to walk is clearly identified with the Lord, in whose light and company he can alone hope to travel safely.

When Paul appealed to the Ephesians to "walk in love" he immediately added the motive and pattern of Christ's example to give the appeal substance and weight: "even as Christ also hath loved us";[3] and when he asked the Romans to forego things legitimate in themselves but possibly injurious to another's conscience, he again urged as both illustration and reason the fact that "even Christ pleased not himself".[4] We have already noticed Paul's way of setting his own life as an example of Christian living, a first lesson in the meaning of following Christ.[5] To the Colossians, he urged the compulsion of Christ's example in the matter of mutual forgiveness: ". . . forbearing one another, forgiving one another, if any man have a quarrel against any: even as Christ forgave you, so also do ye."[6]

John's use of the example of Jesus has the depth and pointedness we always associate with John's teaching. "Hereby perceive we the love of God, because he laid down his life for us: and we ought to lay down our lives for the brethren."[7] "We love him because he first loved us."[8] As we have seen, John was especially concerned to lay down tests by which the pretensions of certain heretical teachers might be examined; and the claims they make to "know God", to be "born again", to be "abiding in him" disproved. One such test runs somewhat paradoxically: "He that saith he abideth in him ought himself also to walk even as he walked."[9] To stay with Christ, we must move with him, in the direction, at the speed, towards the goal he sets. He who would "walk" with Christ must be going Christ's way, and keep in step, and stay the distance —else, he loses the divine companionship. Christ does not stand

---

[1] John 14: 6.
[2] John 8: 12.
[3] Eph. 5: 2.
[4] Rom. 15: 1–3, 7.
[5] 1 Cor. 11: 1; 1 Thess. 1: 6, etc.
[6] Col. 3: 13.
[7] 1 John 3: 16.
[8] 1 John 4: 19.
[9] 1 John 2: 6.

still, and to abide in him we must "walk as he walked"; equally, we shall not walk after his peerless example unless we keep abiding in him, for without his presence our step must falter and our strength decay. In all of which John is saying in his characteristic way that the Christian life is a progressive walk modelled upon the ever-advancing example of Jesus himself.

What especially impressed Peter, again, about our Lord's example to his followers, was his patient acceptance of undeserved suffering: "This is thankworthy, if a man for conscience toward God endure grief, suffering wrongfully. For what glory is it, if, when ye be buffeted for your faults, ye shall take it patiently? but if, when ye do well, and suffer for it, ye take it patiently, this is acceptable with God. For even hereunto were ye called: because Christ also suffered for us, leaving us an example, that ye should follow his steps . . ."[1] Is it altogether fanciful to see some connection between this emphasis of Peter upon the example of Christ's *patience* under persecution and his own vehement and cursing denial, in the same circumstances?

What Paul, John and Peter thus set forth, in appealing to Christ's example to define the walk of the converted man, is likewise suggested by a group of unfamiliar but very interesting titles applied to Jesus in the epistle to the Hebrews and the Acts of the Apostles. He is "the Prince of life",[2] "the Captain",[3] the "Author of eternal salvation" and "of faith".[4] In each passage the meaning hovers between "author, fount, inaugurator" and "leader, pioneer, Prince", and the fitness of these titles for him who is at once the origin and the perfect exemplar of Christian life is apparent. The central thought is still more clearly expressed in the picture of the arena in which Christians must run their race, with the eyes of multitudes of spectators upon them, after laying aside every impeding weight of evil and every clinging garment of sin, running ever "looking unto Jesus" the Leader of the running-team, who has himself endured, and who has won his crown of joy.[5]

We may say, then, in view of this unity of thought amongst various New Testament writers, that the Christian Way is to be defined as following Jesus, understood in the sense of "walking" day by day with the pattern of his life before us, placing our feet

---

[1] 1 Pet. 2: 19f.   [3] Heb. 2: 10.
[2] Acts 3: 15.   [4] Heb. 5: 9 ; 12: 2.
[5] Heb. 12: 1–3.

in his footsteps, so as to ensure at the same time that we are both copying his example and keeping near to his presence. Our Lord, Redeemer, Saviour and Friend is also the Pioneer of our way: the word given by the Angel of the resurrection is fulfilled in a larger sense for all disciples, "He goeth before you", leading his followers home not by instructions from afar, nor by counsel from behind, but by the path that he himself has trod, and with sympathy born of his own experience of the way.

III. TREADING THE WAY

If then conversion means essentially turning from our own chosen road into the Way of the Lord, the way of his example, what precisely does that example mean in daily practice? Familiar though it is, the appeal to the example of Jesus raises all kinds of problems for the young convert. Some, who would make it the whole of Christianity, fail to see how deep and complex are its implications: others, who realise that example without regeneration offers little hope to the struggling soul, sometimes underestimate the power of Our Lord's character to draw us after him. Does following Christ's example ever involve the threefold medieval vow of poverty, chastity, humility, because he was penniless, childless and of the common people? Is withdrawal from all the world's active concerns required of us, as it was of him? Are we to do exactly what he did, leave undone what he left undone, say what he said? External conformity of our lives to his has always attracted, while it baffled, the best of his followers. Is it then enough to ask "What would he do in my place?" In actual fact we make all kinds of allowances and accommodations, because we know he lived in a different world to ours, in a vastly different age, under a wholly different social system, accustomed to Eastern speech, dress and modes of thought impossible for us to imitate: how far should such adjustments for time and place and custom go? *Can* we copy his example? If we can, *dare* we? And if we dare, what do we *mean*?

Such questions are practical enough, and it is the ultimate purpose of all our study of Christlikeness to attempt an answer to them. At the point we have reached we are ready only to accept a hint at the final answer, a hint afforded by the way in which our Lord himself applies the principle of his example. Before recalling his own sayings about it, we might profitably summarise the particular directions in which Paul, John, and Peter applied the example of Jesus. These have to do with mutual love, not pleasing self, forgivingness, laying down one's life for the brethren, patience under persecution, and earnest and resolute endeavour in running the appointed race. It will not surprise us to find that these are echoes of our Lord's own words about the example he has left us.

Three or four times in all did Jesus set forth his own example for the disciples' emulation. Once it was to urge them to bear towards each other the same goodwill and affection which they have observed and experienced in his dealings with them: "A new commandment I give unto you, That ye love one another; as I have loved you, that ye also love one another . . . This is my commandment, That ye love one another, as I have loved you."[1] Motive, measure, scope and endurance, all are in that "as I have loved "! Again, our Lord set before the disciples the example of his own submission to the imperative will of the Father: "I must work the works of him that sent me . . . My meat is to do the will of him that sent me . . . to accomplish his work . . . If ye keep my commandments ye shall abide in my love, even as I have kept my Father's commandments and abide in his love."[2] Neither inclination, nor impulse, nor the pressure of circumstances, shaped his career: the dignity and steadfastness of his soul came from the surrender to a divine compulsion in which he delighted, and which he invites us to share.

In a similar passage Jesus urged the example of his own patient resistance to a hostile world: "Remember the word that I said unto you, The servant is not greater than his lord. If they have persecuted me, they will also persecute you; if they have kept my saying, they will keep yours also."[3] Christ would have them to expect like treatment from like causes, and meet it with like composure and resolution. Most clearly of all, the Saviour said: "Ye call me Master and Lord: and ye say well; for so I am. If I then, your Lord and Master, have washed your feet; ye also ought to wash one another's feet. For I have given you an example, that ye should do as I have done to you."[4] An example of lowly service given not alone in the gracious washing of Peter's, and Thomas' and Judas' feet, but again on Calvary: "Whosoever will be great among you, let him be your minister; and whosoever will be chief among you,

---

[1] John 13: 34; 15: 12.   [3] John 15: 20.
[2] John 4: 34; 9: 4; 15: 10.   [4] John 13: 13–15.

let him be your servant: *even as* the Son of man came not to be ministered unto, but to minister, and to give his life a ransom for many."[1]

In such words we are listening to the Master himself answering our questions as to the precise meaning of his example. The things to which he points belong to no one age or race or land, to no one particular social system or culture: they are timeless and unchanging—to love as he loved, obey as he obeyed, suffer as he suffered, serve as he served. Here is part of his answer to our perplexities: not in outward conformity of our lives to his, but in likeness of inward spirit, motive and ideal; not in external copying, but in the profound attuning of our spirit to his, do we follow his example. Nothing short of this can be called "following Jesus"; and in spite of all the differences between our world and his, it can and must be done. Just how we can be so inwardly transformed as to imitate his pattern from an inward likeness of nature has been suggested in our previous studies, and will be examined more fully later. But let us note very clearly that Christlikeness once again appears to be a larger, more far-reaching ideal than often it is taken to be, and its place in New Testament teaching is very large indeed.

But one point remains: part of our Lord's answer, when we ask the meaning of his example in our day, is to point us to timeless qualities of his mind and spirit for our emulation. The other part of the answer is somewhat unexpected, and illuminating. Again and again in his own sayings, and in the words of his apostles, we are reminded that the example which we follow is not merely something *set before us*, but even more it is something *done to us*. It would be tedious to rehearse again the many verses, already quoted, in which the example of Jesus is appealed to, where this point is illustrated: a few will suffice to show how constantly it is present to the minds of the writers. "Love one another as I have loved *you*"—it would have been enough to say, "As I have loved others". "As Christ forgave you, so also do ye "—why not "As Christ forgave *his enemies* . . ."? "Walk in love . . . as Christ hath loved us"; "He laid down his life for us . . . we ought also to lay down our lives for the brethren". The appeal to his example in suffering might have run: "Suffering . . . take it patiently, for Christ also hath suffered at the hands of enemies," but Peter strengthened the appeal immeasurably when he added "suffered *for us*". Always this

[1] Matt. 20: 26-8.

added thought creeps in when any extended reference to Christ's example occurs. "I have left you an example that ye should do"— not merely what you have seen me do, but what you have experienced at my hands—"as I have done *to you*."

In other words, the motive urged for imitating Christ's example is not simply that of admiration for a splendid life nobly lived, but also that of personal gratitude for what that splendid life did, suffered, and gave, for our sake. The things we seek to copy are not merely things we have seen, but things we have experienced, of the free grace of Christ. The difference is fundamental, not only in the strength of motive evoked but in the spirit in which we seek to follow that perfect pattern. The shallow modern Christianity which rolls up its sleeves and sets out confident of its own strength to imitate the noble example of Jesus, because it has the taste to admire that perfect life, may be near to New Testament Christianity, perhaps, but it is not identical with it. New Testament Christians were very conscious first, that following Christ's pattern involved much deeper transformation of spirit, attitude and quality than mere moral effort could ever achieve; and second, that the great glory and accomplishment of Jesus were not simply admirable features worth copying: they were the unmerited kindness of Christ upon which their whole hope of salvation depended, and without which all "following" would be impossible. They acknowledged the imperative demand that they be Christlike, because it was to the Christ-spirit they owed their very lives, and their hope of mercy.

CHAPTER 4

RISEN WITH CHRIST

THE FOURTH New Testament metaphor to describe the beginnings of Christian life represents conversion as a resurrection out of death. To modern, and especially to Western, minds it is a somewhat astonishing idea; there is some evidence that it would not be quite so surprising to people of the first century, even outside the Church. Even so, the occurrence of such an expression repeatedly in the New Testament reminds us of the deep wonder with which the first Christians reflected upon their experience in Christ. We shall find once more that the thought of Christlikeness lies near the heart of this mode of speech, as of those already studied; but we shall also find, if we are prepared to wrestle a little with the unfamiliar language, that this particular form of the Bible doctrine of conversion underlines more than any other the inwardness of the Christian ideal and the depth of that faith-union with Christ without which all talk of being "conformed to his image" would be idle and unreal.

I. "DEAD"

Two distinct but closely related ideas are combined in this representation of conversion as a spiritual death and resurrection: the sinner's death *in* sin, and the believer's death *to* sin. Both demand our patient attention, not only as being scriptural, but as being traceable ultimately to the teaching of the Master himself. There is in the whole Bible no more sharp or dramatic portrayal of the true effect of sin in human experience than in our Lord's picture of the prodigal son in the far country. In that description the ultimate word is "He was dead, and is alive again, was lost and is found".[1] The story eloquently illustrates the Bible meaning of "dead in sin". All that we associate with death is here implied of the sinner's state —the sense of separation, of being beyond the reach of a love that

[1] Luke 15: 32.

41

is strong as ever but now is powerless, of insensitiveness, alike to duty and affection. Even the finality of death is suggested, in the inability of the lad—until misery and memory combine to change him—to retrace his steps. "He was dead." Elsewhere too Jesus speaks of the broad way, found by many, "which leadeth to destruction"—the opposite of "life".[1]

According to John, Christ came especially to bring *life*, abundant and eternal life, to a world of spiritual death. "I am come that they might have life . . . This is life eternal, that they might know thee, the only true God, and Jesus Christ whom thou hast sent . . . He that believeth on the Son hath everlasting life: and he that believeth not the Son shall not see life. . . . God so loved the world that he gave his only-begotten Son that whosoever believeth in him should not perish but should have everlasting life . . . This is the record, that God hath given to us eternal life, and this life is in his Son. He that hath the Son hath life: and he that hath not the Son of God hath not life."[2] The clear implication is that outside of Christ is—death.

Paul was equally emphatic: "The wages of sin is death";[3] "to be carnally minded is death";[4] "if ye live after the flesh ye shall die . . . he that soweth to the flesh shall of the flesh reap corruption".[5] Paul's own experience had been that "when the commandment came, sin revived, and I died . . . sin slew me".[6] And in consequence he spoke of conversion as "quickening", being made alive again in Christ: "and you, being dead in your sins, hath he quickened together with him, having forgiven you . . .";[7] "And you hath he quickened who were dead in trespasses and sin . . . even when we were dead in sins."[8] Sin *is* death, and there is no deliverance except through resurrection in Christ to life everlasting.

A second group of passages concerns the transition of the believer from this death *in* sin to life in Christ through a death *to* sin. It is important that this idea should not be made mystical or mysterious, or dismissed as beyond understanding. In essence it is no more than the prodigal's "coming to himself" and saying "I will arise

---

[1] Matt. 7: 13, 14.
[2] John 10: 10; 17: 3; 3: 36; 3: 16; 1 John 5: 11, 12.
[3] Rom. 6: 23.
[4] Rom. 8: 6.
[5] Rom. 8: 13; Gal. 6: 8.
[6] Rom. 7: 9, 11.
[7] Col. 2: 13.
[8] Eph. 2: 1, 5.

and go". In that moment the *prodigal* died, and the *penitent* rose from his grave. This is, in fact, implied in the old and familiar conception of *repentance*, putting one way of thinking and behaving utterly behind you, to adopt a new: dying to one life and becoming alive to another. The truth receives sharper definition, and at the same time is pressed upon the Christian conscience with unanswerable authority, in the solemn words of Jesus: "If any man will come after me, let him deny himself, and take up his cross, and follow me. For whosoever will save his life shall lose it: and whosoever will lose his life for my sake shall find it."[1] "He that taketh not his cross and followeth after me is not worthy of me."[2]

Christ's words are echoed in the great declarations of Paul: "I am crucified with Christ: nevertheless I live; yet not I, but Christ liveth in me: and the life which I now live in the flesh I live by the faith of the Son of God, who loved me, and gave himself for me."[3] "Those that are Christ's have crucified the flesh with the affections and lusts."[4] And again, "God forbid that I should glory save in the cross of our Lord Jesus Christ, through whom the world is crucified unto me and I unto the world".[5] Paul had "taken up his cross" and died, for Christ's sake, to all that previously dominated his life, to the law,[6] to sin,[7] to the world,[8] and to self.[9] His words are not to be discounted as "mystical" or emotional exaggeration: he is only developing in his own vigorous language, and with insight born of experience, the truth he had learned of Christ, that to "take up the cross", be "crucified with Christ", "lose his life for Christ's sake" was the only way, and the sure way, to find life abundant. As the matter is presented in the New Testament, every man is either dead in sin, or he has died to sin and risen to life in Christ.

II. "QUICKENED"

It is important to notice that this death to past sin and resurrection to new life in Christ is not something ascribed only to a few, or to those most advanced in Christian life: it is asserted of all who believe. In passages we have still to study, in his letters to Rome, Ephesus and Colosse, Paul based urgent appeal upon the argument that all Christians have died with Christ to sin: the appeal would lose most

[1] Matt. 16: 24, 25.   [4] Gal. 5: 24.   [7] Rom. 6: 11.
[2] Matt. 10: 38.   [5] Gal. 6: 14.   [8] Gal. 6: 14.
[3] Gal. 2: 20.   [6] Rom. 7: 4.   [9] 2 Cor. 5: 15.

of its weight if it applied only to exceptional Christians, and those the best and most mature. "As many of us as were baptised into Christ Jesus were baptised into his death"[1]—and that meant, in New Testament times, every member of the Church. In other words, it is part of the meaning of conversion, and is inherent in the nature of the Gospel message, that all who believe take up the cross and die with Christ. Yet we are saved by "simple faith" in Christ. How can so profound an experience as death and resurrection with Christ be implied in saving faith?

Paul was never weary of insisting that a man is saved by faith alone. But when (as in Romans) the moral dangers of such a Gospel of "easy" salvation by "just believing" were before his mind, Paul proceeded to expound the meaning of saving faith in terms which show it to be, not any less simple and easy to exercise, but yet profoundly significant and transforming. That very faith which is expressed in our first baptismal confession of Christ, is faith in the Christ who died our death, in our place and on our behalf. By that same faith we are saying "Amen" to his death, accepting it, and approving it, as the necessary way of dealing with our sin. We are saying, "My sin *needed* just that: thank you, Lord." And thus, logically, consistently, feelingly, we are committed—by our simple saving faith—to die with Christ to all the sin that put him to death.

A sentence in Second Corinthians[2] is illuminating. "The love of Christ constraineth us; because we thus judge, that if one died for all, then were all dead: and that he died for all, that they which live should not henceforth live unto themselves, but unto him which died for them, and rose again." The transition from a life lived "for themselves" to a life lived "unto him"—in other words, the death of one kind of living and the rise of a new kind—is effected by a certain "judgement"—"we thus *judge*"; and the inference, or judgement, is this: that if one died for all, then were all dead. If we assert that he died in place of our forfeited lives, then we are admitting that our lives were rightfully forfeit: that we deserved to die. We cannot claim the benefits of his death in our place, and then go on to say that of course our sin was not really serious enough to involve death! *We cannot at the same time plead the merit of his cross and repudiate what he there did in our name and on our behalf.* To accept his death as for our sakes is, *to accept his death*, to die with him to all that he died to.

[1] Rom. 6: 3.　　　　[2] 2 Cor. 5: 14, 15.

Of course, in the first days of our Christian life we would hardly express the meaning of our faith in these deep psychological or spiritual terms. But we would say that, tired and oppressed with sin, and longing to put it behind us, we saw that Christ had judged, conquered and atoned for it, on our behalf. Gladly we accepted all that he had done for us, and surrendered utterly to all his will—to his judgement of our past, and his programme for our future. And in saying that, or anything like that, we are saying all that Paul implied: we are admitting that the past, for us, ended on the cross of Calvary, and all began anew. Later on we might express what Jesus did for us in time-honoured words that carry great meaning. We will say that Jesus died as our Substitute, dying that we might not have to die, the death of the sinner under the wrath of God; but he died also as our Representative, dying so that in him we should die, to all that caused his death, to sin and self and the godless world, gladly taking our place beside him on the cross—taking *our* cross, and following him, all the way to Calvary, and to Resurrection.

Saving faith is thus, for Paul, far more than the merely intellectual belief in certain ideas against which James warns us in a famous passage.[1] It is rather a whole-hearted adhesion to Christ, an acceptance of what he did for us so complete and consenting that we adopt his attitude to sin as our attitude, his judgement upon it as our judgement, his death to break its spell as our death. Faith thus implies, or includes, loyalty, love, unity of mind, will, affection, with our dying and rising Lord: by it we take our place beside him in death; by it we accept what he did *for* us and what he seeks to do *in* us; and in this faith-union of loyalty, love, and acceptance, we are transformed. We die "with Christ" and "rise with Christ to newness of life". This was Paul's answer to the charge that his Gospel of salvation by faith alone allows a man to continue in sin.

III. "RISEN"

It is plain that in all this train of thought the idea of the believer's experience as somehow parallel to that of Christ is paramount. The Christian "recapitulates" the life of his Master. As one with Christ, and a member in Christ's body, the Church, he assents to,

[1] Jas. 2: 14–26.

undergoes and so in a profound sense repeats, the great redemptive acts of Christ. He "dies with Christ",[1] is "crucified with Christ",[2] crucified to the world by the cross of Christ.[3] The use of the word "crucified" to describe this moral and spiritual experience of conversion is itself a deliberate echo of the cross of Calvary; in the same way the believer is "raised with him",[4] "risen with him through the faith of the operation of God, who hath raised *him* from the dead".[5] "You . . . hath he quickened *together with him.*"[6] Given their due weight such phrases make it certain that Paul was thinking of the parallel between the Master and the Christian—was thinking, in fact, of the ideal of Christlikeness. But it does not depend on isolated words and phrases: two great passages draw out the parallel in detail.

In the letter to the Ephesians, the correspondence between Christ's resurrection, ascension and exalted session in heavenly places and the believer's quickening from sin's death, resurrection in Christ and raising to heavenly places, is deliberately elaborated. "God raised him from the dead, and set him at his own right hand in the heavenly places, far above all principality . . . and hath put all things under his feet . . . and you hath he quickened who were dead in trespasses and sins . . . even when we were dead in sins, (he) hath quickened us together with Christ . . . and raised us up together and made us sit together in heavenly places in Christ Jesus . . ."[7] We share not only in the resurrection power which brought Jesus from the grave, but in the exaltation over all evil forces, in the victory obtained for us in conflict with "principalities and powers", and in the access granted to him, our Lord and Representative into the holy place on high—we die with him, rise with him, are exalted with him, triumph with him and reign with him. His experience is shared with us: so far are we to follow his steps and bear his likeness !

In the letter to the Romans the same correspondence is illustrated between the death, resurrection and victory of Jesus and those of the Christian, but this time in association with the believer's baptism.[8] "How shall we, that are dead to sin, live any longer therein ? Know ye not, that so many of us as were baptised into Jesus Christ were baptised into his death ? Therefore we are buried with him by baptism into death; that like as Christ was raised up from the dead

[1] Col. 2: 20.   [3] Gal. 6: 14.   [5] Col. 2: 12.   [7] Eph. 1: 20—2: 6.
[2] Gal. 2: 20.   [4] Col. 3: 1.   [6] Col. 2: 13.   [8] Rom. 6.

by the glory of the Father, even so we also should walk in newness of life. For if we have been planted together in the likeness of his death, we shall be also in the likeness of his resurrection: knowing this, that our old man is crucified with him . . . Now if we be dead with Christ, we believe that we shall also live with him. . . . For in that he died, he died unto sin once: but in that he liveth, he liveth unto God. Likewise reckon ye also yourselves to be dead indeed unto sin, but alive unto God through Jesus Christ our Lord." Baptism is thus an acted recapitulation of the death, burial and resurrection of Jesus: but the outward act represents and expresses an inward experience of taking up the cross, dying with Christ to all that is unchristlike, and rising to life in him, with him and for him. This doctrine underlies also the references to baptism in the letter to the Colossians. "Buried with him in baptism, wherein also ye are risen with him through the faith of the operation of God, who hath raised him from the dead . . . If ye then be risen with Christ, seek those things which are above, where Christ sitteth on the right hand of God . . . For ye are dead, and your life is hid with Christ in God."[1]

It is assumed in these passages, as everywhere in the New Testament, that baptism was the conscious act of the baptised himself, on profession of his faith, and so carried moral obligations, voluntarily accepted, to which such strong appeal could be made. It is the faith in Christ crucified which effects the death and resurrection in the believer: Paul nowhere suggests that the ceremony of baptism itself could by its own efficacy achieve anything so far-reaching and so deep. Had he thought so, there would have been no point in the exhortations to the baptised which fill Romans 6. But the faith which baptism expresses does achieve it, only since faith fluctuates and wavers it is necessary continually to reaffirm what our baptism set forth, to stand by what we then meant and what we did, to "*reckon ourselves* dead indeed unto sin but alive unto God . . . to mortify our members which are upon the earth".[2] We are called throughout our Christian life to accept ever more fully that Christ died in our place and stead, for our sins; and in so accepting, to reaffirm that he truly represented us, and to hold ourselves indeed to have died with him, and with him risen to newness of life.

But if the act of baptism does not in itself complete the work once for all, it is not therefore insignificant. It expresses with

[1] Col. 2: 12; 3: 1-3.　　[2] Rom. 6: 11; Col. 3: 5.

dramatic appropriateness what that faith is which we are confessing before men—faith in a Saviour who himself died, was buried and rose again. It expresses with equal clearness both the *experience* which faith has brought to us, of having died with him to sin, self and the world, and our *resolve* that henceforth we shall willingly and of deliberate purpose, count ourselves so dead to sin and alive unto God. In such a public committal to faith in Christ, in all its moral implications, the conscious acceptance of Christ's attitude and experience as the model for our own is plain.

It is possible that the correspondence between our Lord's experience of death-burial-resurrection and our own is carried one step further. If we examine again the passages which describe the "risen" life of the Christian,[1] we shall notice that emphasis is laid upon its "newness", its triumph (over sin and over death), its freedom and its being "hidden with Christ in God". Is it accidental that these are precisely the marks of the risen life of Jesus in the Gospels? That life was *new* in its radiance, timelessness and uniqueness; it was *triumphant* over the sin that crucified him and the death that could not hold him; it was *free* from the limitations he had voluntarily accepted in becoming man, and from the hindrances he had patiently borne from men; and it was *hidden*, in that "the world seeth him no more", all resurrection-appearances being to believers only.

It may be that this is to press the likeness too far: but the essential point is plain, the risen life of the believer is modelled upon the risen life of Christ, and depends upon it. "That I may know him, and the power of his resurrection"[2] was the ambition of Paul. In dying, burial and rising again, so picturesquely set forth in baptism after the apostolic manner of immersion, the believer "follows" the experience of his Lord, transposing his physical experience into an ethical and mystical key, but in a deep and realistic sense always "bearing about in the body the dying of the Lord Jesus, that the life also of Jesus might be made manifest in his body".[3]

The ideal of Christlikeness thus touches Christian experience at its inmost places: with this teaching before us we can never reduce "conformity to Christ" to any merely mechanical or external thing, for its inner meaning runs very deep indeed. With this thought of death and resurrection with Christ in baptism as clue, we shall expect

[1] Col. 3: 1–4; Rom. 6: 1–23.   [2] Phil. 3: 10.   [3] 2 Cor. 4: 10.

that being conformed to the image of Christ will involve a re-orientation of the whole personality, in which, *as to mental and emotional experience* the believer "recapitulates" the experience of his Lord; *as to ethical attitude* he is set at his Lord's own stand-point towards sin, self and the world; and *as to intellectual and moral judgement*, he explicitly adopts the standards and values of Christ himself. Understood in this way, it is surely not exaggeration to say that the Christlike ideal is much more than a metaphor associated with the Gospel, much more than a useful expression of a Christian ethical idea: it is the heart of the evangelical experience, it gives meaning and content to the doctrine of conversion, it lends an ethical quality and direction to the truth of "salvation by faith alone".

IV. "CLOTHED"

The apostle Paul found the truth that God seeks to make us Christlike to be implied in baptism in yet another way, expressing essentially the same idea in rather more homely terms. "As many of you as have been baptised into Christ Jesus have put on Christ."[1] "Put on" is an unexpected phrase: it has to do with "donning" garments, or armour, and is the root of our word "endue". Being "clothed with Christ" is not a familiar manner of speech to us, but it is not obscure. Paul used it again in Romans: "Put ye on the Lord Jesus Christ,"[2] in Ephesians: "Put ye on the new man, which after God is created in righteousness and true holiness"[3] and in Colossians: "Ye have put on the new man which is renewed in knowledge after the image of him that created him."[4]

The new man, or new self, as we have seen bears the image of its creator and so "putting on the new man" is putting on Christ-likeness. Naturally, the "putting off the old man, with his deeds" is either mentioned or implied in all these passages.[5] One passage indeed develops the theme at length, listing "the garments of the renewed soul"—compassion, kindness, humility, meekness, long-suffering, forbearance, forgiveness, and the "girdle of perfection, charity"—a list in the midst of which the appeal to Christ's example is again made quite explicitly.[6] The argument here is the same as in Romans 6: we "put on Christ", or the new nature remade in his

[1] Gal. 3: 27.
[2] Rom. 13: 14.
[3] Eph. 4: 24.
[4] Col. 3: 10.
[5] See Col. 3: 8, 9; Eph. 4: 22 and Rom. 13: 12.
[6] Col. 3: 12–14.

likeness, first of all in baptism,[1] but we must repeatedly reaffirm what our baptism implied: we must "put on Christ" again and again, day by day.

"Putting on the Lord Jesus Christ" means more than "putting on the character of the Lord Jesus Christ" as Dr. Moffatt translates it.[2] As the passage in Galatians shows, it is linked to the whole doctrine of the Body of Christ of which each Christian is an individual member; it is linked also to the significant phrase "in Christ" in which so much of Paul's view of the Christian life is summarised. The believer is "clothed with Christ" as he can be "clothed" with power,[3] or immortality.[4] The outward adornment of the Christlike character is the manifestation of this inward enduement with the Christlike spirit—nothing less than that.

So much is clear, but the connection with baptism is a little less obvious. Later custom may supply an interesting clue. In the early centuries the putting off of the clothes of the baptismal candidates before baptism, and the clothing of them afterwards, sometimes in white raiment, came to be emphasised as parts of the baptismal ceremony. Constantine was buried in his baptismal robes. The evidence for this symbolic clothing at baptism is late, but the need for disrobing obviously existed from the first and there was abundant precedent for reading into it a moral lesson. The Essenes, a small Jewish sect contemporary with the apostles, associated with their bath of purification the wearing of white veils during the ceremony and at the religious meal which followed. The High Priest, in Zechariah's vision, is stripped of his filthy garments and robed anew as preparation for his ordination,[5] and the conception is familiar in the Old Testament. A Christian writer, by the middle of the second century, can use the expression "even so we . . . have been stripped of the filthy garments, that is of our sins". Paul's metaphor may thus be a covert reference to familiar baptismal practice, and if so, his words gain much in vividness and appeal. But in any case the meaning of his teaching is clear: the man in Christ has been "clothed upon" with the Christ-nature, and this is, as it were, an "outside" description of the same process of spiritual reorientation which is described from the inside as death and resurrection with Christ.

[1] Gal. 3: 27.
[2] Rom. 13: 14 Moff.
[3] Luke 24: 49.
[4] 1 Cor. 15: 53; 2 Cor. 5: 1-4.
[5] Zech. 3: 3.

This chapter has carried us far and deep, but always we remain in sight of our central theme. The believer, in conversion, is already transformed after the likeness of his Saviour, entering fully into his Lord's experience, adopting for himself his Lord's attitudes and standards, and being led by "saving faith" through a spiritual crisis in which his inner nature is wholly renewed. He is crucified with Christ, buried with Christ, rises with Christ, puts on Christ, because he has been baptised into Christ. Henceforth he continually reckons himself dead to sin, alive to God, and repeatedly puts on Christ in daily confirmation of his earliest vow. Henceforth too, Christ lives in him. That is the depth of the Christlike ideal.

The New Testament leaves us in no doubt that the purpose of God in saving us through Christ is that we should be refashioned after the image of his Son. Whichever of these great Scripture expressions we prefer—becoming a new creation in Christ Jesus, being reborn into the divine family, turning from our chosen way to follow Jesus, or dying and rising again with him by faith—each points in its own way to the same ultimate end: we are to be re-created after the divine pattern, bear the divine likeness, imitate the divine example, share the divine reaction to sin, as these are seen in the Master himself. Already we have seen enough to convince us that this ideal of Christlikeness is no simple and elementary conformity of our outward behaviour upon the Pattern of Christ's, but a very deep and far-reaching principle which affects mind, emotion, will and the inmost experiences of the soul. Before our studies are finished we shall make an earnest attempt to show what this all means in the concrete situations of daily life, but before so doing we must try to see how the purpose embarked upon in conversion is pursued in the long process of spiritual growth and discipline.

THE PROCESS

CHAPTER 5

GROWING UP

EVANGELICAL emphasis upon the necessity, and the wonder, of conversion is not always accompanied, unfortunately, by equal stress upon the need for spiritual growth and moral development. How many personal disappointments and short-lived enthusiasms are due to that simple lack of balance in evangelism! Conversion *is* a thrilling experience, but it only sets the feet upon the long hard highroad to the Celestial city; new creation is a glorious act of God, but the command is to be fruitful and multiply; dying and rising with Christ is a transforming commitment, but the new life has still be to lived out and the death daily reaffirmed; birth into God's family is a wondrous privilege, but birth must be followed by growth if the soul is not to be stunted and immature.

The point appears obvious, but the place it occupies in the New Testament is evidence of how often it is overlooked. It is hardly an exaggeration to say that the whole New Testament was originally written not so much for the conversion of unbelievers as for the nurture of the new-born Christian, the edifying of the immature Church. Any study of the Christian ideal of personal discipleship must therefore give prominence to the New Testament's teaching about Christian progress. Our interest is especially in the persistent scriptural emphasis that throughout the many-sided process of Christian development God is working out one sovereign purpose—to remake each believer after the image of his Son.

I. THE PRICE OF SPIRITUAL IMMATURITY

Five times the New Testament warns us against failure to grow up in Christ. "Ye therefore, beloved, seeing ye know these things before, beware lest ye also, being led away with the error of the wicked, fall from your own steadfastness. *But* grow in grace, and in the knowledge of our Lord and Saviour Jesus Christ."[1] The *but*

[1] 2 Pet. 3: 17, 18.

55

is important, for it presents alternatives: either you grow, or you fall away. It is either progress or retreat all the time in every Christian life. There lies the *peril* of immaturity. The ungrown believer stands in peculiar danger of slipping back to the error and wickedness of his former life, or of wavering perpetually between the old and the new way of living, "fallen from steadfastness". The advancing Christian, on the other hand, continually leaves farther and farther behind him the enticements to return. To go forward is to be safe.

Closely related to this, but not precisely the same, is Paul's warning to the Church at Ephesus. "That we henceforth be no more children, tossed to and fro, and carried about with every wind of doctrine, by the sleight of men, and cunning craftiness, whereby they lie in wait to deceive; *but* speaking the truth in love, may grow up . . ."[1] Again the *but* presents alternatives. Either we grow up, or we remain emotionally and intellectually unstable; as to our minds, the easy prey to any clever orator with a glib tongue, pretentious authority and specious promises of new thrills—"carried about with every wind of doctrine"; as to our hearts, "tossed" between waves of elation and depression. Spiritual "children" are easily persuaded, and easily cast down; confused and contradictory in judgement, and torn by conflicting feelings; equally unreliable in opinions and in moods. And because emotions, beliefs, loyalties fluctuate, no steady work, no consistent witness, no serious responsibility is to be expected of them. There lies the *weakness* of immaturity, and how familiar the picture is ! "Brethren, be not children in understanding: howbeit in malice be ye children, but in understanding be men."[2]

Instability of this kind arises from too superficial thinking and too shallow experience. So Paul hints in another Corinthian passage : "When I was a child, I spake as a child, I understood as a child, I thought as a child: but when I became a man, I put away childish things."[3] The reference here is quite incidental, it is true. Paul was thinking of the permanence of faith, hope, love, compared with prophecy, tongues, knowledge which pass away in the full maturity of heaven. But the hint of spiritual immaturity (in the light of the rest of the letter) is obvious, and the exact words chosen are significant. I put away the "chatter" of childhood, impetuous, imitative, irresponsible—charming in children, but dreadful in grown-ups ! I put away the "thinking" of childhood, make-believing,

[1] Eph. 4: 14, 15.   [2] 1 Cor. 14: 20.   [3] 1 Cor. 13: 11.

wishful, emotional, rosily optimistic—delightful in children, dangerous in grown-ups ! I put away the "reasoning" of childhood, superficial, short-sighted, self-centred, content with half-answers to little-understood questions, and seeing the whole world only in relation to its own needs—natural in childhood, but foolish in grown-ups !

We have all indulged in childish speech, often talking instead of taking responsibility, making large vows that we too soon forget, airing ill-considered opinions upon all kinds of topics. We have all imagined the world a wholly wonderful place, where right always triumphs, and the possibilities are limitless, and all good things lie round the corner. We have all reasoned with too short perspective and too personal and self-regarding standards: this is only to be expected in the first days of discipleship. But if it is carried forward into later Christian life, if we persistently refuse to learn the more careful, disciplined speech, the more realistic and open-eyed judgement of men and the world, the deeper broader conception of life and God's purposes, then we are heading for disappointment, disillusionment, and unbelief. There lies the *inadequacy* of immaturity: it cannot outface the realities of Christian life in an unchristian world. Progress brings a chastened speech, a sober but deeper faith, a realistic but courageous understanding, enabling us to quit ourselves like men, and be strong.

Spiritual immaturity, however, affects not only our own happiness and security, but also our value and relationships in the common life of the Church. Opposing the party-strife at Corinth, Paul blamed the quarrelsomeness of ungrown Christians. The best children quarrel sometimes, it is their way of asserting themselves, of testing their own powers, of declaring their own importance. Each is naturally self-centred, touchy, and very, very tactless ! So it is, all too often, in God's family. Part of the serious duty of growing up in spiritual life is growing in tolerance, sympathy, understanding, love, and learning that you do not know everything, for God has other secrets to whisper to other hearts, other ways with other men, other tasks for other servants. Part, too, lies in realising that your insights, your experiences, your tasks are not God's sole concern—nor your brother's. The Christian who "just cannot get on" with other Christians, who will never work alongside them, or consent to differ from them in love, but prefers to isolate himself in self-righteous superiority, assured that he knows

all the mind of God, is just a child in the Christian nursery, demanding attention, asserting himself against the rest of the family, and
when he fails to get his own way, sulking in a corner.

So Paul wrote: "And I, brethren, could not speak unto you as
unto spiritual, but as unto carnal, even as unto babes in Christ.
I have fed you with milk, and not with meat: for hitherto ye were
not able to bear it, neither yet now are ye able. For ye are yet
carnal: for whereas there is among you envying, and strife, and
divisions, are ye not carnal, and walk as men? For while one saith,
I am of Paul; and another, I am of Apollos; are ye not carnal?"[1]
Here "carnal" means simply *of the flesh*, whatsoever comes naturally
to our weak and sinful human nature, whatever belongs to the old
life in the flesh, outside of Christ. In the immature Christian, whose
spiritual life is undeveloped, these natural propensities persist with
scarcely diminished power, and the new spirit-born impulses constantly conflict with the established habits of thought and desire.
Especially (in this passage) does this happen in the case of old habits
of self-aggrandisement, pride, self-assertion and quick resentment,
which foster violent partisanship and party-strife. Immaturity is
thus *divisive*, destructive of all true fellowship. Readiness to co-
operate, a deep aversion to quarrels, are distinguishing qualities of
the grown-up Christian.

One more example of this New Testament concern about spiritual
immaturity is found in the epistle to the Hebrews. ". . . We have
many things to say, and hard to be uttered, seeing ye are dull of
hearing. For when for the time ye ought to be teachers, ye have
need that one teach you again which be the first principles of the
oracles of God; and are become such as have need of milk, and
not of strong meat. For everyone that useth milk is unskilful in
the word of righteousness: for he is a babe. But strong meat belongeth to them that are of full age, even those who by reason of
use have their senses exercised to discern both good and evil."[2]
Here again it is not the effect of stunted spiritual growth upon the
believer himself which is chiefly in view, although slowness to learn
("dull of hearing"), inability to distinguish primary principles from
secondary matters, unskilfulness in the Word, and lack of discern-
ment between good and evil in complicated situations, are certainly
serious deficiencies in any Christians, even those of short experience.
What is central in this rebuke, however, is the effect of such

---

[1] 1 Cor. 3: 1-4.   [2] Heb. 5: 11-14.

immaturity upon the individual's value to the Christian community. Considering the time they have been believers they ought to be ready to serve, but they cannot teach—they need still to be taught; their minds so ill-informed, their consciences so inexperienced and confused, they are useless, fruitless, idle passengers in the fellowship, always dependent upon others to carry them, counsel them, encourage them, and never themselves becoming the strength and guide of younger converts. Immaturity is so *useless*: spiritual growth is increase also in capacity—the capacity to learn, to teach, to serve, and to save.

It is hardly surprising that in that "mushroom" Church of the first century there should be many "babes in Christ", children in faith, experience, knowledge and behaviour, sure of one vivid, real, transforming experience of Christ's saving power, but needing to go forward to deeper life. Nor can we of the modern Church think it strange if there were many who tasted that the Lord was gracious, but failed to grow in grace, many who began well but were hindered. Knowledge of our own hearts confirms this five-fold indictment of spiritual immaturity—perilous, weak, inadequate, divisive and useless—as not one whit too strong. However wonderful our initial experience may have been, our present need and our Bibles alike urge us not to be content or complacent, but to rise to the full height of the Gospel's promise, and "grow up into Christ in all things".

II. THE AIDS TO SPIRITUAL ADVANCEMENT

"Which of you by taking thought can add one cubit unto his stature ?" asked Jesus on a famous occasion, deprecating fretfulness about things which are the heavenly Father's care. When physical growth is in question the answer is plain: but it is not safe to apply the same principle to spiritual progress. In Christian experience a great deal can be accomplished "by taking thought". In one sense it is true, "growth" is essentially a natural process: it is the property of living things to grow of themselves, and forced over-development is as unwelcome in young Christians as in young plants. But the spiritual life is a delicate thing, and the climate of the world not helpful; some care and informed attention are essential if maturity is to be reached.

Paul contrasted two general ways in which the "small" Christian

—small in faith, experience and influence—can become a "big" Christian: by being built up, or by being "puffed up"; by really growing, or by merely swelling; by improvement or by inflation. The expression "puffed up" comes from the word for "bellows" (the root-word is actually pronounced "fizz" !) and it has to do with inflating wine-skins, or a bubble. It well suggests what Paul thought of certain self-important, over-assured people who make great spiritual claims but are often somewhat careless about conduct ("Ye are puffed up, and have not rather mourned, that he that hath done this deed might be taken away from among you")[1] and who are given to forming exclusive cliques and factions ("puffed up for one against another").[2] Spiritual inflation arises from the conceit of knowledge prized for its own sake—"knowledge puffeth up . . . vainly puffed up by his fleshly mind" ;[3] from indulging in the criticism of others—"Some are puffed up, as though I would not come to you. But I will come to you shortly, if the Lord will, and will know, not the speech of them which are puffed up, but the power" ;[4] and from dwelling too much on one's "experiences"—a "wilful" humbling of oneself in worshipping angels, "dwelling in the things which he hath seen, vainly puffed up . . ."[5] However it comes, spiritual inflation is an unlovely, repellent thing.

In contrast to it Paul set the thought of "edification", a rather old-fashioned word now, but a valuable one, suggesting something architectural, solid, well-founded, balanced, and (in the original) "homely", or even "home-made", in the mature Christian character. For a full view of Christian progress two metaphors are necessary— the continual *growth* of the soul through the natural development of an implanted divine life, and the steady *up-building* of the edifice of character in conscious and deliberate striving towards deeper faith, experience and virtue.

We are here concerned mainly with the end towards which spiritual progress is aimed, but it may be useful to note briefly the means by which it is achieved, according to New Testament teaching. Much is said in this connection of the corporate life of the Church, and especially of her common worship. Writing to Corinth Paul urged that everything done in the meetings of the Church should be tested by this rule, that each shall be edified by the various parts of

[1] 1 Cor. 5: 2.
[2] 1 Cor. 4: 6; see 2 Cor. 12: 20.
[3] 1 Cor. 8: 1; Col. 2: 18.
[4] 1 Cor. 4: 18–19.
[5] Col. 2: 18 R.V.

the service, by preaching ("prophecy"),[1] "tongues",[2] "giving of
thanks".[3] "How is it then, brethren? when ye come together,
every one of you hath a psalm, hath a doctrine, hath a tongue, hath
a revelation, hath an interpretation. Let all things be done unto
edifying."[4] The building up of souls is thus the determining purpose of worship, as it was of the way the apostles used their authority
(". . . our authority, which the Lord hath given us for edification,
and not for destruction")[5] and generally conducted their relations
with the Churches ("we do all things, dearly beloved, for your
edifying").[6]

For the same over-riding purpose was the whole Christian ministry
gifted by the risen Lord to his Church: "He gave some, apostles;
and some, prophets; and some, evangelists; and some, pastors and
teachers; for the perfecting of the saints, for the work of the ministry,
for the edifying of the body of Christ."[7] This emphasis upon
spiritual growth through the common life of the Church should be
noted carefully, for a reason to be mentioned later. Mutual encouragement and exhortation is similarly stressed as a means for
the upbuilding of young converts. The Thessalonian Church was
commended for this, and urged to continue in it;[8] the Roman
Christians were reminded of the example of Jesus as the motive to
make "every one of us please his neighbour for his good to edification".[9] "It is *love* that builds up";[10] where criticism, rivalry,
argument, rebuke tend to discourage and hinder the growing soul,
genuine goodwill and sympathy, even where it must speak plainly,
tends to strengthen and help forward. Thus "all the body fitly
framed and knit together through that which every joint supplieth,
according to the working in due measure of each several part, maketh
the increase of the body into the building up of itself in love."[11]

This concern for mutual edification works out as a rule of great
practical value in the guidance of conduct: "Let no corrupt speech
proceed out of your mouth, but such as is good for edifying . . .
but speaking truth in love, may grow up . . ."[12] Even more does
it become a firm principle binding the Christian conscience in things
commonly regarded as morally neutral or indifferent. "Let us not

[1] 1 Cor. 14: 3, 4.
[2] 1 Cor. 14: 4, 5, 12.
[3] 1 Cor. 14: 16, 17.
[4] 1 Cor. 14: 26.
[5] 2 Cor. 10: 8.
[6] 2 Cor. 12: 19.
[7] Eph. 4: 11, 12.
[8] 1 Thess. 5: 11.
[9] Rom. 15: 2, 3.
[10] 1 Cor. 8: 1.
[11] Eph. 4: 16 R.V.
[12] Eph. 4: 29, 15 R.V.

therefore judge one another any more: but judge this rather, that no man put a stumbling block or an occasion to fall in his brother's way . . . If thy brother be grieved with thy meat, now walkest not thou charitably . . . Destroy not him with thy meat for whom Christ died . . . Let us therefore follow after the things which make for peace, and things wherewith one may edify another . . . All things indeed are pure . . . it is good neither to eat flesh, nor to drink wine, nor anything whereby thy brother stumbleth, or is offended, or made weak."[1] In the same way concern for our own spiritual upbuilding will direct conscience in doubtful things: "All things are lawful for me, but all things are not expedient: all things are lawful for me, but all things edify not."[2]

Responsible membership in the body of Christ, making for diligence in corporate worship and carefulness in conduct, have then a significant place in this process of Christian growth. So have three other things:

(i) *Nourishing the soul upon the word of God*—"As newborn babes, desire the sincere milk of the word, that ye may grow thereby . . ."[3] "I have fed you with milk, and not with meat: for hitherto ye were not able to bear it . . ."[4] "Everyone that useth milk is unskilful in the word of righteousness: for he is a babe. But strong meat belongeth to them that are of full age . . ."[5] Much spiritual backwardness is due to "malnutrition", and to the loss of desire for Biblical study and scriptural preaching. Yet it is only "the word of his grace which is able to build you up".[6] For this reason one young pastor was warned against contentious and speculative arguments, "Neither give heed to fables and endless genealogies, which minister questions, rather than godly edifying which is in faith . . ."[7]

(ii) *Maintaining a forward-looking habit of mind*—"Not as though I had already attained, either were already perfect: but I follow after, if that I may apprehend that for which also I am apprehended of Christ Jesus. Brethren, I count not myself to have apprehended: but this one thing I do, forgetting those things which are behind, and reaching forth unto those things which are before, I press toward the mark for the prize of the high calling of God in Christ Jesus."[8] The failures of past days, which would discourage us,

[1] Rom. 14: 13–21.
[2] 1 Cor. 10: 23.
[3] 1 Pet. 2: 2.
[4] 1 Cor. 3: 2.
[5] Heb. 5: 13, 14.
[6] Acts 20: 32.
[7] 1 Tim. 1: 4.
[8] Phil. 3: 12–14.

and the successes, which might spoil us, must alike be forgotten in the constant upward striving, single in aim, and with an athlete's dedication of brain and heart and energy, towards God's goal in Christ. The temper of the Christian life is not simply a standing firm in the state of grace into which we entered once for all at our conversion: it is *also* a movement, a steadily advancing trend, a constant progress towards a mark that seems ever to recede as we approach it.

(iii) *Steady and clear apprehension of the goal set before us* is the third significant feature in this process of Christian growth; to this we now turn.

III. THE GOAL OF SPIRITUAL DEVELOPMENT

It is probably true of many hindered, undeveloped Christian lives that much of the cause lies in the lack of any clear sense of direction, of aim, of target. Having found in Christ a seemingly inexhaustible treasure-house of spiritual life and joy, the young believer tends often to regard all his remaining task as the gradual working out of the implications of that experience, looking backward to conversion for all his inspiration, content to take each new situation as it comes and try to understand it in the light of his past discoveries. This is certainly not a wrong way of looking at the matter: but it does need to be supplemented by a forward-looking, expectant, upreaching habit of mind, which has seen a goal ahead, chosen a deliberate aim, and seeks to work to a foreseen end. The sense that we are getting somewhere day by day, or at least that there is somewhere we should be getting, is an important factor in Christian progress.

The passages we have already referred to leave no room for doubt as to what that ideal pattern and end of Christian development is meant to be. Paul pressed "toward the mark for the prize of the high calling of God *in Christ Jesus*",[1] and it makes little ultimate difference if we think of the "mark" as set up for our aim "in Christ Jesus", or of the "prize" as being "found in Christ" at the end, or of the "calling" as coming to us in Christ Jesus. All three interpretations are possible, but each implies at last that the aim and target of the Christian's striving is something which has been set before him in the person of his Master. The end-result,

[1] Phil. 3: 14.

so to speak, of spiritual development, is approximation to what we have seen and heard "in Christ".

So it is with the simple passage with which we began this chapter: "Grow in the grace and knowledge of our Lord and Saviour Jesus Christ."[1] Grace is both something we receive from God, a standing ground of privilege and acceptance ("we have access by faith into this grace wherein we stand"),[2] and a source of strength and comfort ("he giveth grace to the humble").[3] It is also a quality of character nourished in us by God's mercy towards us: generosity, for example ("see that ye abound in this grace also"),[4] or mildness ("let your speech be alway with grace . . .")[5] or whatever virtue in our lives is the fruit of our relationship with Christ. In both senses of the word, the Christian can "grow in grace"—into ever deeper realisation of his privileges in Christ, or into ever clearer reflection in his own character of the grace that has come to him in Christ. So with "knowledge of our Lord Jesus Christ", which could mean the knowledge he imparts, or the knowledge about him. It seems likeliest that we are called to grow in gracious character modelled upon Christ's, and in ever deeper understanding of himself in all his saving power: but the precise shade of meaning does not affect the main point, which here again is plain. The end set before us in all our growth as Christians, is increasing approximation, in grace and in knowledge, *unto Christ*.

Turning finally to the two central metaphors of edification and growth we find the same clear teaching on the aim that is to be held before us. Whether the reference be to the Church[6] or to the individual soul[7] the "building" which we raise is described in several passages as a "temple" or shrine, for the indwelling of God through the Spirit. "Ye also, as lively stones, are built up a spiritual house . . . Ye are God's building . . . Know ye not that ye are the temple of God, and that the Spirit of God dwelleth in you? . . . Ye are built upon the foundation of the apostles and prophets . . . all the building fitly framed together groweth unto an holy temple in the Lord: in whom ye also are builded together for an habitation of God through the Spirit."[8] Within the Church, as within the soul, the glory of the divine Majesty is to manifest itself, and God himself

[1] 2 Pet. 3: 18 R.V.
[2] Rom. 5: 2.
[3] 1 Pet. 5: 5.
[4] 2 Cor. 8: 7.
[5] Col. 4: 6.
[6] See, e.g., 1 Cor. 14: 12
[7] See, e.g., Rom. 14: 19
[8] 1 Pet. 2: 5; 1 Cor. 3: 9, 16; Eph. 2: 20-2.

is to dwell with men, and in men. Others shall see God, and make contact with him, as he makes his abode in the living temples of Christian lives—a breathtaking idea of edification which is very near to our main theme.

Moreover it is repeatedly said that the edifice we raise is based upon Christ himself. Speaking of God's "building", and of himself, Apollos and others as "builders together with God", Paul laid especial emphasis upon the necessity that the human builders do not depart from the original foundation already laid: "For other foundation can no man lay than that is laid, which is Jesus Christ."[1] We "are built upon the foundation of the apostles and prophets, Jesus Christ himself being the chief corner stone; *upon whom* all the building fitly framed together groweth . . ."[2] So Peter: "Wherefore also it is contained in scripture, Behold, I lay in Sion a chief corner stone, elect, precious: . . . the stone which the builders disallowed, the same is made the head of the corner."[3] Foundation-stone and corner-stone are alike in that each controls the design, proportions and situation of the whole edifice. To lay another foundation, Paul suggests, is to begin work upon an entirely new building upon a new design, not God's building at all. The phrase "fitly framed together" probably refers to the need that every part of the edifice shall be matched to its particular place, that the whole may be harmonious and united in plan and alignment, set squarely upon its appointed foundation, not rambling in haphazard fashion over the whole ground. Of course foundation-stone and corner-stone also give stability to the structure: but the main thought appears to be rather that of unity of design: and so once again, though from a rather less obvious point of view, we reach the truth that the whole pattern of Christian development is that revealed and pre-determined in Christ himself.

There remains the greatest New Testament passage on the growth of the Christian: ". . . the edifying of the body of Christ: Till we all come, in the unity of the faith, and of the knowledge of the Son of God, unto a perfect man, unto the measure of the stature of the fullness of Christ: that we be no more children . . . but speaking the truth in love, may grow up into him in all things, which is the head, even Christ . . ."[4] Here again the idea of growth applies both to the individual soul and to the Church as a whole, the Body of Christ. In contrast to spiritual childishness is set the goal of the

[1] 1 Cor. 3: 11. [2] Eph. 2: 20, 21. [3] 1 Pet. 2: 6, 7. [4] Eph. 4: 12–15.

E

"perfect man", the mature Christian, and this is explicitly defined, in contrast to the instability and lack of balance of the immature, as coming "unto the measure of the stature of the fullness of Christ", "growing up *into him*".

Each word here is significant. Christ's character is complete, balanced, rounded, mature, with all powers fully developed, and all qualities perfectly attuned, the whole personality integrated, harmonious, simple. We are to grow unto the completeness— *"fullness"*—of Christ; unto the height and breadth and strength of his example—*"the stature of the fullness of Christ"*; and unto the furthest reaches, down to details and out to the limits of his consistency—*"unto the measure of the stature of the fullness of Christ"*. This is spiritual maturity, to grow into all the measure of his mind, his heart, his will, his moral stature, his mental breadth, his spiritual wholeness, and into all the length and breadth and height and depth of his love. The goal of our growth is Christlikeness: we grow "unto him".

But, finally, concentration upon our own spiritual advancement may well become a form of selfishness. As we saw earlier, the corporate life and worship of the Church, and the claims of our brethren upon our example and encouragement are essential elements of spiritual progress. And here the point receives renewed importance. As it is only "with all the saints" that we can "comprehend the length, breadth, height and depth of the love of Christ"[1]—a significant point not to be lightly passed over—so it is only "in the unity of the faith and of the knowledge of the Son of God" that we can approach Christlikeness. The ideal is no exclusive and private one: *we need each other*. It is the divine purpose that *"all* come . . . unto a perfect man", not merely a chosen few; and to the total maturity of the whole fellowship every separate part of the Body has its own contribution to make. The whole body, exactly fitted and joined together, and made more compact by the muscles and ligaments of every joint, each member performing its due function effectively without interfering with the rest, grows in the growth of its several parts, and not otherwise, building itself up in the unity of Christian love. Clearly there can be no maturity in the Church while its separate members remain childish, but in the same way there can be no real maturity in the individual soul in isolation from the larger Christian fellowship in which Christ has set him. It is

[1] Eph. 3: 18.

important to remember this, lest the Christlike ideal become in our minds too self-centred and individualist: we never grow so well in spiritual life as when we are looking out from ourselves at the needs of other souls and seeking to assist their progress in the things of God.

CHAPTER 6

PROVIDENCE AND DISCIPLINE

IN ONE important respect what was said in the previous chapter about spiritual growth was seriously incomplete, for it looked only at the inward and conscious factors, the spiritual striving and desire, which make for progress. Yet growth is always "conditioned" from without as well as from within, and the outward circumstances have almost as decisive an influence upon the stature of the mature man as the inner aspiration and deliberate self-culture by which he "reaches forth unto those things which are before". Sometimes the outward circumstances in which the Christian life is set influence the soul's growth by direct contribution to its knowledge, strength, grace, enrichment; sometimes their influence is indirect, calling out its native resistance, courage, patience, endurance, and causing the soul to seek refuge and resources in ever closer reliance upon God. Either way, by acceptance or resistance, the Christian's environment plays an essential part in his whole development and maturing.

The Christian's environment comprises all kinds of facts and situations, his daily work, his home and family circle, his education or lack of it, his town or country background, his friends, teachers, neighbours and acquaintances, his books and hobbies, his wealth or poverty, his state of health, and any personal handicap or affliction, together with all that happens to him from without by "accident", inheritance, folly or design. And the shaping of that total life-situation to the needs of the developing spiritual life, and to the larger purposes to which it is consecrated, is the task of divine providence. Allowance must always be made for events and situations which are not God's will at all, but arise through our own foolishness, neglect or sin: for the rest, the New Testament leaves no doubt that God shapes the circumstances of our lives in accordance with his over-ruling purpose in our salvation, that we should be Christlike.

I. The Discipline of Sons

Almost inevitably, when the thought of God's providence is before us, attention fastens upon the unpleasant, the adverse, disappointing, opposing elements of experience, the slings and arrows of outrageous fortune, the sighs and sorrows that seem so hard to reconcile with the promises of God. It is a natural tendency, for the harder experiences are more deeply impressed, and their memory lasts longer: but the result is an unbalanced view, all the same. The happier things of life are equally God's providing, and we are unjust both to our own experience and to him when we speak as though only the disappointments were his appointments. Nevertheless it is the harder things that most obviously affect the shaping of character and the development of the soul, and here our central theme has something very practical and illuminating to say.

For one thing, it sets before the believer, unmistakably and realistically, the prospect of no easier or safer path than his Lord's. If so be that we suffer, we only suffer "with him";[1] "The disciple is not above his master, nor the servant above his lord. It is enough for the disciple that he be as his master, and the servant as his lord. If they have called the master of the house Beelzebub, how much more shall they call them of his household ?"[2] Luke added to this warning an unexpected touch: "The disciple is not above his master, but everyone that is perfect shall be as his master"[3]—as though to say, you cannot choose only certain parts of the lesson set you, evading the rest; to become proficient, like the Master, you must undergo the whole discipline. John connected the same saying of Jesus first to the example of Christ's humility.[4] He recalled it later in connection with the kind of treatment that the disciple may expect from the world: "Remember the word that I said unto you, The servant is not greater than his lord. If they have persecuted me, they will also persecute you; if they have kept my saying, they will keep yours also."[5]

This aspect of the Christian's total life-situation, his being set within a non-Christian society, is among the most important for

---

[1] Rom. 8: 17.
[2] Matt. 10: 24, 25.
[3] Luke 6: 40.
[4] John 13: 15, 16.
[5] John 15: 20.

its effects upon his development, for it determines at once his temptations, his special problems and tensions, his particular opportunities for witness and service of all kinds, and the costliness of his
loyalty. It is in respect of this need to confront the world's antagonism with courage and patience that Peter so often appeals to
the example of Christ, exactly as does John. "This is thankworthy,
if a man for conscience toward God endure grief, suffering wrongfully. For what glory is it, if, when ye be buffeted for your faults,
ye shall take it patiently? but if, when ye do well, and suffer for it,
ye take it patiently, this is acceptable with God. For even hereunto
were ye called: because Christ also suffered for us, leaving us an
example, that ye should follow his steps. . . . For it is better, if
the will of God be so, that ye suffer for well-doing, than for evil-
doing. For Christ also hath once suffered for sins . . . Forasmuch
then as Christ hath suffered for us in the flesh, arm yourselves likewise with the same mind . . . Beloved, think it not strange concerning the fiery trial which is to try you, as though some strange
thing happened unto you: But rejoice, inasmuch as ye are partakers of Christ's sufferings."[1] To one who was "a witness of the
sufferings of Christ"[2] it was a complete answer to all the doubts
and complainings of the persecuted soul that—so Christ suffered.
That sufficiently explains, and sufficiently inspires for further pain
and loss: we are content to be following his steps, passing through
Christlike suffering to Christlike victory.

What is said explicitly of the direct persecution or ill-use which the
Christian may receive from the world, is equally true of every
hardship, disappointment, conflict or duty, of all the toil, weariness,
loneliness, and pain which may contribute to the environment
in which the young Christian finds himself. "It is enough for the
servant that he be as his Master" is the watchword of his faith in
God's providence, and the underlying condition of all God's promises. Indeed the whole doctrine of a providential ordering of our
lives by divine and omnipotent love is only saved from shallow
optimism and complete unreality when the thought of Christlikeness is linked with it. We can expect no easier way than
Jesus trod: that is fundamental, and he never promised otherwise.

Nor could he promise otherwise. There is nothing arbitrary about

---

[1] 1 Pet. 2: 19–21; 3: 17–18; 4: 1, 12, 13.
[2] 1 Pet. 5: 1.

this similarity of experience between Christ and the Christian. *Such discipline is inseparable from sonship—his or ours.* This is the plain teaching of the epistle to the Hebrews. "Consider him that endured such contradiction of sinners against himself, lest ye be wearied and faint in your minds. Ye have not yet resisted unto blood, striving against sin. And ye have forgotten the exhortation which speaketh unto you as unto children, My son, despise not thou the chastening of the Lord, nor faint when thou art rebuked of him: for whom the Lord loveth he chasteneth, and scourgeth every son whom he receiveth. If ye endure chastening, God dealeth with you as with sons; for what son is he whom the father chasteneth not? But if ye be without chastisement, whereof all are partakers, then are ye bastards, and not sons."[1] The argument may sound strange to our modern ears, because of new theories of child-training, but the point is true and important. The undisciplined, untrained street-child of the ancient East was an unwanted, homeless, parentless waif: the lack of discipline proved the lack of love. True parental affection accepts responsibility for moral training of the young, and on this simple fact the writer bases his argument from the discipline the readers are undergoing to the Fatherly cherishing which it implies and proves. Moreover, the discipline of home is well-intentioned; "it yieldeth the peaceable fruit of righteousness unto them which are exercised thereby". Occasionally, with human parents it may be merely the relief of angry feelings[2] but it is never so with God, whose discipline only reveals his loving care and high intent for each growing child within his family.

We may therefore either accept the implications of a position in the Father's house, acknowledged as a son, subject as son to the rules of the household and the training of the family, or we may resent the discipline, evade the chastening, and renouncing our sonship return to the streets, rebellious and homeless, wild and unwanted. What we cannot do, the writer implies, is to claim the sonship and cry out against the chastening. Here again the suffering particularly in view arises from the Christian's situation in a non-Christian environment—the contradiction of sinners, and resistance unto blood; but the thought of chastening is wider, too, and includes "striving against sin", "rebuking" by the Lord, "scourging" and "correcting". All adversity, accepted humbly as the appointment

---

[1] Heb. 12: 3–8.
[2] Heb. 12: 10.

of a Father, has this educational value, and demonstrates the Father's care that his sons shall be worthy of his name.

It is not sufficient, however, to study this passage in isolation from the previous chapters of this great epistle, in which the thought is exceptionally close-knit and interwoven. Any harshness which may yet linger in our minds around the thought of sonship proved by chastening dissolves away when we recall that the writer has prepared for this exhortation by emphasising repeatedly that the discipline inseparable from our sonship was inseparable also from our Saviour's. "Though he were a Son, yet learned he obedience by the things which he suffered; . . . a son over his own house . . . Who in the days of his flesh, when he had offered up prayers and supplications with strong crying and tears unto him that was able to save him from death, and was heard in that he feared . . . being made perfect . . ."[1] Once more the image and example of Jesus is introduced to explain and lighten the experience of the Christian: through infirmity, temptation, prayers and tears, through suffering and obedience even his Sonship was proved and perfected—why not also ours? The writer hints as much even in the midst of his exhortation, for he declares that God chastens us "for our profit, that we might be partakers of his holiness".[2] The providence that shapes our experience and orders our affairs is neither blind, nor careless, nor undirected: it is the Father's training of his "many sons", through good and ill, to make them like his well-beloved, in whom his soul delighteth. And so once more a scriptural train of thought comes round by way of several passages to our central theme: divine providence is a process of discipline designed to make us Christlike.

II. THE KEY TO THE PROCESS

The classic expression of Christian faith in the providence of God is found, however, in familiar, and often too lightly quoted, words of Paul: "We know that all things work together for good to them that love God, to them who are the called according to his purpose".[3] The words are so very familiar, they slip through the mind so easily, that it is essential to try to see them in the setting of Paul's circumstances. This is no comfortable assurance bred of

[1] Heb. 3: 6; 5: 7–9. [2] Heb. 12: 10.
[3] Rom. 8: 28.

cushioned armchairs in a secure and cosy study, no exalted theory of providence spun out of pipe-dreams or debated in some secluded cloister. It is the deep and reasoned conviction of a man with both eyes open to the realities of life, a conviction hammered out, tested and proved in a long and arduous life in which Paul had travelled most of the known world, had suffered far more than most men, and had done battle daily with the sin and ignorance of humanity.

The saying occurs in a context of *thought* which is concerned with infirmities and groanings, tribulation, distress, persecution, famine, nakedness, peril and sword, things present and things to come, all the vicissitudes of life and all the darkness of death—it is with these things in his mind that Paul wrote "All things work together for good . . ." And when we set the saying in the wider context of Paul's experience we remember that he had been treated with suspicion by men to whom he looked for loyalty, he had been let down by unworthy colleagues, he had tasted poverty and hard manual toil, he had seen all the greater towns and cities of the Roman Empire and been roughly handled in most, he had been beaten, plotted against, stoned, shipwrecked, he had fought with affliction throughout a most active career, he had been wrongfully arrested, unfairly imprisoned, unjustly tried, and ever over his life hung the threat of martyrdom—and this is the man who can write deliberately and with full honesty "We know that all things work together for good . . ."

Whatever we do with this saying, therefore, we cannot just dismiss it as the airy optimism of a man for whom life had been easy, or the untested opinion of a man of shallow mind and narrow experience. It is a triumphant declaration of faith, forged in fire, and it demands earnest and careful examination. Especially, perhaps, is it necessary to observe exactly what the Apostle does, and does not, say.

First, that "All things work . . ."—all things have a purpose, and an effect; nothing is futile, nothing accidental, nothing meaningless. This we might call the psychological truth in this great faith: every act a man does, every thought he thinks, every experience he undergoes is registered somewhere in the recesses of his personality. We are "never the same" after any experience—our tears and our laughter, our disappointments and delights, our moods, our holidays, our failures and our omissions, all have gone to make us what we are. Nothing is lost. The dreadful fear that some dark experience is just pointless need not haunt our mind—all things work; we are part of all that we have met, and all that we have met becomes a part of us.

Secondly, Paul says that "All things work together . . ." This we might call the philosophical truth in this great saying. To see life steadily and see it whole brings deeper insight. As it takes the sun and rain, the storm and calm, the heat and cold *together* to give an oak its strength; as it needs the different instruments in an orchestra, the different voices in a choir, the different values in a picture, *together*, to hold the secret of beauty, so with the strong and beautiful soul: joy and sorrow, pain and gladness, success and failure, the things we understand and the things we cannot understand, *together* make faith strong and the soul sweet. Taken to pieces the kaleidoscope of experience may appear but bits of broken glass and tinsel, tawdry and useless, but looked at together, as shot through with the light of a unifying divine purpose, the fragments take on balance and beauty and pattern. It is hard to remember, in the midst of some severe grief, that today's tears balance yesterday's rapture; to recall that success would not thrill so much if we had never tasted failure; to believe that even the high hours of spiritual ecstasy could not by themselves make us saints without the other hours of discipline, duty and darkness in which we learn to trust. But it is true: all things work *together*.

Then, thirdly, Paul adds to the psychological and the philosophic insights the specific note of religious faith: "All things work together *for good* . . .". To understand both the assertion itself, and the limitation "to them that love God", it is essential to give full weight to that statement of God's controlling purpose. Faith in divine providence becomes confused, even disillusioned, because we imagine that God has somewhere promised to make all things work together for our happiness, our ease, the success of our plans, the fulfilment of our dreams. That is not, at any rate, the meaning of this verse. Paul explicitly defines the end to be achieved as "goodness". God's great goal, in all that he permits, appoints, sends or asks of us, is our progress in spiritual life, the promotion in us of "goodness".

But that abstract word is not thus left vague and colourless. The *kind*, and the *quality*, and the *measure* of the goodness God seeks to promote in us are plainly indicated: we are to be "conformed to the image of his Son, that he might be the firstborn among many brethren". This is the "purpose" according to which he has called us; this is the destiny he has marked out for those whom he foreknew would respond to the call.[1]

Hence the limitation of the promise "to those who love God". At first sight this suggests a divine favouritism alien to the universal Gospel. But upon reflection it becomes plain that "all things" do not by any means "work together" to promote goodness in every case. The same experience which will embitter, harden, warp and spoil one soul will sweeten and refine another. Those who love God, those who surrender to his will and lie unresisting in his hands, find this promise true. They accept God's purpose as their purpose, his aim as their aim; they cheerfully consent to his dispensation of things, they trust in his wisdom, lean upon his grace, find comfort in his love; and to these the deepest sorrow only brings a new and clearer insight, the sharpest pain brings new patience and quiet strength, the greatest disappointments bring only fortitude and courage. The more heavily the cross bears upon them, the more Christlike they become. The limits of the great promise are fixed, not by any niggardliness in God's love for his children, but by the nature of our response to the experience life brings. To those who love God all things work together for good *because* they love God, and so loving, surrender to all God's purposes in their lives.

It must be confessed that such a doctrine of divine providence is somewhat more cautious, more ethical, more searching than the rather easy-going assurance that everything will come right in the end, which is sometimes presented as Christian faith. For those who consent, in trustful love, God undertakes to make all things work together towards making them like Christ. That is a faith which may be held intelligently, soberly, and with exceeding comfort, even in the midst of pain and loss and persecution. It is the faith that has inspired heroic courage, nourished unflinching tenacity, and sustained the hearts of generations of afflicted saints. It is a faith which maketh not ashamed.

The key, then, to the pattern of divine providence, and the clue to God's discipline of his sons, are the same: he aims to make us Christlike. With that before our minds we shall not fretfully compare our lives with others', nor complain at the way he leads us. We shall accept with good heart whatever he appoints, content to let him lead us towards the goal for which he called and predestined

[1] Rom. 8: 28, 29.

us. "He doeth all things well", he leads us by true paths, he knoweth the way that we take, and he himself has set the goal. We can trust him utterly to match the discipline of outward experience to the aspiration of inward striving, and so set us forward, ever forward, on the road that leads us to his likeness.

Chapter 7

THE MIND OF CHRIST

IT MUST not be assumed that inward growth and outward discipline comprise the whole process of Christlike development in the Christian soul. God's relation to his children is essentially personal, and between him and us nothing ever happens in a mechanical way or by merely external influence. The response of faith and surrender is indispensable, not only at the beginning of the Christian life but throughout its progress. And in view of the goal towards which our growth and discipline move, this response of faith and surrender must take the form of a conscious and deliberate approximation to the pattern of Christ in all that area of life which is subject to conscious control and deliberate choice.

This approximation to Christ's pattern brings us back of course to the thought of Christ's example, and to the very important practical question of what exactly that example means for everyday life. Our earliest thought is usually that it means doing what Jesus did, and we have seen that this is close to the mediaeval idea of the imitation of Christ, which found expression in vows of chastity, humility, poverty and pain by which Christians sought to reproduce in themselves the outward semblance of Christ's life. The intention is irreproachable, but for practical guidance the rule is far from sufficient and even misleading. Consistently carried out it would forbid all secular work after thirty years of age, all domestic joys and responsibilities, all concern directly with social evils and national or international affairs, all recreation, art and science, and so on. It would isolate the Christian completely from the world's thought and life, abandoning the teeming life of mankind to wholly unchristian forces; it would justify strong denunciations and huge claims to divine authority, and a wooing of martyrdom even when unnecessary. Unfortunately such consequences are not unknown, but the results do not commend themselves to the general Christian conscience. Rather they reveal the underlying mistake: we are not able to stand in Christ's shoes; our time, our circumstances, our

77

responsibilities are all different, and only with the greatest reservations, adjustments and exceptions can we think of doing what he
did who was the unique divine Redeemer, the Lord and Saviour of
the world.

The second interpretation of Christ's example which usually
appeals to thoughtful young believers is that of "doing what Jesus
would do in my place". A splendid rule it is, often sufficient, always
inspiring. It brings Christ and his standards right into daily life,
and makes his Lordship a real and effective factor in spiritual experience. To consider every new decision, and review every established habit, in the light of "What would Jesus do?" does give a new
dimension to Christian character and discipleship. Unfortunately
the answer is not always clear, and sometimes we catch ourselves
ascribing to Jesus the mere projection of our own wishes and opinion.
In time we realise that the rule rests mainly upon imagination, and
it is often exceedingly difficult to imagine Jesus—whom we know as
a Jew of the first century, living in an Eastern province of a totali-
tarian Empire, with a unique world mission and a unique relation
to God—transported as it were two thousand years in time into the
western world of today, into our democratic situation (with all its
new rights and corresponding responsibilities), and doing our job,
living in our home, standing in our shoes. Maturing reflection
finds itself again having to make so many reservations and exceptions
that the rule of "doing what Jesus would do" begins to break down
and we seek a third interpretation of Christ's example.

We cannot do better than adopt that which the New Testament
itself suggests in the profound and penetrating phrase—"having the
mind of Christ". Understood in the New Testament way this
principle relieves us both from the externalism of trying to model our
life on the outward features of Christ's, and from the effort of
imagination that seeks to transport Christ into our situation. Instead it bids us learn to think as he thought, to feel as he felt, to
love what he loved, to seek what he sought, to catch his spirit and
cultivate his qualities—to be Christlike at the heart of us—and then
to bring that Christlike mind and heart to bear on our very different
circumstances and in our vastly different time. It bids us be ourselves, naturally and spontaneously living in the contemporary scene
—but the "selves" we are being will not be those we drifted into or
inherited, but those Christ has refashioned after his own image
and in his likeness.

This is the essence of Christlikeness—"having the mind of Christ". It may sometimes mean in practice that we do not do anything like the things Jesus did. We may enter into relationships (such as marriage) which he did not share, and perhaps undertake things we cannot imagine he would do: but we shall in fact be nearer his likeness and closer to his example than in any other way. And the example of Christ will mean something perhaps deeper and more searching than we have ever thought. In this respect the mediaeval classic of the spiritual life, Thomas à Kempis' *Imitation of Christ*, is much nearer the truth of its subject than might appear. If from its title we expect a study of the example of Jesus we are disappointed: what à Kempis seeks to do is to reproduce in his reader the inner thought and feeling and attitudes of Jesus, leaving the expression of this refashioned inner life to the individual conscience within its own situation. This, we shall try to show, is very close indeed to the New Testament idea of possessing the mind of Christ.

It must be admitted frankly at the outset that this interpretation of the Christlike life will appear vague, indefinite and elastic beside some other methods of directing Christian behaviour. A set of well-defined rules or commandments is in the end a much more comfortable guide; for the requirements are then precise, the demands usually negative, and the limits of obedience are fixed. The difficulty is that no table of commandments, no Christian casuistry, no infallible decisions of the Church, no system of Christian ethics, can be framed which will apply to all the infinitely varied circumstances of different lives. Nor has the imposition of rules from without, by some authority before which the will must bow, ever succeeded in making sinners into saints, or saintliness very attractive.

In any case, the inescapable fact is that the Master left us no such code of directions for making people good by rule. A spirit, an attitude, an outlook, a set of judgements, a scale of valuations, a group of ruling ideas—these are clear and distinctive, though never rigidly defined, and in them the Christian conscience finds its controlling principles *and its freedom*.

Moreover, the guidance offered by this interpretation of the example of Jesus is more definite than might be thought. The New Testament passages concerned fall into two groups according as they relate to mainly intellectual or mainly moral questions. Having the mind of Christ has reference both to the Christian's understanding and to the Christian's qualities of character—though it must be clearly borne in mind that the line of distinction is often very faint and sometimes disappears entirely.

I. THE MIND OF CHRIST IN UNDERSTANDING

Many keen and devout Christian people, even when they are enthusiastic students of Scripture, do not always appreciate the large place which is given to the mind and understanding in New Testament Christianity. Some indeed maintain towards "intellectualism" and "head-knowledge" a wary suspicion which though well-intentioned is often very shallow and dangerous. So deeply devotional a letter as that to the Ephesians is constantly occupied with the Christian's mind—the wicked are vain in mind, darkened in understanding, alienated from the life of God through the ignorance that is in them, doing the desires of the flesh and of the mind. But Christ's grace has abounded towards us in all wisdom and prudence, having made known to us the mystery of his will, long hid but now revealed, and we have been renewed in the spirit of our mind, have "learned Christ", been taught in him, as truth is in Jesus.

Thus the apostle's prayer for us is that God would give a spirit of wisdom and revelation in the knowledge of him, the eyes of our understanding being enlightened, that we may know . . . that we may be strong to apprehend . . . and to know the love of Christ which passes knowledge. It is this revelation of the mystery which has given Paul his understanding, and his commission to make all men see. It is the aim of Christian ministry that all shall come in unity of faith and knowledge unto a perfect man, not tossed about with every wind of doctrine, nor deceived with empty words, and that all shall walk not as unwise but as wise, not as foolish but understanding what the will of the Lord is. Finally the Christian's armour includes a helmet of salvation to protect the Christian's head, and, the only offensive weapon in the list, the sword of the Spirit which is the Word of God. This is an impressive array of references to the place which wisdom, understanding, right-thinking, occupies in Christian life, especially from so short an epistle.

But it is not only in Ephesians that this emphasis occurs: in the sister-epistle to the Colossians the wicked are enemies and alienated from God *in mind*. Paul's prayer is that his readers will be filled with the knowledge of God's will in all wisdom and spiritual understanding, and his task is to teach and admonish every man in all wisdom. He desires for all the full assurance of understanding, that they may know the mystery of God, even Christ, in whom are hid all the treasures of wisdom and knowledge. He warns again about being misled by persuasiveness of speech, mere philosophy and vain deceit, urging that they be established, rooted and built up in the faith; he calls them to set their mind on things above, to let the word of Christ dwell in them richly in all wisdom, and to walk in wisdom towards them that are without.

In Romans[1] we are bidden not to be conformed to this world but to be transformed by the renewing of our mind, and in Corinthians, as we shall see, the spiritual wisdom spoken among the spiritually mature and conferred by Christ, who is made unto us wisdom, is set against the empty, foolish "wisdom" of this world. John's view of Christianity revolves mainly round the Truth in Christ; Peter too describes the unregenerate state as one of "former ignorance" and the process of conversion as purifying the soul by obedience to the truth.[2] James discourses on the Christian wisdom to the same effect.[3]

This somewhat tedious recital of texts is worthwhile if it helps to emphasise the important place given in the New Testament to the Christian's thinking. While it is not hard to understand the fear of over-intellectualism, and the distrust of merely theoretical interest in Christ, there can be little doubt that much modern evangelical Christianity would be immeasurably deepened if this scriptural emphasis were restored. And it is after all in close accord with the place of repentance—*"rethinking"*—in the evangel, and with the original description of Christians as "disciples"—*scholars* in the school of Christ.

The reorientation of the mental life, the new impulse, direction and illumination given to everyday thinking, is then an essential part of salvation. But nothing so far noted has indicated clearly the precise direction of that changed mind which Jesus effects in his followers. Doubtless the general meaning is clear enough: Christ is Teacher, and his word of truth becomes the law of Christian

---

[1] Rom. 12: 2.
[2] John 1: 14; 14: 6; 1 John 1: 5, 8; 2: 21, 27; 3: 19; 5: 20; 1 Pet. 1: 13, 14, 22; 4: 1.
[3] Jas. 3: 13f.

F

thinking, "bringing every thought into captivity to Christ".[1] At first the Truth is received, believed, as something addressed to us, as it were from outside ourselves; then it becomes a law or principle of conduct over us—we love the truth, speak the truth, do the truth, are girt about with truth; finally it becomes a part of us, abiding in us, possessing and refining our nature, and we are said to be "of the truth".[2] Nevertheless this is still somewhat general and undefined. When we seek more precise description of the transformation which comes to the growing Christian's mind, we run against this challenging, provocative phrase "we have the mind of Christ".[3]

This expression, we must remember, is used only once in the New Testament in this connection, but the situation which evoked it lends added importance to that single occurrence. There were at Corinth those who boasted a superior wisdom; with typically Greek love of theoretical discussion, they believed that the simple evangel of the Church—"the preaching of the cross"—was but the ABC of spiritual wisdom, and that this must be left behind by those who were capable of passing on to the mature, perfect wisdom which could read the "deep things of God". An intellectualist division was thus added to the other causes of disunity in the Corinthian Church, and an intellectual pride to its numerous shortcomings. Paul's reply to this claim was, first, to distinguish sharply between the wisdom of God and the wisdom of this world—by which men had failed to know God, which counted the preaching of the cross foolishness, which formed no sure basis for Christian faith, and which was incapable of apprehending spiritual realities.[4]

Secondly, Paul claimed that the Christian message, founded upon the cross and illumined by the continual teaching of the Spirit, is itself the highest divine wisdom, hidden from the wise of this world but revealed unto the spiritual man.[5] To possess this spiritual wisdom is to have "the mind of Christ".[6] The importance of this contrast between the Christian's thought and outlook and the wisest in paganism is obvious, and the distinctive mark of the Christian

---

[1] 2 Cor. 10: 5.
[2] 1 Pet. 1: 22; 2 Thess. 2: 13; Rom. 2: 8; 2 Thess. 2: 10; Eph. 4: 15; 1 John 1: 6; Eph. 6: 14; 1 John 1: 8; 2: 4; 3: 19; 2 John 1: 2.
[3] 1 Cor. 2: 16.
[4] 1 Cor. 1: 10—2: 16, especially 1: 23 ,21; 2: 5; 2: 13, 14.
[5] 1 Cor. 2: 6–15.
[6] 1 Cor. 2: 16.

mind is that its "thoughts are the thoughts of Christ" (Moffatt). So once again we are faced with the focal conception of so much New Testament teaching: the distinguishing feature of the Christian's mind in contrast with the world's thinking is that his has been reconstituted, disciplined, taught, illuminated after the pattern of Christ's own thinking till it may be called "the mind of Christ".

The matter was not one of merely intellectual or speculative importance, however; the Corinthian Church was exercised about certain very practical and everyday problems, concerning which the existence of a small group claiming superior insight and loftier principles made for serious disagreement and discord. Some of these problems had been posed to the apostle by letter and by messenger,[1] and in the first epistle to the Corinthians we are privileged to see Paul applying this spiritual wisdom—the mind of Christ—to these immediate questions of faith and conduct. The method of reply is of paramount importance for understanding what Paul meant by "having the mind of Christ". In dealing with successive questions the apostle appealed to the common tradition of the life and sayings of Jesus[2] for his supreme "directives"; he appealed also to the Old Testament Scriptures for confirmation of his opinion.[3] He argued, reasoned and exhorted, clearly assuming that the Christian outlook and attitude will commend itself to a reasonable mind and alert conscience. And over all he exercised his own experienced judgement, very clearly distinguishing his own opinion from the authoritative word of the Master,[4] but convinced that he too (no less than the wiseacres of Corinth !) had the Spirit of God to aid him.

What better illustration could one wish of the meaning of "having the mind of Christ" ? The exercise of spiritual judgement, informed and controlled wherever possible by the actual words and deeds of Jesus, resting upon scriptural insights, appealing to reason and the believers' innate sense of right, and directed and illumined at every point by the Spirit of Christ—this is the mind of Christ as it relates to understanding.

Beside this story from Corinth we may usefully place two from the Acts of the Apostles. Facing the problem of the admission of the Gentiles to the Church, a Church Council in Acts 15, after consultation about the facts, prayer, quotation of scriptural directives and reflection upon the Gospel, issued its conclusion with the words—

[1] 1 Cor. 7: 1; 1: 11.
[2] 1 Cor. 7: 10; 11: 23; 15: 3.
[3] e.g. 1 Cor. 2: 16; 14: 21 etc.
[4] 1 Cor. 7: 12, 25, 26, 40.

"It seemed good to the Holy Ghost and to us . . ." When Paul and Silas faced, repeatedly, closed doors and frustrated plans, "the Spirit of Jesus suffering them not"[1] to follow their expected programme, a combination of circumstances, a vision, and inward compulsion made them "assuredly gather" that God had called them to go forward into Europe.

In practice, therefore, the early disciples reached their great decisions in the light of existing circumstances but under the compulsion and illumination of the words and Spirit of Jesus. They exercised their own judgement, thoroughly informed about the thought and actions of Jesus, utterly submissive to his authority, open to the direct leading of his Spirit, and making appeal constantly to the general Christian mind and conscience. If the phrase is used therefore (in this connection) only once, we may yet claim that "having the mind of Christ" is an idea reflected in many parts of the New Testament, and that it summarises a whole process of mental and spiritual discipline by which all that is known of Christ is brought to bear upon new problems as they arise, with reverence and freedom, and in the assurance that the Master will make his truth plain and his will known to those who truly seek.

II. The Mind of Christ in Character

We have already urged that the distinction between Christian understanding and Christian character must not be too sharply drawn, for spiritual insight is as much a matter of virtue as of thought, and in Christian terms, "to see" is often an attribute of the heart. Yet it is convenient to consider separately, and from an ethical rather than intellectual point of view, two other passages in which the Christian's "mind" is the subject of discussion.

In his letter to the Romans Paul drew upon his own Judaist experience to illustrate with unanswerable clarity the outstanding weakness of the Jewish law as a way of salvation—its complete inability to deal with the inner self, its desires, thoughts, lusts and covetousness. The intense conflict created by the clash of outward rules of discipline with inward fires of passion and desire is nowhere more acutely analysed or more vividly described than in Romans 7, and when Paul passed on to describe the superiority of the rule of the Spirit in the life of the Christian man, it was to this same problem

[1] Acts 16: 7.

of the inner life that he first addressed himself. The condemnation of the law is done away in the sacrifice of Christ for our sin:[1] the guilty soul is declared righteous, acquitted and released. But by that same faith which unites us to a dying and risen Saviour we ourselves are committed to die and rise, together with him, towards all that is sinful, carnal and alien to God.[2]

This being accomplished through our faith-union with Christ, the law itself is seen to be fully fulfilled in us, for the old desires are dead with Christ and we "mind" no longer the things of the flesh but the things of the spirit. "Minding"—that is "directing the spiritual faculties of attention, affection and activity towards"— the things of the flesh brings death, as the result of the conflict and self-disintegration it occasions; but "minding" the things of the spirit brings life and peace.[3] This new attitude of mind is the fruit of the rule of the Spirit of life in Christ Jesus. It is the result of the Spirit of Jesus dwelling in us; and that same Spirit, Christ's "other self",[4] becomes the Guide and "thought-controller" of the Christian man—else we are none of his.[5]

In all this profound analysis of the experience of salvation it is plain Paul gave prominence to the new total attitude of the Christian's "mind", including his conscience and will, towards the things of the flesh and of the spirit. This new attitude he ascribed, firstly, to the "recapitulation" by the believer of Christ's own dying to sin and rising again, so reproducing the mind of Christ towards sin and towards God;[6] and, secondly, to the Spirit of Jesus at work in the believing soul.[7] It is needless to point out again how near the thought keeps all the time to the basic New Testament idea of Christlikeness.

Turning finally to an easier, but sublime, passage in Philippians[8] we find Paul using this phrase "the mind of Christ" in closest connection with the story of Bethlehem, and the great doctrine of the incarnation. As so often with Paul, a profound declaration of Christian truth arises from a comparatively trivial cause. A tendency towards quarrelsomeness, personal rivalry, odious comparisons, in the Church at Philippi made Paul appeal for the cultivation

[1] Rom. 8: 1f.
[2] Rom. 6: 1f; Eph. 2: 1f; Col. 3: 1f; see above, chapter 4.
[3] Rom. 8: 6.
[4] John 14: 17, 23, 25; 16: 13, 14.
[5] Rom. 8: 2, 5, 9–11, 14.
[6] Rom. 6.
[7] Rom. 8.
[8] Phil. 2: 1–11.

in their fellowship of that spirit which will make such collisions and incompatibilities impossible. He would have them of the same love, accord and outlook, doing nothing from selfishness or conceit, but in lowliness of mind each counting the other as better than himself, and looking not merely to his own interests, but to the interests of others.[1] And this appeal he grounded upon the high example of Jesus as revealed, not as we might expect in the lowly service of his ministry to others, but in the divine condescension which brought him from the glory to the cross, step by step emptying himself of his grandeur, his just claims and rightful glory, and stooping to become man, and as man to become obedient even unto death. "Have this mind in you, which was also in Christ Jesus: who, being originally in the form of God, counted it not a thing to be grasped at to be on an equality with God, but emptied himself, taking the form of a bondservant, being made in the likeness of men; and being found in fashion as a man, he humbled himself, becoming obedient even unto death, yea the death of the cross . . ."[2] Little indeed can be added to such a passage: its meaning is clear, its bearing upon our theme obvious. "Having the mind of Christ" includes the cultivation of that disposition, those qualities, attitudes and selfless impulses which we adore in him and to which we owe our whole salvation.

In answer to those who ask for something more definite and detailed for daily guidance than "a set of judgements, valuations, thoughts, and dispositions, attitudes and impulses"—even when deliberately modelled on the life of Jesus—we noted earlier that, except in the most obvious matters of conduct, detailed rules of universal application are impossible. We may now add one further consideration, very relevant to our whole theme. It is one of the novel and characteristic insights of Christianity that motive, and intention, are of the essence of any act; and the disposition, the general trend of intentions, are of the essence of character. Our Lord's criticism of the Pharisees lay especially here, for while they valued highly the overt acts of prayer, almsgiving, fasting and the like, he saw beneath the act the unworthy motive, the contrary disposition, and held the act to be thereby devalued.[3] In the same way Jesus criticised the traditional law for the externalism which concerned itself only with deeds—of adultery, murder, revenge—

[1] Phil. 2: 2–4 R.S.V.
[2] Phil. 2: 5–8 R.V. and margin.
[3] Matt. 6: 1–18.

and ignored the moral quality of lust, contempt, anger, and hatred.[1]

These are typical examples of an approach to moral questions which is entirely characteristic of the New Testament, and the need for this emphasis is not wholly past. It is because it sees so deeply into the heart of man behind the façade of respectable, and even admirable, deeds, that the Christian faith asserts the need for regeneration and thorough renewal before man's salvation can be complete. In claiming therefore that the essence of following Christ's example lies in the possession of the mind of Jesus, intellectually and morally, we are in complete harmony with the underlying assumption of the Gospel that the quality of the isolated deed is less important than the quality of the mind and heart from which it sprang.

We will not delay here to consider how the cultivation of the mind of Christ is to be pursued. That must occupy our final chapters, and should wait upon our next two studies where the human effort is set against the background (without which we should soon be discouraged) of the work in us of the Holy Spirit, and the sure promise of God that the high goal shall certainly be reached. Here it must suffice to say that no-one can hope to possess the mind of Christ with reference to understanding and spiritual wisdom who has not pondered, long and intimately, the Master's portrait in the four Gospels, memorising his words, vividly picturing each deed, prayerfully and with intelligent care seeking the abiding truth in each situation and saying. And no-one can hope to possess the mind of Christ with reference to his dispositions, attitudes and qualities of character, who has not in addition dwelt long and intimately in his presence. There the portrait "comes alive", the truth is drawn out in living characters, and the soul refashioned. But that brings us to the threshold of our next subject: the image of Christ and the experience of the Holy Spirit.

[1] Matt. 5: 21.

Chapter 8

THE SPIRIT OF CHRIST

I T COULD hardly be expected that the process by which the Christian believer is transformed into the image of his Master could be a simple or one-sided matter. Just as the inward development of the new life by its own natural growth is assisted by the outward discipline of God's providence in the circumstances of life, so also the conscious and deliberate cultivation of the mind of Jesus is assisted by the personal ministry of the Spirit of Jesus in the believer's heart. Thus the inward and the outward life, the endeavour of the soul itself and the action of the Spirit upon him, all are shaped to one aim. It is especially necessary to emphasise the place of the Holy Spirit in the process, not only by way of encouragement, but in order to correct any impression that Christ-likeness is just a backward-looking conformity to a distant memory: it is very much more than that—it involves the *reincarnation* of the very Spirit of Jesus in each surrendered soul.

I. THE SPIRIT AND CHRIST

Most truths of Scripture reach their final meaning only as they find their focus and fulfilment in Christ. This is especially true of the doctrine of the Spirit. In the earliest days the Spirit was believed to confer superhuman gifts, powers and experiences upon certain individuals, for a brief time, for a limited purpose, with little regard to the character of the recipient, and with sometimes strange results. The special skill, wisdom, courage or strength of artists, craftsmen, poets, soldiers or even local prodigies like Samson, are so explained.[1] Neither Samson nor Saul seem to be in any condition of character to receive special favours from God, while the results—Samson became especially violent, Saul danced naked on the hillside—are to say the least not the highest ways in which the Spirit's presence may be shown.

[1] Exod. 31: 3; Num. 24: 2; 27: 18; 11: 26; Judges 13: 25; 14: 6, 19; 15: 14; 1 Sam. 10: 10–12; 19: 23–4.

Under the teaching of the great prophets the emphasis changed. The Spirit was shown coming upon men chosen of God for a life-work, and he was pre-eminently the Spirit of wisdom, of truth, of prophecy, the source of revelation, the giver of visions, the interpreter of events and even of dreams, the One through whom the word of God comes to God's spokesmen. The man in whom God's Spirit is, is in God's counsel; he knows God's secrets and speaks God's truth.[1] At the same time some response on the part of the man possessed by God's Spirit becomes necessary—some qualification of insight, of consecration, faithfulness and moral courage, for the prophet must be in harmony with the message, so far as possible.

Still more significant for our theme, however, is the way in which the prophets related the Spirit of God to the person of the Messiah: it was the anointing of the Spirit which equipped the Messiah, and the outpouring of the Spirit which marked the Messiah's reign. Thus Isaiah promises that the Spirit of the Lord shall be upon Messiah, the Spirit of wisdom and understanding, the Spirit of counsel and might, the Spirit of knowledge and of the fear of the Lord—all the equipment required to *rule*; and the Spirit shall anoint him to bring good tidings to the afflicted, bind up the broken-hearted, proclaim liberty to the captives, the opening of the prison to them that are bound—all the equipment required to *save*.[2] Messiah shall be endowed with the Spirit without measure, and his character will be the perfect vehicle for the Spirit's unhindered activity—he shall not strive nor cry, meekness and gentleness shall mark his method, righteousness and truth shall be his girdle, peace and salvation his aim.

It follows that the Messianic age will be the age of the Spirit, when God will remove the stony heart of his people, and give them a new heart and a new spirit—"I will put my Spirit within you";[3] when not only the prophets specially chosen shall know God but all shall know him by direct inspiration;[4] when "I will pour out of my Spirit upon all flesh; your sons and your daughters shall prophesy, your old men shall dream dreams and your young men shall see visions. Even upon the menservants and the maidservants

[1] Jer. 23: 21–2, and throughout prophets.
[2] Isa. 11: 1–3; 61: 1–4; Matt. 1: 20; Luke 1: 35; Matt. 3: 16; Luke 3: 22.
[3] Ezek. 36: 25–8.
[4] Jer. 31: 34; Isa. 11: 9; 59: 21.

in those days I will pour out my Spirit" saith the Lord.[1] A correspondence between the Spirit-endowed Messiah and the Spirit-indwelt
people is plainly foreseen: in this respect already the Messianic
community is to be like its glorious King.

When in New Testament teaching the truth of the Holy Spirit
comes into clearer light, it is this association of the Spirit with the
Christ that is the controlling thought. "The Spirit of God" becomes
almost as often "the Spirit of Christ"; we read that "the Spirit of
Jesus suffered them not"; "God hath sent forth the Spirit of his
Son into our hearts"; "if any man have not the Spirit of Christ he
is none of his"; and in a passage where the Lord Christ has been
the centre of thought Paul suddenly closed with the pregnant remark
" Now the Lord is the Spirit, and where the Spirit of the Lord is,
there is liberty".[2] To the same Church, too, Paul spoke of the exercise
of spiritual judgement, in one passage as "having the mind of Christ",
in another as "possessing the Spirit".[3] Christ dwells in our hearts
by faith, Christ in us is the hope of glory, we are the temples, and
the body, in which Christ dwells: but this is by his Spirit, we are
temples of the Holy Ghost, God's Spirit is in the inner man, and
the Spirit of God dwells in us. When Luke opened the Acts of the
Apostles with the statement that his former book (the Gospel of
Luke) related all that Jesus *began* both to do and teach before he
was taken up, and then proceeded to record what Jesus continued
to do and teach through the Spirit given at Pentecost, he too was
clearly thinking of the Holy Spirit in terms of the continuing presence
and power of Jesus, risen and glorified.

It is, however, in John's Gospel that this link of the Spirit of
God with the person of Jesus is fully declared. There Jesus speaks
of the coming of *another* Comforter, to *replace himself*, so that at
his going to the Father the disciples shall not be left comfortless.
The promised Spirit of truth shall not speak of himself, but shall
take of the things of Christ and show them unto us. Clearer still
are the surprising words: "the world cannot receive him, for it
does not know him. But *ye know him*, for he *dwelleth with you*,
and shall be *in* you . . . I will not leave you comfortless, *I* will
come to you . . . at that day ye shall know that I am in my Father,
and ye in me, and I in you; we will come to him and make our abode

---

[1] Joel 2: 28–9.
[2] Acts 16: 7 R.V.; Gal. 4: 6; Rom. 8: 9, 14; 2 Cor. 3: 17.
[3] 1 Cor. 2: 16; 7: 40.

with him, . . . these things have I spoken unto you being yet present with you, but the Comforter, which is the Holy Ghost, whom the Father shall send in my name, he shall teach you all things . . . I tell you the truth, it is expedient for you that I go away, for if I go not away the Comforter will not come unto you, but if I go I will send him unto you." In all these sayings the Spirit is One who comes in Christ's place, to fulfil Christ's ministry in the disciples; he is Christ's "Other Self", and in his coming we have Christ with us still.

It is tempting to say that the Holy Spirit *is* the risen and glorified Lord still present with his Church, but we must remember that the New Testament speaks of *both*, not of one; and that we know of Christ and of the Holy Spirit more or less independently (in theory, at any rate) and only later combine the ideas. But with this theologising we are not here concerned: what is important is that we shall always think of the Holy Spirit, as the New Testament does, in terms of Christ. One consequence of this will be that the Spirit will ever be thought of as a Person, never as a mere supernatural power or divine influence coming upon us we know not how or why; and our relationship to him will always in the same way be thought of as a personal relationship of faith, desire, obedience and surrender, and never as something mechanical, magical, or crudely sacramental. A second consequence of thinking of the Holy Spirit always in terms of Christ will be that we shall realise more than ever that he is the Holy Spirit, whose first and highest purpose is to make those in whom he dwells *holy*—after the likeness of Christ himself.

II. THE SPIRIT AND CHRISTLIKENESS

One interesting feature of the New Testament's thought of the Holy Spirit and the risen Lord is that on the one hand everything in the Christian's life is ascribed to Christ himself—the Christian life consists of the apprehension of Christ, the identification with Christ, approximation to Christ, and expectation of Christ, all sustained and experienced "in Christ". Yet on the other hand it is equally possible to show that everything in the Christian life, from the first "conviction" to the final glory, is "of the Spirit". It is illuminating, and very humbling, to gather together the many references to the Spirit in the life of the believer, and realise how truly "every virtue we possess and every conflict won, and every thought of holiness are his alone". The Christian is born of the Spirit, has access to God through the Spirit, worships, is led, taught, comforted, sanctified, delivered, made free, quickened, intoxicated, sealed, sustained, empowered and glorified by the Spirit. But among the many ministries of the Spirit to the Christian believer the one which comes to have outstanding importance in the mind of the apostles is his progressive endowment of the Christian with all the beauty and grace of Christ himself. We are even able to watch the steps by which this emphasis emerged in New Testament thinking.

Just as in the Old Testament the Spirit was first thought of as the source of intellectual and physical prowess, and only later was he seen in close relation to the inner spiritual life and character of men, so in the New Testament a similar progress of thought is discernible, though to a lesser extent. At Pentecost the signs of the Spirit's presence which strike the beholder and the reader are the gifts of tongues, of miraculous healings, of abnormal eloquence, power of speech, and boldness of witness; the same is true also of the experience of the Samaritans and of Cornelius.[1] At Corinth too the more spectacular gifts of the Spirit were prized beyond degree: they came behind in no gift—healing, ecstasy, tongues, government, prophecy, teaching and all the rest of the supernatural equipment bestowed by the Spirit upon the infant Church.[2]

Such signs and wonders became the accepted evidence of conversion and superior spirituality. But the result at Corinth was deplorable: not only did such semi-miraculous endowments come to assume an importance far greater than Paul would allow, they led directly to disorder. The meetings of the Church came to resemble clamouring mobs of excited individualists, all wanting to pray, to speak in tongues, prophesy, sing at the same time, and in aggressive self-assertion, while the same people could be gluttonous at the love-feasts, drunken at the Lord's Table, and tolerate incest and litigation among their membership.[3] So little did the gifts of the Spirit have to do in their minds with Christian character and behaviour.

This was, however, but the beginning. Soon the possession of the Spirit was seen to imply far more than signs and wonders and

---

[1] Acts 8; and 10.
[2] 1 Cor. 1: 4–7; 12: 4–11, 27–31.
[3] 1 Cor., chapters 5, 6, 11–14.

miraculous gifts. For one thing the need of repentance and faith, by which Christ's attitudes to sin, the flesh and the world were accepted by the believer, was seen to be the condition without which experience of the Spirit's indwelling was impossible. For another, Paul's reflections upon the inner experience of conversion led to new insights. The conflict of law and inclination, of spirit and flesh, of the mind and the passions, producing tormented division within the soul, was in his experience the one great bitterness and despair from which Christ had set him free. And this liberation was possible only as the "rule of the Spirit of life in Christ Jesus set him free from the rule of sin—and death",[1] as he steadfastly set his mind to the things of the Spirit, "minding the things that are above", and living not in the flesh but in the Spirit.

We are here clearly on a level of thought very different from that which so fascinated the Church at Corinth: the Spirit is seen not so much as the source of wonderful and exciting experiences and powers, but as the spring and nerve of the new character. This is precisely the message which Paul, with some sternness, sent to them. He insisted that the disorder and division were not of the Spirit at all, but of their own making. The spirits of the prophets are subject to the prophets and they must do all things decently and in order, not pleading the excuse of irresistible impulse or "leading". All gifts of the Spirit must be evaluated in the light of the common good, for they are gifts to profit withal, and for the use of edifying the whole fellowship.

Further, while possessing special gifts is all very well in its place, there is a more excellent way: "Though by the endowment of the Spirit I am able to speak with the tongues of men and of angels, to exercise faith that removes mountains, to understand all mysteries and all knowledge, to prophesy with eloquence and power—if I have not *love* it profiteth me nothing." Again we note the *valuation* of the gifts—without love they mean nothing, achieve nothing, signify nothing. "Follow after love" then; desire spiritual gifts if you will, but even then those that are good for the use of edifying.[2] But *pursue* love in the clear conviction that without it all other manifestations of the Spirit are misleading and useless.

Thus slowly but surely the *gifts* of the Spirit fall into the background, relegated by the logic of the Christian conscience to subordinate place, and the *fruits* of the Spirit come into prominence:

[1] Rom. 7: 7—8: 11.   [2] 1 Cor. 13: 1—14: 12.

righteousness, peace, joy in the Holy Ghost *are* the life of the kingdom; to walk in the Spirit, be led of the Spirit, live in the Spirit means to "bear the fruit of the Spirit—love, joy, peace, long-suffering, gentleness, goodness, meekness, faith, self-control".[1] The proof of the presence of God's Spirit in any life is seen to be the gradual emergence of spiritual character and outlook: the manifestation of the Spirit is seen no longer in slaying Philistines with the jawbone of an ass, or dancing naked on the hillside, but in a unique type of character, a Christlike piety, a strenuous cross-bearing loyalty and service, an unquenchable endurance of faith, and a progressive approximation towards the image of Christ.

This last development of thought is suggested in several places. There can be little doubt whose character is being described in the list of the fruits of the Spirit, nor who sat for the portrait so exquisitely painted in 1 Corinthians 13. "It pleased God to reveal his Son in me" is a striking phrase which at least suggests that the inner revelation of Jesus *to* the soul must have as its counterpart the outward revelation of Jesus *through* the soul.[2] The metaphor of the Body, of which individuals are severally members, and in which Christ is incarnate afresh, likewise implies that Jesus now seeks to accomplish in and through us what once he did through his own body in the days of his flesh.

Again: "Christ liveth in me",[3] as the explanation of the life Paul now lives in the flesh, is a clear indication that the indwelling of the Spirit of Christ involves an outward resemblance to Christ himself, in the quality of life and work. Inevitably, as we by personal purity become more transparent, and his Spirit controls more completely thought, feeling and will, the likeness of Christ must shine more clearly through, till all the beauty of Jesus be seen in us. There is one passage, however, which focuses this thought with perfect clarity and sets the Christian's experience of the Spirit—and of worship at its highest—in direct connection with our subject.

In his second letter to Corinth Paul contrasted the old dispensation of things under Moses with the new revelation in Christ, emphasising the greater glory of the new in several significant respects—it brings acquittal rather than condemnation; it is permanent, not temporary; it is not concerned with that which must be veiled from common sight (as was the transfigured face of Moses) or was veiled by hardness and unwillingness to see (as was the heart

[1] Rom. 14: 17; Gal. 5: 16–25.   [2] Gal. 1: 16.   [3] Gal. 2: 20.

of Israel) but with that which had been perfectly and permanently unveiled—the glory of the Lord. When a man turns to the Lord, "the veil is taken away . . . But we all, with unveiled face reflecting as in a mirror the glory of the Lord, are transformed into the same image from glory to glory, even as from the Lord the Spirit."[1] The thought here is so condensed that precise translation is difficult, and various renderings and marginal suggestions are the result. But the general meaning is perfectly clear. The veil is done away completely, from the face of Christ and from the worshipper's heart (it is not quite clear which Paul means, but both are true): and Christian worship is a matter of full access to the holiest, the way into the Holy Place being made manifest, and boldness to come right to the throne of grace being given to every believing heart. Thus in the hour of deepest communion and adoration we are granted full vision of our Lord and see his glory.

This "beholding the beauty of the Lord" is one essential element of Christian worship, as it was of the Psalmist's devotion. But a second element is inseparable from it. As Moses' face caught something of the glory of the divine presence and "shone", so in the hour of worship the glory we behold is "reflected as in a mirror" in ourselves. If this does not happen, then worship is fruitless. If the divine truth we hear, the beauty we adore, the holiness we venerate, the strength we lean upon, the love we rejoice in—in the hour of communion with Christ—remain wholly outside of us, become no part of ourselves, then worship will leave us little blessed. Transports of delight, without transformation of mood and outlook and character, are not Christian worship. To behold his glory is to mirror his beauty—however little—and to be changed into the same image.

Indeed in this deep matter of the soul's approach to God in Christ it is hard to say which is the prior principle—that only those like God, the pure in heart, shall see God; or that only those who first see his glory can ever hope to be like him. As the deepest human understanding is the fruit of sympathy, so increasing reflection of the divine image is both the condition and the fruit of growing knowledge of the Lord. But repeated experiences of this kind can have only one result, the slow transformation of the soul into the likeness of him whose image we reflect, for the deep abiding result of hours spent in devotion, prayer and communion is the inner

[1] 2 Cor. 3: 18 R.V.

refinement and sanctification of all the springs of thought and character and will, step by step, lesson by lesson, stage by stage until his perfect beauty shines forth in us.

And finally—for the condensed passage includes all these suggestions—the operating power in this experience of transforming worship is the power of the Holy Spirit. The basic attitude of the soul, at this moment, is less that of striving than of surrendering, less that of reaching upwards than of being receptive, letting the winds of God blow through the mind and heart, allowing the divine Spirit to enter in fullness of possession and power, to rebuke, suggest, inspire, constrain, renew, until the soul grows great with his strength and sweet with his purity. Here, at this point of personal devotion and renewed surrender, we reach the heart of the process by which the soul is made Christlike. Growth, providence, discipline, and striving would be insufficient without this. And here too we see the fulfilment of that varied ministry of the Spirit of Jesus in the believing soul—all else leads up to this, that he shall transform us, step by step, into the image of the Lord, reproducing in us the character of Jesus.

III. The Spirit and the Christian

The point has already been made that the basic attitude of the soul, in response to the Spirit within him, is not that of striving but of surrendering. It is well to ponder this a little longer. In modern times the stress has so often been laid upon the need for Christian striving, for noble aspiration and high resolve, for ardent response to challenge and heroic endurance expressed in toilsome service, that there is sometimes about modern Christianity a tension, a weariness, a sense of burden and strain, which is quite different from the radiant sufficiency of New Testament living. Many reasons could be given for this, but among them must be included the tendency to think more of what we do for Christ than of what he has done and will do for us.

In trying to bring our present-day drive, and efficiency, and intensely "practical" techniques, into our "religion for modern men" we have often overlooked, or undervalued, the first principle of the inner life, which is faith—in all its many-sided meaning, as waiting upon God, humble receptivity before the eternal Life, self-abnegation before the throne of God, confession of need rather than assertion of our worth, trust in God's sufficiency rather than the demonstration of our own. Of course there is room and need in Christian life for the most eager striving, service, conflict and endeavour: but the first and most necessary condition is that we shall receive the grace and strength and inner sufficiency without which all our noblest striving is likely to be mere beating of the air. This applies most urgently to our main theme: only God can make us Christlike. Left to us the task is hopeless, even self-contradictory. It applies especially to this aspect of our theme, for one of the great weaknesses of present-day Christianity is that it centres far too much in ourselves and far too little in the Holy Spirit, and is often shallow, frustrated, despondent, very earnest but not very radiant, in consequence.

Some confirmation of this judgement may be seen in the fact that the great New Testament doctrine of the Spirit is crystallised in three direct injunctions, each of which is directed not towards our greater activity and endeavour but towards our giving greater freedom and opportunity for the Spirit to do his work in our lives. This again may well call for energetic steps on our part: but the immediate need is that hindrances and obstacles shall be cleared and the Spirit of God given right of way along every avenue of our experience. The initiative, the power, are his: our highest achievement may be simply to cease obstructing him.

This at any rate is the meaning of the threefold apostolic exhortation "Receive ye the Holy Ghost . . . Quench not the Holy Spirit . . . Grieve not the Holy Spirit".[1] The first is initially fulfilled at the outset of Christian life—"If any man have not the Spirit of Christ he is none of his"—but repeatedly in the course of Christian progress the reminder is necessary. We slip so easily into the habit of leaving out of our thinking the present ministry of the Spirit within the Church and within ourselves. In our attitude to the Bible we forget the Author is at our side to interpret and fulfil his word. In our bondage to ancient formulae of the faith we forget the Spirit of Truth is with us yet. In some of our methods of evangelism we forget that all depends upon the conviction of the Spirit directly upon the heart of the listener. In our dismal prophecies of retrenchment and dwindling influence of the Church we forget that the living Spirit of Christ is still abroad in God's world in the twentieth century. In the acceptance of a poor and rather joyless

[1] John 20: 22; 1 Thess. 5: 19; Eph. 4: 30.

level of Christian experience we forget that the Spirit has much more of Christ yet to show unto us. In these and countless ways the word we need is so often "Receive ye the Holy Spirit—take him into your reckoning, count upon him in your experience, make room for him in your plans".

But equally we need the second injunction: not to quench his operation in our lives by habits and assumptions and rigid modes of behaviour hallowed perhaps by long use but not necessarily the best possible or the way in which the Spirit would have us behave. In laying this exhortation upon the Thessalonian Church Paul adds, "Despise not prophesyings". He is urging that freedom be given for the manifestation of the Spirit in the life of the Church, that the prompting of God's Spirit shall not be stifled, that the fire of God's Spirit in the hearts of believers shall not be extinguished, that gifts like that of speaking forth the word of God, though in broken language and undisciplined speech, shall not be discouraged.

So Paul urged that the life of the Church shall be so organised, and the tone of the Church so keyed, that freedom of expression shall be allowed for the individual upon whose heart the divine fire has been kindled and in whose soul the divine word has come to birth. Of course this needs care, and Paul immediately adds that we should test all things and retain only the good. But the need of care must not be allowed to extinguish entirely that freedom of thought and of response by which alone the presence of the Spirit can be revealed. We must not be so sure we know all the truth that he can teach us nothing; we must not be so sure of the way things should be done that he can guide us nowhere; we must not be so fixed in outlook and method and tradition that he can show us nothing new. The listening ear and the willing, adventurous heart are essential to a life filled with the Spirit.

Yet even this is not so important as the third demand: that we "grieve not the Holy Spirit of God". Unquestionably the deepest reason for our so shallow experience of the Spirit's power and joy is unwillingness to face the searching ethical conditions involved. The "Holy" Spirit is not so named for nothing, and holiness is a word long since quietly but firmly dropped from our vocabulary. The command to grieve not the Spirit comes in the midst of a passage concerned with untruthfulness of speech, anger, compromise, dishonesty, stealing, careless conversation, bitterness, wrath, clamour, backbiting, revenge, grudges, uncleanness, covetousness, foolishness—and leaves no doubt at all as to what is meant by grieving the Spirit. Our experience of the power and joy of the Holy Spirit depends very much more upon obedience than upon theological understanding, and until we are willing for a return to holiness the pentecostal experience of the Spirit of holiness will remain a wistful memory, and a standing rebuke to our frustrations. In this supreme matter of being made progressively Christlike by the indwelling Spirit of Christ, the ultimate secret is the same as in every other aspect of the Gospel: he will—if we are willing.

CHAPTER 9

THE CHRISTIAN HOPE

ONE OF the most distinctive and attractive features of New Testament Christianity is its undiscourageable hopefulness. In strong contrast to the mood of brave, wistful despondency common among ourselves, the zeal of the first Christians was fed by an abounding confidence in the future, and in all the good it held for those who were Christ's. It is not enough to say, by way of explanation, that their faith was new, undimmed by the disillusionments of twenty centuries; not enough to paint dark pictures of our age as though their situation were easier than ours. The Roman Empire and the first century were by no means friendly to the new faith: and the more we know of the political, moral and religious conditions in which the early Christians witnessed the more we are compelled to wonder at their courage, daring and assurance. The shadow of literal, physical persecution throws the incurable optimism of the Christian faith into brighter relief—and the Christian faith *is* incurably optimistic. With its message of a love that would not abandon men, of a Saviour who counted no cost too great, of a cross which dealt finally with the deepest of problems, of an empty tomb proclaiming victory and life for evermore, it could hardly be otherwise.

"We are saved by hope", declared the apostle Paul, and "all experience worketh hope"; "we rejoice in hope" as those who know that their "hope will not be put to shame". To be without Christ is to be "without hope"—the direst of extremities—but to be "in Christ" is to be "begotten again unto a lively hope"; and that hope is an "anchor of the soul" in the day of shaking. Hope is one of the three "abiding things", and by it the Christian mind is armed against the cynicism and pessimism of the world—"for a helmet, the hope of salvation". One way in which the whole purpose of Christ's dying and rising again is defined is "that your faith and hope might be in God", and in the closing pages of Scripture Christ appears as the Lamb of God, in triumph "in the midst of the throne"

100

with the sealed book of the future in his hands, and possessing authority and power to unfold the world's destiny—for the Lord Jesus Christ is himself "our hope".[1] It is clearly no exaggeration to describe hopefulness as one constant hall-mark of truly apostolic Christianity.

Hope is, however, more than the happy inference of faith arguing its future from the blessings of the past—more than a mood of confidence leaning forward. Christian hope fastens upon certain firm and far-reaching promises, certain foreseeable "moments", four in number, upon which to focus expectation: the hope of the kingdom, the hope of everlasting life, the hope of glory, and the hope of Christ's coming. Of these the first concerns our theme but a little, the second and third we have glanced at already and need only recall, the fourth fittingly closes this study of the process by which—according to New Testament thought—God seeks to make us Christlike.

I. THE HOPE OF THE KINGDOM

The hope of the kingdom is an essential element of the forward-looking faith of the Christian man. It derives of course from the Old Testament promise of Messiah and the messianic community: the ancient hope of an elect people, under the divine vicegerent, dwelling in a transformed earth cleansed and reconciled and redeemed to its Maker.[2] Sometimes conceived in narrow and nationalist terms which glorified Israel among the nations, the kingdom-hope was also interpreted (as in the later chapters of Isaiah) in universalist and spiritual fashion—embracing the Gentiles, and demanding for its preparation that all men "return unto the Lord, and he will abundantly pardon". This deeper note formed the theme of the great forerunner of the Messiah, John the Baptist, who announced that the kingdom is at hand, and that those who failed to prepare for it by repentance would find it to be a reign of judgement and wrath.[3]

On this note too our Lord opened his own ministry,[4] but the warning of imminent judgement was now replaced by gracious

---

[1] Rom. 8: 24; 5: 2; 5: 4, 5; Eph. 2: 12; 1 Pet. 1: 3; Heb. 6: 19; 1 Cor. 13: 13; 1 Thess. 5: 5; 1 Pet. 1: 21; Rev. 5: 1–10; 1 Tim. 1: 1.
[2] Isa. 9: 6–7; 11: 1–10; Micah 4: 1–7; Dan. 7: 1–14.
[3] Matt. 3: 1–12; Luke 3: 1–17.
[4] Mark 1: 14–15.

invitations telling of the attractions of life under the rule of God. To enter the kingdom is like stumbling upon treasure hid in a field; like the thrill of satisfaction that comes to a collector of gems on finding in the market one pearl above price; it is like an invitation to the wedding of a prince, offered to beggars sleeping beneath the hedges; like the welcome to a great feast in a wealthy house. Yet still the call is to repentance and faith as the way of entrance into the life ruled by God. For the coming of that kingdom, in which the will of God will be done on earth even as it already is done in heaven, we are bidden to pray daily; while the analysis of the good life in the great sermon on the mount, and the parables of well-doing, consecration and service which are spoken to the disciples towards the close of the ministry, are alike descriptions of the practical outworking of that divine rule in the conduct and experience of everyday life.[1]

The message of the king, and of the kingdom, thus fills the Gospel stories; we do not always realise that it continues to find echoes in the Acts of the Apostles[2] and repeatedly in the epistles.[3] As the gospel-witness moved out of Jewry into the Gentile world the idea of the divine rule in human hearts was *translated* into language more familiar to non-Jewish ears—the Master and his willing slaves, the divine Lord and his "ecclesia". Beneath the metaphors the meaning of course remains precisely the same, the submission of the soul to the rule of Christ as God's appointed vicegerent or king-Messiah. The concern of the epistles no less than of the Gospels is to describe the outworking of the life of obedience to the divine rule in all the varied circumstances and responsibilities of the early Church.

Now amid all the parables, metaphors, exhortations, warnings, counsels, arguments and rebukes only one perfect illustration emerges of what it actually means to live at every point under the rule of the kingly Father: the life of Jesus. He himself could say —and he only—"My meat is to do the will of him that sent me";[4] "I do always those things which please him".[5] Thus, yet once more, we run upon our main contention, that the heart of the Christian

---

[1] Matt. 11: 28–30; 13: 44–46; 22: 1–14; Luke 14: 16f; Matt. 8: 11; 6: 10, 11; 5: 1–16 etc.; Matt. 25 etc.
[2] Acts 1: 3, 6; 8: 12; 19: 8; 14: 22; 28: 23; cf. 17: 7.
[3] Rom. 14: 17; 1 Cor. 4: 20; 15: 24, 50; 6: 9, 10; Gal. 5: 21; Eph. 5: 5; Col. 1: 13; 4: 11; 2 Thess. 1: 5; 2: 12; Heb. 12: 28; Jas. 2: 5; 2 Pet. 1: 11.
[4] John 4: 34; 6: 38.
[5] John 8: 29.

life, in the classic New Testament descriptions, lies in correspondence between our daily character and conduct, and the character and conduct of Jesus. Like so many facets of Christian truth, the doctrine of the kingdom is seen to find its inner meaning in *Christlikeness*.

This correspondence between the life of the Christian under God's rule and the life of the Vicegerent himself, as embodying that rule, is especially emphasised in one passage which our familiar translation makes a little too easy. "There was a strife among them, which of them should be accounted the greatest. And he said unto them, the kings of the Gentiles exercise lordship over them; and they that exercise authority upon them are called benefactors. But ye shall not be so: but he that is greatest among you, let him be as the younger; and he that is chief, as he that doth serve . . . Ye are they which have continued with me in my temptations. And I appoint unto you a kingdom, as my Father hath appointed unto me; that ye may eat and drink at my table in my kingdom, and sit on thrones judging the twelve tribes of Israel".[1] Here, the "kingdom" appointed to the disciples is more accurately "dominion, royal power and privilege". It is defined in the following words as the right to eat and drink at the king's table and to sit on thrones judging (as Court Assessors) the twelve tribes of Israel.

Mark too records this promise that some shall sit "on my right hand and on my left hand",[2] but again on the very significant condition that it is not a privilege to be contended for, or to be sought secretly behind the backs of others, as James and John had attempted to do: it is to be "given to those for whom it is prepared". The preparation is plainly described: it consists of "enduring continuously with me in my tribulations", "drinking the cup that I drink of, being baptised with the baptism that I am baptised withal". The honours of the kingdom are not to be won more easily by the disciple than by the Master. He appoints them to the disciples on the same terms "as my Father hath appointed unto me".

For each of us the hope of the kingdom rests to this extent upon our sharing, so far as may be demanded of us, in the tribulation and sacrifice of Jesus. We too must find exaltation through abasement, honour through service, working towards the final goal of a world subdued to the will of God not by force but by gentleness, not by dominion but by sacrifice. And this must mean that from us

[1] Luke 22: 24–30.   [2] Mark 10: 35–45.

are demanded the same decisions, the same rejections and acceptances, that were demanded from Jesus in his wilderness temptations. The kingdom must come, not by the easy way of promising material prosperity for all, turning the very stones into bread; not by the popular spectacle and sensuous thrill of the supernatural; not by the methods of the kingdoms of this world, the iron rod and martial conquest; but by the way of persuasion, service, appeal, rejection, and death. Just as the *meaning* of the kingdom is Christlike obedience to the rule of the kingly Father, so the *way* to the kingdom—we are so slow to learn—is and must ever be *the Christlike way to Christlike power.*

II. THE HOPE OF LIFE EVERLASTING

The hope of the kingdom is the constant inspiration and goal of the Christian society at work in the world; the hope of immortality is likewise the inspiration and goal of the individual believer, contemplating the ultimate issues of life and love and sorrow. Without it, as Paul says, our faith, our preaching, our redemption would be vain. Doubt about it makes nonsense of the total Christian valuation of life and history: "if in this life only we have hope in Christ, we are of all men most miserable".[1] If God is good, and life is to be meaningful—not just a tale told by an idiot, full of sound and fury, signifying nothing—then death *cannot* be the end.

It is not, however, simply a conviction of its moral *value* that supports the Christian affirmation about immortality. The basis of that hope lies partly in the promises of Scripture, and in the power of God.[2] It lies partly, also, in the instinctive and intuitive "intimations of immortality" which have sustained such a hope in every living religion in every age. It lies partly, for some minds, in certain philosophical insights and arguments about the nature of mind, spirit and morality. In Old Testament faith the basis of the belief, at its highest point, lies in the present experience of the saint that God is good, merciful and faithful *plus* the conviction that present fellowship with God cannot be destroyed by the mere accident of physical decay: God will not let his servant perish.[3] For the Christian, however, these arguments, except perhaps the last,

---

[1] See 1 Cor. 15: 14, 17, 19.
[2] Mark 12: 18 and foll.
[3] This is the thought expressed in Ps. 16: 5–11; 49; 73; 139; and 23.

are little more than confirmation of the one sure ground of hope—
that Jesus rose, and lives, and is alive for evermore. That fact,
together with the general principle everywhere apparent that the
Christian's life corresponds to his, adds up to the sure confidence
that he that believeth shall never die.

With impressive unanimity the New Testament writers appeal to
this central argument for the Christian hope. "Because I live ye
shall live also" is John's record of Christ's promise, making the
fact of Christ's eternal life both the basis and the cause of the
Christian's immortality.[1] The same point is made equally clearly
in what is perhaps the greatest of all sayings of our Lord on this
theme: "As the living Father hath sent me, and I live by the Father:
so he that eateth me, even he shall live by me",[2] and it underlies
the whole teaching of John concerning the eternal life possessed
here and now by every believer—"God hath given to us eternal life,
and this life is in his Son".[3] Life "everlasting" is but the unbroken
continuance through death of that life already communicated
through the risen Lord to all who believe: it is his life imparted to
us. We live because he lives.

This also is Paul's thought. It is "the life also of Jesus which
is made manifest in our mortal body"[4] and "he which raised up
the Lord Jesus will raise up us also by Jesus".[5] The argument of
Romans 6, that the Christian is planted together with Christ in
death and resurrection, applies in the first instance to the present
experience of the "risen" life in victory over sin: but before the
chapter ends the planting together in the likeness of his risen life
is seen also to involve ". . . the end, everlasting life". This is taken
up again in the eighth chapter: "If the Spirit of him that raised up
Jesus from the dead dwell in you, he that raised up Christ from the
dead shall also quicken your mortal bodies . . ." [6]

In Philippians we meet the same argument again: the hope of the
apostle is to share in Christ's resurrection power—and not only in
present triumphant living but in the final resurrection of the dead.[7]
The message of comfort sent to the Church at Thessalonica marshals
the same ground of faith: "I would not have you to be ignorant,
brethren, concerning them which are asleep, that ye sorrow not, even
as others which have no hope. For if we believe that Jesus died and

---

[1] John 14: 19.
[2] John 6: 57.
[3] 1 John 5: 11.
[4] 2 Cor. 4: 11
[5] 2 Cor. 4: 14.
[6] Rom. 8: 11.
[7] Phil. 3: 10, 11, 20, 21.

rose again, even so them also which sleep in Jesus will God bring with him"[1]—if we believe that Jesus rose . . . even so ! It is but another way of saying the same thing when Paul speaks of Jesus as the "firstfruits"—the sample and pledge and guarantee of all who shall rise "in him".[2]

Turning finally to Peter's solitary reference to the hope of immortality, we find the same pattern of thought, briefly expressed: God "hath begotten us again unto a lively hope *by the resurrection of Jesus Christ from the dead*".[3] Given the general truth that the experience and character of each believer are modelled ideally upon Christ's, it follows that his resurrection in triumph from the grave carries with it, inevitably, our own final victory. In all these passages, though in varied modes of expression, the same motif persists: Christlikeness is the final goal of all God's dealings with us, and this necessitates the hope of life eternal. As surely as we died in him, and live in him, so surely shall we rise in him and triumph in him, and Christlikeness be complete.

III. THE HOPE OF GLORY

So far we have considered only the *fact* of eternal life; with the New Testament in our hands we may dare to go further and ask a little about the *form* of that life beyond. It need hardly be said that we are here on delicate ground, and need to keep strictly to the words of Scripture, speaking only with reverent caution and without dogmatism. We have already seen that the "hope of glory" occupies no small place in New Testament thought, and that its meaning includes far more than "brightness and bliss".[4] The "glory" is closely associated with the divine pattern of creation, the image of God; as the image was marred, so the glory was lost, but recovery of the glory is promised us in Christ—"the hope of glory". This hope is shared by Nature herself, in whom the curse of Adam is to be exchanged for the liberty of the glory of the children of God; and so will end Nature's subjection to the bondage of corruption and decay.[5]

It remains only to show how this thought is developed in three important passages, in connection with the form of the "body that shall be".[6] The passage just quoted, from Romans 8, emphasises

---

[1] 1 Thess. 4: 13, 14.　　[3] 1 Pet. 1: 3, 4.　　[5] Recall Rom. 8: 18–21.
[2] 1 Cor. 15: 20.　　[4] Chapter 1 (page 20).　　[6] 1 Cor. 15: 37.

that complete redemption lies still ahead. For complete redemption involves the adoption of the whole man, spirit and body, out of this realm of corruption into the realm of "glory". Already we have the firstfruits, the redemption and adoption of the spirit; but the body awaits its full salvation, because in it too the divine image is to be restored, and it too will share the liberty, incorruption and glory of the fully redeemed world.[1]

These thoughts are closely followed also in Philippians 3. Here Paul followed an impassioned description of worldliness with the assertion that the Christian's citizenship belongs not to this world but to heaven. We are a "colony" of heaven set down in this unheavenly realm. We might have expected Paul to proceed with a call to take advantage of the colonising opportunities so afforded; instead he moved at once to the statement of the Christian hope: "For our citizenship is in heaven; from whence also we look for the Saviour, the Lord Jesus Christ: who shall change our humiliating body that it may be fashioned like unto his glorious body, according to the working whereby he is able even to subdue all things unto himself."[2]

Philippi was a Roman colony on the Greek mainland, and very proud of it. Such a colony may be thought of, as in chapter 2, as an advance-base for strategic operations—"holding forth the word of life" to the surrounding peoples; or it may be considered as a perilous foothold in enemy country, besieged by foes and needing above all to be delivered. Here it is of deliverance that Paul is thinking, and we note especially that at once the thoughts of the body, of glory, and of likeness to Christ, spring to his mind. "The body of our humiliation" is our present physical frame, seen in its frailty, its susceptibility to temptation, its mortality, its weakness as the partner of the spirit. Paul did not, and would not, write of the body as "vile". "The body of his glory" is the present "body" of the ascended Lord, the vehicle by which—beyond all our imagining —he made his presence known to the disciples on Easter morning, to Stephen, and to Paul at Damascus. As in the previous passage so here, this transformation of the body into the likeness of the Lord's glorious body is seen as the consummation of the whole process of redemption: "we wait for the *Saviour*".

The third passage is the famous, and crucial, fifteenth chapter of First Corinthians, where after vigorously asserting the importance

[1] Rom. 8: 23; cf. 1 Cor. 15: 49.   [2] Phil. 3: 20, 21; cf. R.V.

of the resurrection-hope, Paul dealt with the "common sense" objection that the body is in fact destroyed at death. "How are the dead raised up, and with what body do they come ?" Paul replied that the familiar process of sowing and reaping sees a complete transformation from one body—that of the seed—to another, that of the full-grown plant, while identity and continuity of life remain. The same living creature will have different bodies at different times. The universe is full of these differing bodies—beasts, birds, fishes, sun, moon and stars all differ among themselves and each has the type of "body" befitting its sphere. Writing today, Paul might have drawn even closer analogies from the identity of the individual person through all the changes of his bodily form from the period before birth on through childhood and adolescence into manhood, while the chemical structure of his physical frame is constantly changing. Sameness of being—the identity of the person —does *not* depend upon sameness of body.

Thus in the resurrection individual identity survives the crisis and change of death—as it survived the crisis and change of birth—and inherits a new type of body adapted to the new level of existence. The change is no more "unimaginable" than the conditions of this present life would be to the unborn infant approaching the mystery of birth. But the new, divinely wrought body of the risen life differs from the present body in certain specified ways. The present body, as age, disease or injury destroys its powers, corresponds to the seed sown "in corruption", but the new body is raised in incorruption. The present body is sown in dishonour, the lifeless clay being no longer the fitting object of love or regard, but the new body is raised in glory. The present body, again, is sown in weakness, the new is raised in power. And the present body is "natural", in the deep sense in which Paul used this word: it is framed and adapted for the life of the "natural man", the animal soul; but the new body is framed and adapted for the pure life of the spirit. The present body belongs to earth and bears the marks of its earthly habitat, the new body belongs essentially to heaven. Finally, the present body bears the image of the earthy, the impression of Adam and the whole material world of the first creation, but the new body shall bear the image of the Heavenly Man, and that spiritual realm to which he belongs by nature and as of right.[1]

So far we may go with the New Testament to help us. Of course

[1] See 1 Cor. 15: 35–49, especially 42–5.

we are here in the realm of devout speculation and apocalyptic, where all seems metaphor and hint, rather than clear knowledge. To many it may seem strange that Paul should be concerned about the fate of the body, for the modern habit is to think only of the immortality of the soul. It is the difference between the Greek and the Hebrew outlook. Greek thought distinguished sharply between body and soul, and some held the body to be essentially evil and temporary, while the soul sought escape from it into the realm of spirit. From this point of view the immortality of the soul is everything, the body is better left behind.

To the Hebrew mind, on the other hand, the whole physical creation was of God, and the body itself God's handiwork, fearfully and wonderfully made; human personality was regarded as a unity, an animated body, and the soul was the divine life inbreathed into the body and inseparable from it. To Hebrew thought there is something horrible in the suggestion of a "naked" or unclothed[1] soul (a "ghost" or shade), and there is no difficulty at all that he who first made the body[2] and still fashions each new person in the miracle of birth[3] should fashion again a new mode of existence suitable to immortal spirits. There was no difficulty in the idea, and real need for it. For individual personality and personal relationships had come to have great significance in Hebrew thinking, and life hereafter possessed a greater reality and hope if by means of a resurrection body some personal identity and relationship could be felt to outlive the grave.

Greek thought undoubtedly influenced the later faith of the Church, but it was the Hebrew outlook that Christianity first inherited. And it is significant for our theme that when the early Church sought for an analogy by which to explain this "spiritual body" fitted for eternal life, self-identical yet transformed and glorious, they found it in the stories of the appearances of the risen Lord, and so carried yet one step further the great truth of Christlikeness. The hope of glory is in fact the hope of bearing his divine image not only spiritually and progressively here on earth, but essentially and finally hereafter in heaven—to share "the body of his glory" and "bear the image of the heavenly Man".

---

[1] 2 Cor. 5: 1-4.
[2] Emphasised in Gen. 2: 7; Job 33: 4.
[3] Ps. 139: 13-16; Job 10: 8-12.

IV. THE HOPE OF HIS COMING

No account of the Christian hope could pretend to be even nearly complete without some reference to the great central expectation which sustained the faith and service of the apostolic Church, the hope of the advent. It is neither possible nor necessary to expound that hope in its fullness, but at one important point it is closely relevant to our theme.

The first Christians were vividly aware that they stood "at the fullness of the times", with page after page of the ancient prophecies finding fulfilment around them. But they knew too that something remained, promises of the messianic glory and power, pictures of the final triumph and the fully redeemed world, prophecies of the establishment of the throne of David unshakably, for ever. The story remained unfinished: and this sense of more to come was sustained and deepened by the promises of Jesus himself. He had spoken of the coming of the Son of Man on the clouds of heaven, appearing as the lightning, and unheralded, so that the only possible preparation is continual faithfulness in the work appointed for his absence.[1] Jesus too had repeatedly introduced into the memorable parables of service, vigilance, and judgement the note of approaching crisis, and the theme of the returning Lord,[2] while the last unforgettable moments with him had been charged with hints of the great consummation still to come.[3] The Communion service, with its recurring reference to "My Father's kingdom" and possibly already the phrase "until he come", helped to stimulate the intense personal affection which cherished the eager hope of his bodily presence again. In days of persecution and rejection the longing to see Jesus finally vindicated in obvious and public victory added to the earnest expectation that he would soon return in power.

We can form little idea, after the long waiting centuries, of the intensity and urgency of this advent hope in the early Church. It seems that at Thessalonica the apocalyptic excitement interfered with the more normal business of life, both within the Church and in the earning of one's daily bread. It coloured quite seriously the counsel of the apostle on matters of marriage and slavery.[4] It

[1] Mark 13: 26; Matt. 16: 27; 24: 30, 42f.
[2] Wheat and Tares, Dragnet, Talents, Bridesmaids, Sheep and Goats.
[3] Acts 1: 6–11; also Matt. 28: 20—" unto the end of the *age*".
[4] 2 Thess. 2: 1–3; with 3: 5–12; 1 Cor. 7: 29–31; 1 Cor. 7: 17–24 and 29.

helps to explain the attitude of the early Christians to the State, to questions of the reform of society, to matters of Church organisation, and perhaps also the strange delay in committing to writing the matchless stories of the Master. The apostolic Church, at the first, simply had no long perspective of history stretching ahead of it : the advent was around the corner, "the Lord is at hand".

The passage of time, widening experience and deeper reflection combined to make necessary a certain reassessment of this advent expectation. The Pastoral epistles offer counsel directed towards the building up of Christian homes and families, and the closer organisation of the Church, with clearly defined officers. Some care is taken too about the accurate preservation of the sacred tradition of teaching.[1] Already, in Philippians, Paul's anticipation was rather that he would depart and be with Christ, than that Christ would return to him[2]—though certainly the advent hope was not lost.[3] The deep reflection of the Gospel of John brings into new prominence thoughts that could not but temper somewhat the excitement of those who lived in daily anticipation of Christ's return—for John repeatedly stressed that the Master *had* returned in the Spirit[4] as the risen Lord, and that Jesus had already been manifested in glory—indeed John wrote of the total act of death-burial-resurrection-ascension as the "glorifying" of Jesus.[5]

Undoubtedly the emphasis changed. The "physical" return of Jesus became less important (though, of course, Christians never lost the sense that the risen, returning Lord is "personal"); and the conception of his being glorified became in time a little less worldly and more truly spiritual. Faithfully too the early Church treasured those sayings which forbade too close prying into supposed dates and divine programmes of events.[6] But the hope of his appearing remained, the hope of meeting him again, of knowing him as they were known, and of fellowship "face to face". And this hope spurred their efforts, cheered their hearts, nerved their endurance and sustained their faith through years of incredible labour and unceasing menace.

[1] 1 Tim., chapters 3 and 5; 1 Tim. 5: 14; 4: 3; Titus 2: 4, 5; 2 Tim. 1: 13; 2: 2; Titus, chapter 2; 3: 8.
[2] Phil. 1: 19–25.
[3] Phil. 3: 20; 1 Tim. 6: 14; 2 Tim. 4: 8.
[4] John 14: 16–26, especially verses 18, 21, 28; 16: 7–14; cf. 17–19, and 22. See chapter 8.
[5] John 1: 14; 2: 11; 7: 39; 12: 16; cf. 16: 7.
[6] Mark 13: 30; Matt. 24: 36; Acts 1: 7.

It is this spiritual value of the advent hope that most concerns us here. The intense gladness and buoyancy of apostolic faith was largely due to their assurance that they lived in the last days; the New Age had dawned, the Day of the Lord was imminent. A keener edge was given to the Christian conscience by the knowledge that any moment might be the last, that he would suddenly appear, and the servants left to "occupy till I come" would be called to account. Christians are the children of the Day, renouncing the wantonness of those who prefer the darkness and the shades of night. The hope of the return became in these ways an active stimulus to zealous service and sanctification, as well as a source of comfort and patience.[1] It is still true that where the message of his coming is neglected or denied something of the apostolic quality of Christian living is always wanting.

But the advent hope and its abiding value for Christian hearts are nowhere better expressed, nowhere more simply and movingly stated, than in John's first epistle: "Beloved, now are we children of God, and it is not yet made manifest what we shall be. We know that if he shall be manifested, we shall be like him; for we shall see him even as he is. And everyone that hath this hope set on him purifieth himself, even as he is pure".[2] Here, for the last time, we run again upon our subject, assumed and asserted as the crowning moment in the whole process of divine salvation: we shall be like him. As dimly seeing him in the high hours of worship in the Spirit gradually transforms us into his image,[3] so the perfect vision shall find us wholly like him. This is the divine promise—the long process shall succeed, the purpose of our salvation shall be fully accomplished —even in the wayward and the slow to believe: we *shall* be like him. But the promise is no excuse for slackness, it is the incentive to persistent sanctification and daily growth into his likeness: to possess this hope is to purify oneself as he is pure.

We could not expect the way to such a goal could be swift or easy, nor the steps towards it simple and obvious. Christ finds us far from his likeness—sinful, weak, rebellious and self-centred. His mercy is immediate, his forgiveness sure: the life he imparts, the Spirit he gives, the miracle he works in us are ours—at once—in the

---

[1] Rom. 13: 11–14; 1 Thess. 5: 1, 8 and 4: 13–18.
[2] 1 John 3: 2, 3 R.V.
[3] 2 Cor. 3: 18.

first sincere outreach of our faith towards himself. But the process then begun is deep, and wide, and many-sided. The life then imparted grows by its own nature towards his maturity *if we let it.* The outward circumstances of our lives are shaped by divine providence, and the inward experiences of our hearts are framed by divine discipline, to the same end, *if we co-operate.* We are called to the daily cultivation of the mind of Christ, in all spiritual wisdom and character, that we may approximate ever more closely to his image; and meanwhile the Spirit of Jesus himself labours within us to fulfil the same high purpose. Ever ahead lies the Christian hope, beckoning to a kingdom, to eternal life and glory, to a rendezvous with the returning Lord, in which the completion of the purpose is divinely guaranteed. "He that hath begun a good work in you will perform it until the day of Jesus Christ. . . . He is able to keep us from falling and to present us faultless before the presence of his glory with exceeding joy."[1] Here hope can rest: "As for me, I will behold thy face in righteousness: I shall be satisfied, when I awake, with thy likeness".[2]

[1] Phil. 1: 6; Jude 24.　　　[2] Ps. 17: 15.

THE PORTRAIT

CHAPTER 10

CONTEMPORARY IMPRESSIONS

IT HAS been our endeavour, while describing the process by which God would make us Christlike, to keep a true balance between those parts of the process which are—so to speak—in God's hands, and those which are to a greater extent in our own. The natural growth of the spiritual life, properly nourished and unhindered, the shaping of our outward circumstances and inward experience by divine providence and discipline, and the many-sided ministry of the Spirit of Christ within us—these we may say are the steps which God takes in bringing us toward the goal. Obviously some co-operation, in diligence, trust and surrender, are required of us, but the main work in these respects is God's.

On the other hand, the deliberate and conscious holding before one's spiritual vision of this great Christlike ideal, the persistent attempt to read the secret of God's way with us in this light, and the cherishing of the transforming Hope, are ways in which we ourselves are called to help forward the great task of making us "in his image". But as we saw in chapter seven the central duty which is laid upon us all in this whole series of studies, the imperative call to our conscience which this whole truth makes, is that we shall diligently, earnestly and persistently cultivate "the mind of Christ".

It is not necessary to emphasise again that this means much more than the outward copying of the conditions of his wonderful ministry—echoing his words and deeds and renunciations with literal exactness; more, even, than the devout effort of imagination to "see" him in our place and under our responsibilities. It is a matter of *inward* resemblance of outlook, aim, spirit, disposition, attitude, nature, judgement, valuation and faith, and it affects matters of spiritual wisdom no less than matters of moral character. For this, the careful, devout and patient study of Jesus himself—the matchless portrait of the Master in the four Gospels—is the only possible method. But one or two cautions are necessary.

117

For one thing, we shall not make progress in the knowledge of Jesus, in this inward way, unless all our study of his story is carried forward *in his presence*. We cannot know him merely through printed words upon a page, even inspired words upon a sacred page, without the opening of the heart to his own incoming, to illumine the story and apply the truth.

Secondly, we must study in order to do: "He that willeth to do . . . shall know" is the law of all spiritual understanding.[1] It applies especially to our subject—the Christian ideal is no mere theory for academic debate. Then, we must be careful about the use of imagination in the study of the Gospel stories. Reverent reconstruction of the circumstances in vivid and dramatic form does help to explain and enforce the written word, but sometimes it tends to replace it, and we "imagine" what is not there. We must beware too of building too much upon a narrow foundation of isolated texts or single sayings; what we seek is the broad picture of the Master's character, the portrait that emerges from the many deeds and utterances and records, seen in balance and perspective, undistorted and undimmed.

And our final caution shall be that no theological presuppositions shall be allowed to hide the Master from us. This is specially important. Some feel so jealous for the indispensable truth of the divine Sonship of Christ that they try to evade, explain away or "spiritualise" the plain statements of the Gospel writers, as though Matthew, Mark, Luke and John were not themselves the best defenders of his unique glory who ever took pen in hand.

"'Jesus therefore being wearied with his journey sat thus on the well . . .'[2] . . . but of course he was the Son of the eternal, unwearying God, and he never grew tired: John means he *looked* tired, or seemed to the woman to be tired, or was really weary of the sin of men and the hardness of men's hearts. . . .'" This type of exposition approaches very nearly to handling the word of God deceitfully. It fails utterly to take the measure of the amazing act of condescension and self-emptying[3] by which the eternal Son took upon himself the nature of man in all its weakness, frailty and limitations. No doubt the eternal Son could not grow weary, nor be tempted, nor suffer, nor die—but the eternal Son incarnate *did* these things, not in pretence or in disguise, but in painful reality and utter truth. That is the miracle of the incarnation: we do not

[1] See John 7: 17.   [2] John 4: 6.   [3] Phil. 2: 7 R.V.

enhance it, but deny it, when we fail to give full weight to the Gospel accounts of his incarnate life, when we let our doctrinal prejudices or fears obscure the portrait, and fail to see him as he really was.

These cautions may seem a little forbidding, but it is a serious undertaking we set ourselves when we would "see Jesus". Not a few familiar and treasured misconceptions may have to be surrendered, and certainly the "Christ made in our image" must be forgotten. The vague sentimental "conception of Jesus" must be made clear and definite, the popular misrepresentations must be corrected. We shall try for different points of view, seeking first to see Jesus through the eyes of others, his contemporaries: then to summarise our own impressions of his character. But we know a man not only by the impressions he makes on others and the outstanding qualities of his character, but by the ideas that govern his thinking, the attitudes that characterise his relation to others and to things, the basic assumptions upon which his general outlook rests. Reverently and with care we shall seek to see Jesus in all these ways, praying that in the end we shall know him a little better, and be much clearer in our own minds as to what it means to be like him.

We begin, then, with contemporary impressions of Jesus, the things about him which primarily impressed the crowds, the many suppliants for his mercy, his enemies, and his friends.

I. In the Eyes of the Crowds

It would be interesting to estimate the impression which Jesus made upon the great majority of his hearers by gathering together the varied comments upon him which are preserved by the Evangelists—"Never man spake like this man—Who is this ?—When the Christ comes, will he do more than this man ?—We never saw it on this fashion—Have any of the rulers believed upon him ?" Yet these are isolated remarks that for one reason or another were remembered afterwards: it happens that we have a surer guide to popular feeling about Jesus, in the considered reply of the disciples to Jesus' own question "Whom do men say that I the Son of man am ?"[1] The answer is illuminating: "Some say that thou art John the Baptist; some, Elias; and others, Jeremias, or one of the prophets."

Of course this falls short of the Christian's faith; as the sequel shows, Jesus himself would not let men rest in that view of himself.

[1] Matt. 16: 13f; cf. Mark 8: 27f and Luke 9: 18f.

But as a summary of the popular, "interim" impression it is valuable. And indeed there was no higher title, save only that of Messiah, which the people could give to Jesus. For many years the living voice of prophecy had been silent in Israel, until John had stirred echoes of the old days when God spoke directly through chosen men. To call Jesus "prophet" was to rank him among the greatest of the heroes of Judaism, and to acknowledge, though it be confusedly, that divine authority lay in him. No open claim to Messiahship having yet been made, the use of the prophet's title to express what men felt about Jesus implied no rejection—yet—of a higher possibility: it was a true estimate so far as it went, and a tribute of the highest honour.

But even more significant is the division of opinion among the people as to whether Jesus resembled more closely Elijah, the stern, unyielding, uncompromising prophet before whom even Ahab trembled and Jezebel fell (and so at the same time, John the Baptist, himself a prophet in whom men recognised "the spirit and power of Elias")—or whether he was not more like Jeremiah, the sad and sensitive prophet of the decline and fall of Israel, a man of exquisite tenderness and humility, burdened for his people's sufferings, reluctant to speak the message given him and unwilling from first to last to be God's spokesman in an evil time.

Elijah is linked in all minds with years of drought imposed to bring a nation to its knees; with fearless challenge to decision upon Mount Carmel, and the slaying of four hundred prophets of Baal; with equally fearless denunciation of King Ahab for his tyrannical oppression of the "little man" Naboth; and with the destruction of the students of the "schools of the prophets" who set their official status derisively against the inspired independence of Elijah.[1] Yet the people thought Jesus was Elijah, returned from heaven whither the chariot of fire had taken him without death.

Jeremiah is known to most Bible students, unjustly, though not without some truth, as the weeping prophet. His inner conflict of fears and self-mistrust, his reluctance to prophesy hard truth, his sympathy for his erring people, his intense wrestling with God, his indomitable courage in fulfilling his unwanted task in spite of peril and apparent failure—all this endears him to us as one of the most "human" (and to some of us as quite the greatest) of Old Testament figures. And the people thought Jesus was Jeremiah.

[1] 1 Kings 17, 18, 21; 2 Kings 2: 23.

Here plainly is the authentic popular impression of Jesus—confused, contradictory, insufficient. Fastening upon one point with certainty: He has God behind him, he is a prophet, they are divided as to which quality is most prominent, the fearless truth, authority and challenge of Elijah, or the tender, sensitive graciousness of Jeremiah ! Yet we will not press the reply of the disciples to Jesus too far: this double impression of grace and truth, of authority and humility, is confirmed in other ways.

At Nazareth, at his first sermon, men "wondered at the *gracious* words that proceeded out of his mouth"[1] and the word signifies something of charm, attractiveness and comfort. But the sermon proceeded to unwelcome truths, still persuasively argued from the Old Testament lesson, and anger was kindled. The "gracious words" forgotten, they "thrust him out of the city and led him to the brow of the hill that they might cast him down headlong". Jeremiah had become Elijah, in the span of one sermon ! But while a crowd may urge and demand and shout that something should be done, the inner ring of individuals hesitate and nudge each other to begin. When in the centre of that timorous inner ring there stood one with the personal dignity and quiet fearlessness of Jesus, whose glance subdued and whose words were swords—then the outer fringes of the crowd might shout as they would, he walked serenely through the midst of them "and went his way". Could any testimony be more eloquent to the innate authority and "presence" of Jesus, combined with winsomeness and grace ?

The people, we are told, heard him with delight—with *pleasure*: and yet said of him, that he taught as one having *authority*, and not as the scribes.[2] Men used of him the words of Isaiah: "He shall not strive, nor cry; neither shall any man hear his voice in the streets. A bruised reed shall he not break, and smoking flax shall he not quench";[3] yet it could also be written that none "dared" ask him any more questions.[4] When the Jewish leaders send "officials" to arrest Jesus, they return with the task undone, and the moving tribute "Never man spake like this man"[5]—a significant testimony from men of official standing and legal authority, of a type not usually susceptible to persuasive speech. On the other hand, when a Roman Centurion wishes a favour from Jesus he makes the request that Jesus shall not come to the house but speak the word

---

[1] Luke 4: 22.   [3] Matt. 12: 19, 20.   [5] John 7: 46.
[2] Mark 12: 37; Matt. 7: 29.   [4] Matt. 22: 46.

only, for "I *also* am a man set in a position of authority: I too say to one 'Go' and he goeth, and to another 'Come' and he cometh".[1] From such a man, this is perhaps the most convincing testimony of all, to that note and bearing of authoritative power which men acknowledged in Jesus.

We are being faithful, then, to the broad picture of the Evangelists when we say that the prevailing popular impression of Jesus was one of mingled authority and graciousness, power and gentleness, alike arising from a divine commission similar to that of the prophets of old. Here, at the very outset, is a practical matter of everyday behaviour in which the ideal of Christlikeness condemns at once the careless, exaggerated, irresponsible, impassioned and inaccurate speech which too often passes unnoticed amongst us.

Our Lord's authority implies more than a certain accent of speech, and his graciousness more than kindliness of conversation, but it was in these that men recognised his prophetic power (as well as in his deeds) and in these we can be like him. Scripture has much to teach about accuracy and gentleness in what we say;[2] "speaking *truth* in *love*" is part of growing up into the fullness of Christ's stature. The solemn prohibition of oaths in the mountain sermon[3] originally had nothing to do with processes of law, but was concerned with the haggling of the market-place where men called God to witness that some cheap and shoddy merchandise was worth three times what the seller himself had paid for it! "Let your Yea be Yea, and your Nay, Nay; whatsoever is more cometh of *evil*"—the evil of an accepted low standard of truthfulness, a conventional over-emphasis which convinces no-one, a habitual exaggeration which makes quiet, plain-spoken truth a novelty. As for *loving* speech, the New Testament's frequent lists of the ugly sins of the lips—railing, clamour, slander, jesting, lying, "corrupt communications", cursing, blasphemy and the rest—show how much even apostolic Christians had to learn of Christlike conversation. A reputation for strict and sober truth in judgement and in business, for fair and kindly comment in personal relations, adds immeasurably to the power of our witness for the Lord: men will note in us what they felt in him, the deep authority of a guarded tongue.

---

[1] Luke 7: 8 (literally).
[2] E.g. Matt. 12: 37; Col. 4: 6; Titus 2: 8.
[3] Matt. 5: 33–37.

II. IN THE EYES OF THE SUPPLIANTS

No-one ever gazed at Jesus with more earnest attention and eager enquiry than the countless needy folk who turned to him for healing, comfort, restoration and forgiveness. Through their eyes, perhaps, we might see him more clearly than through any other, but that would be possible only if we sat where they sat. Of the many things which they might tell us concerning him who met their need, and kindled hope and faith within their hearts, one especially stands out, and to it they would unitedly bear witness: "Out of his fullness have all we received, and grace upon grace."[1] The words are John's, and his meaning goes beyond our present purpose. But they serve to express what so sharply emerges from all the stories of miracles and ministry, comfort and help. Jesus possessed an overflowing fullness of spiritual resources adequate for every demand made upon him, sufficient for every opportunity presented, an inexhaustible reserve of patience and of power that in itself imparted confidence and rebuked the half-belief that hesitated to ask for help.

"Lord, if thou wilt, thou canst . . ."[2]: that is the impression he left upon the suffering, and it is revealed in numerous ways. The Syro-Phoenician woman, pleading for her daughter, was not put off by Christ's reference to the limitations of his ministry, for she knew there was more in him than Israel could exhaust, and the very crumbs that fell from the table he spread were precious.[3] A stricken woman pressed through the crowd, assuring herself that he need never know that she had touched him, for such is the fullness of his grace and power she needed only to touch the hem of his robe (with that queer mixture of superstition and faith which God graciously accepts) to be healed.

Jesus "overflows", so to speak.[4] Mothers coveted for their babes the caress of his hand, the spoken blessing, because they knew that something dwelt in him that could enrich their children's lives. His own mother, in a simple domestic emergency, when the whole future happiness of a peasant couple was so nearly overshadowed on their marriage day by a public exposure of their poverty, out of her experience of this Son of hers, calmly advised "*Whatsoever* he saith unto you, do it".[5] Such things remind us of details we usually

[1] John 1: 16.   [3] Matt. 15: 21–28.   [5] John 2: 1–11.
[2] Matt. 8: 2.   [4] Mark 5: 25–34.

take for granted: how calmly he—a carpenter—faced the raging
storm and trod the waves; how quietly, with no ostentation or
drama or striving for effect, or seeming effort, the miracles were
done; how *adequate* he was, never tiring, never spent, while a
suppliant remained.

And we—with him beside us? How different a story! We are
so often fully burdened with our own sorrows, absorbed in our own
affairs, immersed in our own spiritual conflicts, wholly occupied
with our own doubts, so much more ready to look for help than to
give it. Yet of his fullness have all *we* received, and he promised
it shall flow not only *into* but *out of* us.[1]

> O fill me with Thy fullness, Lord,
> Until my very heart o'erflow
> In kindling thought, and glowing word
> Thy love to tell, Thy praise to show.

III. IN THE EYES OF HIS ENEMIES

It may seem strange to admit the slanders of Christ's enemies as
evidence of the kind of man he was, and we must handle the evidence
with care. But even a slander, if it gains currency at all, must be at
least conceivably true, must contain at least enough of truth—or of
resemblance to truth—to lead intelligent people to repeat it. To be
dangerous, slander need not be true but it must be possible: and
thus two things said about Jesus by his enemies provide further
sidelights upon his character. They said that he was "gluttonous
and a winebibber", and they said that he was mad.[2]

Had the former been said about John the Baptist it would have
been laughed out of existence: it was in fact partly in contrast
to the known austerity and asceticism of John—and his discipline
of fasting[3]—that the charge arose. Whereas John was essentially
a man of the wilderness, alone and aloof, Jesus moved among men
as a genial, friendly, sociable and warm-hearted man, around whom
even the children gathered unafraid and to whom the common
people extended invitations to sit at their tables and visit their homes.
Here was no haggard, burdened, unsmiling man, despising the
world and his fellows! He could be criticised for *not* fasting, and

---

[1] John 4: 14; 7: 37–39.
[2] Matt. 11: 18–19; Luke 7: 34; Mark 3: 21.
[3] Matt. 11: 18, cf. Matt. 9: 14.

when Levi was called to be a disciple[1] his first thought was to invite Jesus to his home and let his old friends and colleagues in the tax-gathering business meet the new Master in a feast of farewell. How vividly that reveals what Levi thought of him, and of his attitude to the class from which the new disciple came. This again was made occasion for criticism—he eateth with publicans and sinners, a winebibber and a glutton ! But we may be thankful for the glimpse thus given of a Master in whose company the friendly enjoyments of sociable people were not killed.

We may digress for a moment to mention here, however briefly, the Master's gift of humour. On the whole the Bible contains sur-prisingly little humour, perhaps because there was little in the Jewish character: what there is in Scripture is wholly in Christ's own words. Unfortunately a customary assumption that religion must be solemn, combined with the sonorous language of the Authorised Version, effectively hide these sallies of Jesus from modern readers. But who that heard his description of the Pharisee straining out from his drink with the fringe of his shawl the microscopic insect that has fallen into it, then proceeding to swallow whole the ugly mis-shapen bulk of a full-grown camel, "head, horns, long neck, one hump, two humps, knobbly knees, hoofs and all" *without noticing it !*—who that heard it for the first time would not have shared the laughter of the delighted crowd ? So with his picture of a neighbour officiously giving first-aid to a friend in trouble with a speck beneath his eye-lid, all unconscious of the *baulk of timber* that sticks out of his own eye-socket, interfering with his vision.

Was that not a smiling tilt at Martha's over-lavish hospitality that betrayed her into criticism of Mary's truer sense of values— "Only one course is necessary, Martha, and Mary has chosen her plateful—don't let us snatch it from her" ? And was that not a playful final quip, after the superb discourse on not taking thought for tomorrow: "After all, haven't you got enough of trouble today to worry about, without adding tomorrow's" ? (If this last sen-tence is taken seriously, it is hard to reconcile it with the lesson on faith, much less with our Lord's usual attitude to life.)[2] These are but examples of a simple, glinting humour that now and again lends added point to his utterance and fresh winsomeness to his teaching. But the Pharisees—and not the Pharisees alone !—do not welcome it.

Luke 5: 27–32.   [2] Matt. 23: 24; 7: 3–5; Luke 10: 38–42; Matt. 6: 34.

Such at any rate Jesus is shown to be by the malicious exaggeration of his foes: a man with "the enjoying nature" rather than a hermit, recluse, or ascetic. This is his Father's world, this his Father's time, and he his Father's child. That is why he could appear so often among his friends with his call to peace, and his characteristic greeting, "Be of good cheer!" If we have given ground for the world's accusation, that the Master is the enemy of all life's lovely things, that the world has grown grey with his breath, then our responsibility is heavy indeed. But the fault is wholly ours, not his: "Man of sorrows" though he was, he victoriously hid his aching heart and bequeathed to us and to all who will take it, an inheritance of *joy*.[1]

The charge that Jesus was mad—"beside himself"[2]—may have been merely a cheap and idle sneer: but it was more probably a reflection of something much deeper, and in the eyes of his enemies much more mysterious, than an occasional oddity of behaviour. Insanity was in the ancient mind allied not simply to genius but to "possession", whether by divine powers or by demons. Modern expressions such as "like one possessed", and "lunatic" still preserve the age-old association of the disordered mind with the invasion of alien powers. That such implication was behind the charge levelled against Jesus is confirmed by its close connection in the same passage with the more explicit charge of working in league with (or under the possession of) the Prince of demons.[3] A similar feeling that in Jesus dwelt powers and agencies not of this world lies behind the strange explanation by which Herod sought to account for the miracles: Herod in all probability did not believe in angels or demons, but that a supernatural, or at least a supernormal, force was at work in Christ he could not deny; he declared therefore that Jesus is John the Baptist "risen from the dead, and therefore mighty works do show themselves forth in him".[4]

He is mad—he is possessed—he is John resurrected: the accusations seem to us absurd, and unworthy of attention. Yet they were dangerous charges, especially the one that suggested co-operation with the devils he exorcised. And the real danger lay once more in the semblance of truth (one might almost say in the element of truth) that made the rumour possible. For undoubtedly there was that about Jesus, beyond his personal authority and power, which

[1] John 15: 11; 17: 13 etc.
[2] Mark 3: 21.
[3] Mark 3: 22, 30.
[4] Matt. 14: 1, 2.

"did not belong" to the normal scheme of things; something not of this world, an air, an energy, an outlook and standard of values which seemed out of key with ordinary judgements and motives. Despite his genial friendship and homely approachableness there was yet in Jesus such a quality that "when you thought of him the thought of God was never far away".

In their malice and unbelief the enemies of Jesus do but bear witness unwillingly to the truth that he himself confessed in the upper room, "I am not of this world".[1] Even this quality is an essential feature of the full delineation of Christlikeness. To grow like him is to grow steadily more unlike our former selves, our "normal" selves, and many of our fellows; it is to keep step with a distant drum; to do, say and decide odd things; to be in the eyes of many inexplicable, eccentric, other-worldly. Not that we can ever forget, with his example before us, the needs and responsibilities and opportunities of this world; but we face those needs, responsibilities and opportunities no longer as those who are thoroughly at home here, or as those facing the world's problems with merely human weapons and resources, but as those who belong elsewhere and travel to distant horizons. Like our Master we are in, but not of, this world.

Two other impressions which our Lord made upon his enemies need not be considered fully here because their real significance will occupy us later: but it is well to notice them in this context of reluctant admissions. One was that Jesus was—*dangerous*. "What do we? for this man doeth many miracles. If we let him thus alone all men will believe on him: and the Romans will come and take away both our place and nation. . . . Perceive ye how ye prevail nothing? behold the world is gone after him. . . . They sought to lay hold on him, but feared the people: for they knew that he had spoken the parable against them."[2] The effeminate and colourless Christ of artistic tradition would not be worth crucifying; the historic Jesus on the other hand was such a potential danger that educated, calculating, experienced leaders of Jewry and of Rome thought it safer, even at considerable risk of popular uprising, to put him to death.

Linked with this is the testimony of his enemies that he was also —*courageous*. Herod, who marvelled at his silent dignity in peril, Pilate, who likewise was deeply impressed with the bearing of his

[1] John 17: 16.   [2] John 11: 47; 12: 19; Mark 12: 12.

enigmatic yet transparent prisoner, and the centurion of the cross, who must have seen many men die, in battle and upon gibbets, yet felt that the manner of Christ's death showed him to be "truly a son of the gods"—together they bear witness that Jesus was outstanding even among stubborn Jews and stoic Romans as a Man of superb physical courage and self-control.[1]

Both these traits in the story *must* be allowed for when we seek the complete picture of the Man, Christ Jesus. For in both respects the real Master differs greatly from the conventional conception of him, in ways that seriously affect the meaning of his example for us, and to a degree that partly accounts for the moral flabbiness of much modern Christianity.

IV. IN THE EYES OF HIS FRIENDS

In one sense, of course, all the knowledge we have of Jesus is due indirectly to the deep impression he made on the minds and hearts of those who grew to understand, trust and love him with their uttermost devotion. It was they who treasured his words, and deeds and even his gestures[2] and who gave their lives that he might be known. Much might be written of the significance of their attitudes towards him: of the significance, for example, of Peter's weeping bitterly when Jesus turned and looked upon him;[3] of Mary's presence in the garden in the morning twilight, clinging pathetically to the last place where she had seen him;[4] of the perplexed minds and desolate hearts of two walking to Emmaus, to whom his death had meant the bottom falling out of their world.[5] Significant too is the uncomprehending but dogged loyalty of Thomas electing to return with Jesus to the perils of Judea rather than let him go alone;[6] the intuitive understanding of Mary breaking the treasured alabaster of ointment "against the day of his burial";[7] the spiritual sympathy of the disciple whom Jesus loved and who reclined on his breast at supper; and the belated but very brave adherence of Nicodemus, Joseph, and James the Lord's brother, in the hour of greatest peril. These things must ever be remembered when we are recalling the

[1] Luke 23: 8–9; Matt. 27: 12–14, cf. Matt. 27: 54 and Luke 23: 47.
[2] Mark 3: 5; 7: 34; John 1: 42, "looked steadily", cf. Mark 10: 21.
[3] Luke 22: 61, 62.
[4] John 20: 11, 14, 15.
[5] Luke 24: 14, 17, 19–21.
[6] John 11: 7, 8, 16.
[7] John 12: 7.

slowness, the ambition, or the unbelief of the first disciples. It is they themselves who tell us of their faults, in order to help us see how wonderfully he dealt with them: beyond all else these men loved him, with a quality of love that is eloquent of his worthiness to be loved.

But from the many things that might be said we choose one particular impression which Jesus left upon his friends, because it is one of the most significant, though often overlooked. When the wealthy tax-gatherer Zaccheus, on his first acquaintance with Jesus, had sat at table with him for only a short while—the conversation is unrecorded, and only the criticism of the bystanders reveals what kind of man Zaccheus was reputed to be—suddenly the professional misdeeds of a lifetime were blurted out, fourfold restitution of exorbitant exactions was freely offered to the wronged, and the whole outlook and habit of a confirmed materialist, in whom social approval, patriotism and religion had hitherto been sacrificed to ambition, were totally changed. What no amount of public ostracism or Pharisaic scorn had ever achieved was accomplished at once *in the company of Jesus.*[1]

When the woman of Samaria had sat awhile with Jesus on the well-head in Sychar, the hoarded secrets of a long career of unhappiness and sin were brought into daylight and her heart was changed and cleansed in the course of a brief conversation.[2] A woman taken in adultery was brought forcibly into his presence, doubtless embittered, emboldened and afraid: but when his searing words—"He that is without sin among you, let him first cast a stone at her"—had shamed her accusers into silent withdrawal, she, who might have been thought first to slip away, lingered on to speak with him. She waited, a wholly changed woman, until the bowed head was lifted, and she received the gracious words of kindness, warning and pardon.[3]

So it was with Peter. After his first meeting with Jesus, in which the promise implied in the new name given him had quickened the wish to be a better man, Peter found he could not achieve his aspiration; habit and inclination proved too strong for moral resolutions of reform. When next he met with Jesus it was to lend him the fishing-boat for a pulpit: and the meeting, and perhaps the message, stirred again the deep longings awakened in his heart. The sermon over, Jesus instructed the disciple group to launch out for a catch of fish, but Peter reminded him that they had toiled

[1] Luke 19: 1–10.   [2] John 4: 5–30.   [3] John 8: 1–11.

I

all night and found nothing. But with Christ in command failure is always turned to success, and fruitless struggle becomes a victory. Peter read the meaning with painful clarity—and fell upon his knees protesting "Depart from me, for I am a sinful man, O Lord".[1] The inner secrets of struggle, longing and failure lay all exposed, and the Master had answered, by the parable in a miracle, what Peter wanted to say but dare not.

So again it was with Nathanael. When Philip brought him from the place of meditation under the fig-tree (a favourite refuge among the more thoughtful and retiring pious of Jewry) Nathanael was greeted, to his great astonishment, with words from Jesus which echoed precisely the thread of his reflections upon the story of Jacob at Bethel,—the trickery and guile which necessitated Jacob's flight from home, and the gracious promise of the ascending and descending angels still caring in mercy for his wayward soul. "Whence knowest thou me?" is Nathanael's involuntary question, for yet again the thoughts of the heart had been revealed, and Jesus had probed the inner world of a man's secret self-communings.[2]

When these and similar incidents are pondered together, it becomes evident that those who had reason to know him best discovered in Jesus a searching, austere insight that exposed one's inner sinfulness—or piety—and brought hidden things to light. More often than not, an astringent purity that was both confiding and cleansing won from his friends a heartfelt confession; and sometimes, as with Zaccheus, there was an instinctive sense of what was morally fitting to the friendship of such a one. There was about Jesus something inexorably straight and clean, in whose presence the shameful and the false could not live, but must either slink away or stay to be forgiven. The woman of Samaria attempted to give a name to this quality, in declaring "Sir, I perceive that thou art a prophet"; Nathanael, by saying "Rabbi, thou art the Son of God, thou art the King of Israel"; Peter, by his "Depart from me, O Lord". But, however we define it, there was certainly about the portrait of Jesus seen through the eyes of his friends an antiseptic quality of moral insight and truth that constituted an unspoken demand for righteousness, for penitence and for sincerity. None who lingered in his presence failed to be cleansed by his company.

[1] John 1: 42; Luke 5: 1–11. (The interpretation suggested seems the only one which really accounts for Peter's unexpected reaction and which sets John 1: 42 in clear relation with Luke 5: 1–11).
[2] John 1: 45–51.

In imperfect ways, and in infinitely lesser degree, something of this kind is possible to those who grow in Christlikeness. Most of us cherish the memory of some saintly parent, teacher or friend in whose presence our secret regrets and hidden falsehoods seemed "dragged out of us" by their kindly sympathy and faithful sincerity in dealing with our souls. It must be emphasised that such an influence is almost wholly unconscious: to seek it is to make it wholly impossible. We become merely critics of our fellows, and judges— or what is worse, self-appointed father-confessors,—if we set ourselves to examine the secrets of our brethren. But it remains true that here again is part of the matchless portrait, and as we cultivate the mind of Christ and are transformed into his image so will others increasingly testify that God has used us deeply in their lives.

Though this chapter has been long it is, of course, very far from a complete account of Jesus seen through the eyes of his contemporaries. We have sought only to suggest one method by which we can seek to know the lineaments of the Master, and to offer some illustrations of its use. It is an indirect method, but it has special value for that reason: for by it our personal predispositions and preferences are to some degree set aside and we are led to see Jesus from unaccustomed points of view. But incomplete though it is, even as an example of one particular method of "seeing Jesus", we cannot but feel humbled by the glimpses of his greatness, and the height of that ideal to which we have been called.

CHAPTER 11

OUTSTANDING FEATURES

IT MAY be said that in one respect we have a slight advantage over many of Jesus' contemporaries when we seek to see clearly and in true perspective what manner of man he was. Whereas they usually saw him on isolated and particular occasions, we with the Gospels in our hands can see more easily the whole picture; and with our knowledge of all that followed we can appreciate a little more fully the true significance of what we see. Of course we lose a great deal in other ways, and the effort of reverent imagination needed to make the stories vivid to our minds is never easy. All the more reason is there, then, to make the most of our slight advantage, to be careful to keep in mind the whole story, and observe the balance of truth, when we are attempting to describe the impression Jesus makes upon ourselves.

So rich and profound a character as Christ's cannot, of course, be summed up in phrases, or "outlined" and analysed in mere words. Inevitably we make selection among the features of the portrait that could be listed, and the selection will vary not only with different believers but at different stages of each believer's spiritual progress. One thing after another in the matchless story seems to be the crucial matter, and again and again as insight deepens and our own character develops we revise our mental picture of Jesus. No description therefore can ever be final: and for the same reason no one else's description will ever satisfy us. Yet if we are to share our thoughts about Jesus something must be said, and so we choose four outstanding features of the impression Jesus makes upon ourselves, as the four corners of a portrait-sketch of One who truly "beggars all description"—his strength, his tenderness, his purity, his love.

I. THE STRENGTH OF JESUS

We begin here with the "robust manliness and steel-tempered will power" of Jesus because this may truly be said to be the foundation

132

from which all else in Christ's nature derives its strength. The
true quality of Christ's tenderness, the intensity of his holiness,
the meaning of his love, can only be understood against the background of a nature immensely powerful, vigorous and strong.

Popular ideas about Jesus are probably nowhere further from the
truth than just here. Deliberately we set that borrowed phrase
"robust manliness and steel-tempered will power" alongside the
childhood hymn, true enough but far from adequate, "Gentle
Jesus, meek and mild . . ." The traditional picture of Jesus,
treasured not only in the stained glass of the churches but in the
imagination of many Christians, makes Jesus a mild and almost
effeminate personality, insipid, soft and sentimental, a womanly
man, burdened with sadness and (so one would sometimes imagine)
ever on the verge of tears.

Two facts alone should make the inadequacy of that conventional conception of Jesus obvious to even the most casual reader
of the Gospels: one is that Jesus did gather around him, hold, and
fire with undying enthusiasm a group of strong, virile and essentially
masculine disciples, men of no effeminate nonsense, men like Peter,
Thomas, Levi, James, and Paul—and that is deeply significant.
The other fact is, that Jesus was crucified. If Christ really were the
kind of man so many pictures suggest, it is difficult to see how he
ever came to exercise any power over his own generation, how he
could ever become an influential factor in history, or why anybody
should think him dangerous enough to kill him. His cross is the
final tribute of his enemies to the strength and vigour of his character: they knew him to be a man to be reckoned with, and to be
guarded against.

Turning again therefore to the New Testament story, and seeking
to adjust our thought to what is actually written, we are immediately
in danger of seeing nothing but his strength. Each saying, each
action, each move, considered in this light, seems to remind us of
the quality of the Man with whom we have to do. The Evangelists
seem to say, with Pilate, "Behold the Man". For instance, they
appear intent on emphasising at all points *his moral courage*. They
show us One never timid before his enemies, never hesitant before
his questioners, never careful of his watching accusers. He acted
according to his conviction, spoke as conscience bade, without
considering the effect on his own safety or reputation. He called
a publican into the circle of his disciples, in defiance of prevailing

opinion, and visited the house of Zaccheus of Jericho as readily as that of Simon the Pharisee.[1]

While in no way holding himself aloof from the Pharisees, or setting himself in antagonism to them as a class, Jesus nevertheless even while accepting their invitations would neither trim his own behaviour to their prejudices nor evade the issues that divided him from them. At "a certain Pharisee's" house Jesus sat at meat without first performing the ceremonial washing which Pharisaism demanded, in part no doubt because in the intimate circle of the disciples the custom was never observed. In a "chief Pharisee's" house he spoke unanswerably on the vexed question of the Sabbath; and on another similar occasion, in defence of a woman, seemingly of his company, whom the host had ignored, he uttered the most scathing denunciation of a flagrant breach of the elementary rules of Eastern hospitality—"Simon, did you *see* this woman ? . . . you offered me no kiss of welcome, no water or towel, no oil for anointing . . . she, a sinner, puts you to shame, though it was at your own invitation I sat at your table !"[2]

His attitude to the crowds he sought to win is equally expressive of independence and certainty. While never ignoring or despising "the multitude", but rather yearning over them,[3] he refused to pay lip-service to popular religious ideas, and avoided the use of the title Messiah because it would arouse unthinking excitements and provoke misunderstanding. He was prepared to disappoint the people by refusing a sign,[4] and again by repudiating revolution.[5] He charged them with following him for unworthy motives[6] and would not abate his claims to keep them.[7] Even when the crowds began to desert him, he only turned sadly to his inner circle of disciples and said "Will ye also go away ?"[8] Here surely is no reed shaken by the wind of popular feeling, but a moral courage that goes its own way assured of its own integrity.

The same strength is seen in *the deliberate policy of his ministry*. His message was one of challenge and candour: his very invitations discouraged impulsiveness. The path that leads to life is narrow and lonely,—the gateway restricted. The righteousness demanded in the kingdom is higher, not easier, than that of the Scribe, and demands a "becoming as a little child" so radical as to involve

---

[1] Matt. 9: 9–13; Luke 19: 7 and 7: 36f.
[2] Luke 11: 37–40; 14: 1–6; 7: 44–6.
[3] Matt. 9: 36; Mark 6: 34.
[4] Matt. 12: 38, 39.
[5] Matt. 22: 18.
[6] John 6: 26.
[7] John 6: 41, 43, 52, 60–6.
[8] John 6: 66–7.

rebirth with a new nature. The type of person who will find blessed-
ness in the kingdom of God is the precise opposite of the type
who prospers in the world, and he must expect to be persecuted.

Nor will outward allegiance alone, or the profession of words,
avail anything, for it is the state of the heart and the detailed obedience of conduct which alone ensures acceptance. Those who think
of following him had better sit down to consider if they can see
it through, like a wise builder planning a tower or a king contemplating war. And they had better prepare beforehand for self-
denial, and daily self-crucifixion, bringing their own crosses. No
guarantee against trouble was offered, for the same storm of wind,
rain and flood beats upon the wise man's house as upon the fool's
—only in the outcome is the difference seen. And so the impulsive
were deliberately sent back: while no one postponing decision
or hankering after the old life was fit for the kingdom.[1] This whole
policy of truth and heroic challenge puts to shame the sentimentalism
and emotional excitement of some evangelism, and expresses a
moral and intellectual strength which is unfamiliar to much modern
Christianity. It is the method Jesus deliberately chose in the wilderness, and which led inevitably to the cross.

The strength of Jesus is seen no less in *the physical and mental
endurance* which the story reveals. Early rising, sleepless nights,
busy days, long journeyings, homelessness sometimes, and the
constant drain of physical and nervous energy[2] add up to a strenuous
though short career. The odd remark of certain bystanders "Thou
art not yet fifty years old" may suggest that the strain told in his
appearance and added years to his look.[3] The incessant mingling
with sick, demented, deformed men and women imposed upon
his sensitive heart—more than once the groan of his own soul's
sympathy escaped him—a burden that told.

Still more demanding were the constant collisions with popular
thought, and the accusing, tempting trials of strength and of wisdom that faced him in the last days in Jerusalem.[4] The failure of
the crowd to understand, the inability of the disciples to appreciate
his inner meaning, the falsity of Judas, the expediency of Caiaphas,

---

[1] Matt. 7: 13, 14; 5: 20; 18: 3; John 3: 3; Matt. 5: 1–12; 7: 21–3; Luke 14:
25–33; 9: 23–4; Matt. 16: 24; 7: 24–7; Luke 9: 57–62.
[2] E.g. Mark 1: 35; Luke 6: 12; Mark 10: 1, 32, 46; 11: 1, 15; Luke 9: 58;
Mark 5: 30.
[3] John 8: 57.
[4] Mark 11: 27; 12: 13, 18, 28; Matt. 22: 15, 34f.

the cowardice of Pilate all imposed strain upon the spirit of Jesus, yet he moved amidst it all never doubting, never unnerved, never despondent. John the Baptist questioned the message he had delivered, the disciples hesitated and counselled caution,[1] but "he steadfastly set his face to go to Jerusalem",[2] knowing all the time the fate that awaited him. He had the patient endurance that only strong souls know.

The conventional, popular idea of Jesus omits all reference to *his anger*. The Gospels, written by men who knew him far better than we, do not hesitate to tell of the deep indignation that sometimes roused his soul and overflowed in burning words. When the disciples drove back the mothers and children seeking his blessing "he was very indignant" as the original has it, and rebuked them publicly and sharply.[3] The priestly families of Judea took advantage of their power to reject blemished sacrifices or Roman coins from use within the Temple, to establish a monopoly of market and money-changing within the sacred precincts, thereby exploiting the pilgrim-worshippers and denying to the devout Gentile the only place of prayer allotted to him.[4] Jesus drove forth the beasts and overturned the tables, uttering words of such searing accusation and scorn that for a time none withstood him, but all scattered before his anger. In the Synagogue, zeal for the letter of the Sabbath law made the Pharisees indifferent to the eager longing and urgent need of a maimed man—and before healing him Jesus "looked round about upon them with anger",[5] being grieved for the hardness of their hearts.

Something of this anger at callousness towards the sufferings of others breathes in the parable of Dives and Lazarus,[6] and it was expressed beyond doubt in the great and terrible chapter of denunciation in Matthew 23. This incisive attack opened with the damaging distinction between the *authority* that Scribe and Pharisee undoubtedly bore, and the danger of following their *example*. With scorn he described the love of outward homage and flattering titles which the crowd well knew marked the rising Pharisee; their hindrances to true religion; their skill in lending money to illiterate widows (unable to read the bonds they sign) and so obtaining mortgage of their houses—the while covering their rapacity with ostentatious prayers. He castigated their misguided zeal in proselytising,

---

[1] Luke 7: 19; John 11: 8.   [3] Mark 10: 14.   [5] Mark 3: 5.
[2] Luke 9: 51.   [4] Mark 11: 15–18.   [6] Luke 16: 19f.

their morally blind casuistry, their lack of perspective in religious judgements, their hypocrisy, which made them a hidden spring of uncleanness in society, their blind opposition to the truth and to the message of God; and he foretold their doom. All this was declared in words of vigorous indignation that help to explain why the ruling classes of Jewry counted him a danger and a foe.

The anger of Jesus has in it nothing of self-defence, retaliation, or nursed resentment: he was not roused by infringement of his personal interests, but by inhumanity, by hypocrisy, by worldliness under the cloak of religion. And in such anger we feel his strength.

Finally, though we are not here concerned with the details of his story, we should note the strength revealed in Christ's *deliberate programme of action*. After many months of ministry in Galilee, with occasional visits to Jerusalem, Jesus retired to Caesarea Philippi to examine the disciples as to the impressions made upon the crowds that have followed him everywhere, and upon themselves. Peter's confession that he was the Christ brought a swift and calculated change of programme. Immediately Jesus left the circuits of Galilean villages and made straight for Jerusalem, teaching and healing those who came to him, but no longer practising itinerant preaching.

At Jericho he received from blind Bartimaeus the first acknowledged public recognition that he was "Son of David"—hitherto the idea had been avoided or silenced. Then followed the astonishing five-fold challenge to the nation to make up its mind about his claims.[1] Under the shadow of the city he raised Lazarus, and the crowds, swollen now by pilgrims from every quarter of Palestine, were set excitedly arguing about himself and his intentions.[2] In this atmosphere he rode into Jerusalem as Zechariah foretold but in such form that his claim was unintelligible to a Roman court[3] though perfectly understood by Jews. At the gate of the city, where every year pilgrims had seen the figtree beside the road, he left a standing parable of the doom that awaits anything—nation, institution, Church, individual,—that makes great profession without bearing real fruit. A people accustomed to the acted parables of the prophets understood his meaning very well.[4]

Next day he challenged the priestly authorities in their own

[1] Mark 10: 46–52.
[2] John 11: 1–44, note 45–53; 12: 10–11, 18.
[3] John 12: 10–19.
[4] Mark 11: 12–14, 20; Matt. 21: 19, 20.

stronghold, the Temple courtyard, driving out their representatives and denouncing their avarice. And then, with deadly insistence, he unfolded and supplemented a passage of their own Scripture, beloved of every Jewish heart proud that his land was indeed the vineyard of the Lord, and prophesied the destruction of the vineyard-servants, and the giving of the vineyard to others—to Gentiles. "And the chief priests and the scribes sought the same hour to lay hands on him . . . for they perceived that he had spoken this parable against them".[1]

Crowded thus into the last five days were five hammer-blows at the nation's conscience, delivered at the Capital and the Holy Place, in the high season of Passover—no wonder they felt bound to act at once, dropping the original caution, "not at the feast, because of the people".[2] For events were in his hands, not theirs, and he was most definitely to be reckoned with,—and removed.

His courage, his candour, his endurance, his anger, his programme of assault—all speak his strength of purpose, his vigour of character. "His was a commanding personality, and no-one dared take liberties with him." We desert the records and dishonour him, when we cling to the idea that Jesus was a genial and indulgent sentimentalist. He was stern in challenge, terrible in denunciation, clear in warning, swift to oppose falsehood, definite in demands, feared as well as loved. Yet ever that strength was under control, serving the interests of truth, or of others, never of self, and none need fear it but those who preferred evil to good, their own way to God's.

Lack of this feature in the prevailing idea of Jesus has wrought real havoc with the type of Christianity that has served as model in much Christian work. Our preaching has so often lacked the strength of deep thought and moral challenge, our Churches fear discipline, our opposition to the vested evil of the world is pitiable, our evangelism is from weakness instead of from strength—too often resembling an appeal from a hard-beset Church to the outsider to "come over and help us". Much of this arises because we have forgotten the strength of Jesus and the uncompromising, martial spirit of the early Church. God needs strong servants, Christlike in the vigour of deep conviction and indomitable courage: men and women strong in the strength which God *supplies*, through his eternal Son.

[1] Luke 20: 1–18 and note 19.   [2] Matt. 26: 5; Mark 14: 2.

II. THE TENDERNESS OF JESUS

It is well to dispose at once of the thought that the tenderness of Jesus is in any sense the opposite of his strength. It is truer to say it is that strength's perfection. Tenderness is not by any means the same thing as weakness: rather, only the really strong can be truly tender. For the essence of gentleness lies in the curbing of strength to avoid injury to the weak; in the dedication of strength to the assistance of the helpless; in the assertion of strength in defence of the sensitive and vulnerable. It is not the weak who can help the weak, but the strong, where strength is compounded with sympathy, sensitiveness and concern.

The tenderness of Jesus then is the tenderness of power held in reserve. We are to see how wondrously his strength was tempered, sweetened, poised and controlled by superb sensitiveness to others' feelings and exquisite gentleness of manner and of action. Proof here is hardly necessary: the need, and the difficulty, is to describe what is accepted and familiar in ways that will make the truth vivid to our hearts.

One characteristic of the soul sensitive to others' needs is the ability to "sit where others sit", and so to do those small but eloquent things which seem obviously right when done but which are so often overlooked. The life of our Lord abounds in examples of this "sympathetic transference" from one's own point of view and feeling into that of another soul. He felt, despite the crisis of his own affairs, the conflict of panic and loyalty that tore the disciples in the Garden of Gethsemane, and with a word—"If ye seek me, let these go their way"—he at once asked the soldiers' permission, and gave his own, for their flight.[1] He foresaw and forbade the discourtesy that could so easily wound the humble folk who would invite into their homes his messengers, travelling two by two around the villages of Galilee, if when some more imposing and wealthy home was opened to them the disciples moved their quarters— "Into whatsoever house ye enter, first say, Peace be to this house . . . And in the same house remain, eating and drinking such things as they give . . . Go not from house to house."[2]

After a long tiring day of high teaching, Jesus will not, like the disciples, let the crowd depart hungry to seek food where they

[1] John 18: 8; Mark 14: 48-50. [2] Luke 10: 5-7.

may: their ordinary comforts also are his concern, and he feeds them in the wilderness ere he bids them go.[1] Despite the crowds who press upon him he finds room for attention to the children— and surely not merely that he might get on the right side of the mothers![2] In the darkest hour of his own agony he thinks of his mother's need of another son's care.[3] Nor should we take for granted the way Jesus adapts his teaching to the capacities of his humblest hearers. He adorns the truth in the simplest of tales, and yet he never "condescends" to lower intelligence, for he leaves much to be pondered over, with his "He that hath an ear, let him hear" and "Why even of your own selves judge ye not what is right?"[4]

Such illustrations of his insight into the feelings of others are everywhere, but especially perhaps in the *manner* of the miracles. This is a very moving feature of his ministry to the sick. He is always adequate, powerful, calm, and yet he is never distant, unfeeling, aloof, never preoccupied with his own cares, nor with the effect the miracle is going to have upon others. The sufferer absorbs his attention, and with amazing understanding the method of the miracle serves the individual need.

Thus, for a striking example, the miracle at Cana of Galilee[5] seems to some unnecessary; it is curiously roundabout (and, since it is secret, ineffective) if its sole purpose was "to reveal his glory". Jesus did not usually act for this reason. But if we get inside the story, and see the situation created in a tiny village by the (apparently unexpected) arrival at the wedding feast of several young men of hearty appetite; if then we try to imagine the effect *on the young couple* of the public disclosure of their poverty, and foresee the village gossip which they would never quite live down—"after all, they started badly, they couldn't really afford to get married!"— then we begin to see why Mary turned quietly to Jesus with a motherly concern for the young people, and why attention was diverted from what he was going to do. We see why none of the guests, not even the mystified master of ceremonies, is enlightened about it—"but only the servants which drew the water knew" (and they knew already the predicament of the house!). But what delicacy and tender concern is revealed in *the way* he did it.

---

[1] Mark 6: 35–44.
[2] Mark 10: 13–16.
[3] John 19: 26.
[4] Mark 4: 9, etc.; Luke 12: 57.
[5] John 2: 1–11.

The same is true of the raising of Jairus' daughter. Here also there is mystery and it seems true to say, with all reverence, that Jesus fosters the mystery. To this day scholars debate whether the girl was dead or not. According to Mark[1] the first message brought to Jesus was that she lay "at the point of death" and he was asked to come and "heal" her. The second message said she was dead, and there was no use in troubling Jesus further. Matthew condensed both messages into one: "My daughter is even now dead, but come and lay thy hand upon her and she shall live." Luke explained in his own words that "she lay adying" and gave the second message as Mark, "Thy daughter is dead, trouble not the Master." All this, with the presence of the professional mourning women, and the scornful laughter that greeted his assertion that she slept (Luke adds "knowing that she was dead" to explain their laughter), would seem to leave no doubt that the girl had really died. Yet observe what happened: arriving at the house Jesus at once dismissed the mourners sternly, with the word that "*She is not dead*, but sleepeth".

Is that to be taken literally, or did he mean that since he was going to restore her the present condition would end in "waking"? The same word was used to describe Lazarus' death,[2] about the reality of which there can be no doubt, and the word became the regular word among Christians for death-with-the-Christian-hope. It is not certain how Jesus' words are to be understood—and that is probably as he intended. For (the next strange feature of the story) he allowed only the parents (who had to know in any case) and three disciples of the inner circle (whom he could trust) to go with him to the bedside, as though intent upon preserving secrecy. And then, in tender words which rang in Peter's memory throughout his life, and passed thence into Mark's Gospel, he took the girl's hand and said, "Get up, girlie"—the words are impossible to translate acceptably because they are the kind of idiomatic, family-language which defies being put into print. The point is important, for the girl awoke as she had for every day she could remember, with the same words in her ears, her mother beside her, and in the astonished silence that held the circle, before the girl could sense their fright, he broke in with the suggestion of breakfast—she was hungry. Then he charged all "straitly" that no one should know of it.

[1] Mark 5: 22–43, cf. Matt. 9: 18 and Luke 8: 41.
[2] John 11: 11–13.

Why all this secrecy, and how is it possible to keep it secret ? *Simply that the girl might not know she had been dead ;* simply that she might return to normal life, knowing only that she had been very ill, that the Prophet had come and wakened her, and that though many seem to have thought she had died it was really only the last deep sleep that made her better ! And for the village—let them draw what conclusion they like. He has provided the excuse for saying she was only asleep after all, as he said ! Is this all just fancy ? Is there any other explanation of his curious behaviour, or of the strange command to keep the matter secret, when all the district knew ? Is it not that here, again, the perfect understanding by Jesus of the inner feelings and needs of those whom he is helping has shaped the miracle itself in a way puzzling to us but clear to those who knew.

There is no need to insist upon this admittedly imaginative interpretation, for the point itself is well established that in the way he did his miracles, as well as in the compassion that prompted them, Jesus revealed the most perfect sympathy with the inward distress of the sufferer. For the demented man of Gadara,[1] too confused in mind to give even his name, and speaking now in the singular, now in the plural, about "himself", Jesus had time for quiet talk and enquiry in which the man gained confidence. Then, the miracle done, with the same clear insight into the man's need, he would not let him run away from the place of his fears but sent him back among his friends and kindred—to grow strong in mind and faith.

For the blind, whose faith must rest for the most part on the assurance in his voice,[2] Jesus provided the conventional medicaments of clay and spittle laid upon the eyes, to help quicken expectancy and confidence—though he needed no means to convey his power. In one case, where the man had memory of sight[3] he took the sufferer away beyond the town to a quiet place for the first overwhelming moments of the cure. The deaf and dumb were regarded oftentimes with horror and almost with fear, but Jesus would wait, and with infinite patience engage in the tedious language of signs in order to communicate to a soul otherwise cut off the purpose he intended and the faith he desired,[4] again taking the supplicant aside alone for the interview.

[1] Mark 5: 1–19; Luke 8: 26; Matt. 8: 28.
[2] Notice John 9: 12, 36, 37; 10: 3, 4, 5; for the clay John 9: 6; Mark 8: 23.
[3] Mark 8: 22f.
[4] Mark 7: 32–5.

The tender "My daughter, my son, thy faith hath saved thee" set at rest the fear and confusion in many a trembling soul, and we must refuse even to try to say what volumes of sympathy and understanding were conveyed to the bitter loneliness of the outcast leper when his gentle fingers rested on the loathsome, unclean flesh. Lest we imagine that all this meant nothing to his own heart, recall again that at the healing of the dumb he was heard to sigh, at the cure of the epileptic boy his burdened heart found utterance,[1] and at the grave of Lazarus a shuddering groan escaped him, and "Jesus wept".[2] Surely he hath borne our griefs and carried our sorrows, with the inward sensitiveness of a divine sympathy.

Even so, it is not with the suffering, but with the sinful that his exquisite tenderness is fully seen. The chief temptation of the strong is impatience, or contempt, for the weak and the erring: but it is written of Jesus that "a bruised reed shall he not break, and smoking flax shall he not quench".[3] Twice we see him face to face with a woman known to be sinful, while proud, self-righteous Pharisees watch for his reaction. To the one he had no word at all of rebuke or question, but seeing her repentance in her tears said only "Daughter, thy sins *are* forgiven thee—go in peace". To the other, having first sent out her accusers with smarting consciences, he said simply "Neither do I condemn thee, go—and sin no more".[4] Here is strength, setting itself between the fallen and the accusing finger of society, while entering fully into the inmost pain of the soul in shame.

Jerusalem, boasting its divine election and destiny, was preparing for him its cruellest form of death, yet he could not think of her approaching punishment without breaking down.[5] Judas, a confidant and friend, had sold him to the authorities and sealed his treachery with a kiss, yet Christ had for him, even in the Garden, only the infinitely gentle, infinitely sad word, "Friend, why . . . ?"[6] Thomas, one of the twelve, despite the promise and the report of the resurrection, stubbornly refused to believe—"except I see the nailprints" —and when Jesus came to him, instead of rebuke there was only the gentle reminder, after his test was patiently met, that "Blessed are those who have *not* seen, yet have believed".[7]

---

[1] Matt. 17: 17; Mark 9: 19; Luke 9: 38f.
[2] John 11: 33, 35.
[3] Matt. 12: 18–20.
[4] Luke 7: 36–50; John 8: 1–11.
[5] Luke 19: 41–2.
[6] Matt. 26: 50.
[7] John 20: 24–9.

One further illustration of Christ's gentleness with sinners will suffice—the moving, subduing story of his dealing with Peter. When first they met Jesus had spoken of the new man he could make of Peter[1] and apparently Peter had tried, and failed, to respond to that quickening promise. When next they meet it is beside the lake and a miracle of successful fishing speaks transforming things to Peter's soul,[2] culminating in the kindling imperative "Follow me". There ensued the great confession, followed at once by the great rebuke,[3] and a steady discipline in which Peter's exuberant, impetuous spirit was slowly harnessed by Jesus. Then the solemn warning of the imminent forsaking, to which Peter presumptuously replied, "Though all forsake thee, yet will not I." Jesus answered bluntly that before the cock should crow Peter would thrice deny that he had known him. And so it was: beside a fire of coals in the courtyard of the High Priest's house, with oaths that echoed the old life before he met the Master, Peter denied that he had ever known the Lord. Immediately, a glance of grief and love from the eyes of Christ broke him down in shame, and going out into the night Peter hid from the rest, and was not with them through the dark weekend.

But on Easter Day the risen Lord sent a separate, personal message to him—"Tell Peter"—and later sought him out for an interview nowhere described.[4] Yet still the shameful denial had not been erased, as truth and honour and Peter's future usefulness demanded that it should be. Then came another scene upon a lakeside, after another miraculous catch of fish, and beside another fire of coals. Drawing Peter apart from the rest Jesus gently questioned him, but the name was the old, original name of the earliest days: "Simon, son of Jonas, do you love me" (as you said you did) "more than these do?" Vividly remembering, Peter again declared the love, but avoided the boast. Repeating the question, Jesus himself this time omitted the comparison—"Lovest thou me?" And so a third time. The parallel with the threefold denial struck sharply home to Peter: he was "grieved", and protested, but humbly and brokenly, by the Lord's own knowledge of his heart, that spite of all "I love thee". Only then was given the heartening promise that next time

[1] John 1: 42.
[2] Luke 5: 1–11; see page 129 above.
[3] Matt. 16: 13–20; 21–3.
[4] Matt. 26: 31, 33–5; Luke 22: 31–4; Matt. 26: 58; and 69–75; Mark 14: 66–72; Luke 22: 54–62; Mark 16: 7; 1 Cor. 15: 5; John 21: 1–19.

he is tested, he will be steadfast even unto death; and so back again to the old beginning, a chastened new beginning, with another "Follow me".

Could anything be more exquisitely delicate in dealing with an erring soul—more intimately understanding, more gently firm? Denial and shameful weakness cannot be merely overlooked, nor sentimentalised over, nor politely "forgotten"; it is not by pretence or evasion that great apostles are made. But there is no word of direct reproach, no stern "Peter, I warned you", no punishment. Tenderly and faithfully the erring disciple is led to recall the beginnings, to remember his boasts, to retrace his steps, to erase his denial with renewed vows of love, and then to take up the tasks again, not expecting to be spared further and severer testing, but ready for it, and still, as of old, to follow. The strong and true, but infinitely gentle Jesus woos, and wins, and holds for ever one whose self-reproach might have wrecked his high career.

This then, too, is part of the portrait: this too it means to be Christlike. Most of us are afraid to be gentle, lest it be taken for weakness. We are ourselves so uncertain of our strength we fear to compromise our own position, and the respect of others that we know is given to the brusque and forceful. Jesus shows that the gentle man is great. Strong in his tenderness, and tender in his strength, he sets us the high pattern of his own example, and gives us his Spirit, of whom one fruit is ". . . gentleness".[1]

III. The Purity of Jesus

We have already noted, among the impressions left by Jesus upon his contemporaries, the experience shared by numbers of his friends that there was about Jesus something inexorably straight and clean, in whose presence the shameful and the false could not live. They felt in him an antiseptic quality of moral insight and truth that constituted an unspoken demand for righteousness, for penitence and for sincerity. It is difficult both to name and to analyse this quality: *purity* seems too narrow and inadequate a word; *holiness* suggests to modern minds something distant, supernatural and cold. Without insisting on the name we shall do our best to describe a *cleanness* of nature and of will that is beyond common experience, and well-nigh beyond imagining.

[1] Gal. 5: 22.

K

Inevitably in this connection we think of the complete absence from the mind and character of Jesus of all those things which defile and warp human nature, rob the soul of its innocence and make it corrupt in itself and a menace to others. But this is only half the truth. His was a strong deep positive purity that was not only victorious over all life's defilement, but seems ever to have been out of range of the coarser temptations that afflict most men. Certainly Jesus was tempted: the Evangelists record it, Jesus admitted it, the epistle to the Hebrews based on the fact his fitness to be High Priest, "having been tempted in all points like as we are".[1] And the wilderness experience was no pretence; the ministering angels testify to its intensity,[2] as do also the vehemence of Christ's words to Peter[3] and the anguish of Gethsemane.[4]

But this also must be noted: the temptations, though painful, came in his case ever from without—from the task in hand, from the stubbornness of the disciples, from the alternative ways of accomplishing his task that presented themselves, from the approach of the cross—never from within his own heart. He could say (as we so rarely can) "The Prince of this world cometh and hath nothing in me"—no foothold with the fortress of his soul.[5] Nor was the issue ever in doubt. His was no prolonged struggle, no gradual conquest, no falling and rising again; he shook off the temptation from his soul with clear and prompt decision that left not the slightest stain or scar. He was tempted; he remains "the Holy One of God".[6]

Those who lived nearest to Jesus were the loudest in their testimony to his absolute purity of heart. They expressed it in varied ways: they said he had no experience of sin ("knew no sin"), that he was faultless in his conduct ("did no sin"), that he somehow dwelt above sin ("he was without sin"), that sin had no place at all in his thought or feeling ("in him was no sin").[7] The final reason for their belief in the sinlessness of Jesus was doubtless the fact that though no man ever had a more tender conscience, nor a keener awareness of what sin was, nor a deeper hatred of all forms of concealing sin, yet they never once heard from his lips a confession of

[1] Matt. 4: 1–11; Luke 4: 1–13; Luke 22: 28; Heb. 4: 15.
[2] Matt. 4: 11.
[3] Matt. 16: 23.
[4] Luke 22: 44; cf. Heb. 5: 7.
[5] John 14: 30.
[6] Mark 1: 24.
[7] 2 Cor. 5: 21; 1 Pet. 2: 22; Heb. 4: 15; 1 John 3: 5.

sin, a prayer for forgiveness, an expression of unworthiness, an apology or a plea for grace and mercy. He who taught us to pray daily for forgiveness[1] and bade us copy the publican's penitent cry for mercy[2] needed not to set example in either.

This fact undoubtedly lies behind the confident assertions of the sinlessness of Christ: but is it not obvious that before they could have believed it, or testified to it, they who had known him so intimately must have known that nothing in their memory of him made the idea incredible, the faith impossible? From personal, constant acquaintance with him they knew he ever acted as one free from the inner sense of sin: and—most significant of all— within days of his death they addressed to him their prayers, offered him their worship, surrendered to him that absolute obedience that only God may demand. The truth goes far deeper than the assertion of Pilate "I find no fault in him"; deeper too than his own question "Which of you convinceth me of sin?";[3] the disciples recognised in Jesus that quality of intrinsic holiness which through long centuries of revelation and discipline Israel had been taught was the character of her God.

All this we normally take for granted. The difficulty here again is to make the familiar truth vivid to our hearts in terms of life and character—remembering we are called to be Christlike.

Certainly the purity of Jesus means that he was utterly free from *passion*. There seems to be something almost irreverent even in referring to the normal meaning of purity, in connection with Jesus. His whole bearing soars infinitely above the lusts and passions that rage in other hearts. We shall see that he pressed the command of absolute purity right into the inmost regions of the mind, and condemned the unclean thought and desire as sharply as the outward act. We know too that he gave to marriage and to womanhood an altogether new dignity and sanctity.[4] It is significant that the men who lived three years with him, and found it possible afterwards to worship him as God's Son, never tell us in so many words that he was pure in this sense—it simply never occurred to them that any could doubt it.

Yet Jesus knew very well the intense struggle which this problem of purity, the central problem of all character-building, involved

[1] Luke 11: 4 (cf. verse 3); Matt. 6: 12 (and cf. verse 11).
[2] Luke 18: 13, 14.
[3] John 19: 6; 8: 46.
[4] Matt. 5: 27, 28; 19: 3–9.

for other men, and he was never so stern against sins of passion as society sometimes is. In himself we see the true Christian ideal, so often misrepresented both by unbelievers and believers: a nature harmonised, perfectly attuned to a spiritual key, in which each power and each element plays its appropriate part, without violation and without conflict. It is not repression, nor self-torture, nor unnatural, self-deceiving pretence at innocence—it is self-harmony: the perfect balance of the whole nature under the control of the Spirit. In him this is the highest fruit of self-control: in us, the highest fruit of his control of us.

Similarly, under the greatest provocation, we never see Jesus in danger of losing his temper. His strong nature was often stirred, and as we have seen he could sometimes be angry. But he was always perfectly and rigorously in control: his deep feeling was never out of hand, nor did he need ever to retract a word or excuse a deed when the feeling had passed. The truth is that, in spite of appearances, passion is not strength, and poise is not weakness. In Jesus we see a vigorous and deep nature, capable of being profoundly moved, but so disciplined and balanced that its whole strength was ever "at call", held in strategic reserve, as it were, ready for obedience to the purpose of the moment, but never squandered in exhibitions of passion or allowed to dominate the moment.

From another side, the purity of Jesus means surely that he was free also from *pride*, which, like passion, possesses amazing power to warp and defile the human soul. It is almost impossible to present a worthy idea of the humility of him who could say "I am meek and lowly in heart",[1] for humility (like pride) has myriad forms. We see his lowliness in the frank admission which Jesus always made of his feelings, his needs, his sorrows, his wish for the friendship and sympathy of the disciples[2]—"Ye are they which have been with me in my temptations"; "With desire have I desired to eat this Passover with you before I suffer"; "Could ye not watch with me one hour?"; "I have a baptism to be baptised with, and how am I straitened until it be accomplished!" No proud man ever lays bare his heart like that.

We see it too in the willingness to adopt the speech and illustrations familiar to ordinary people, in his patience with the stupid and the

---

[1] Matt. 11: 29.
[2] Luke 22: 28 and 15; Mark 14: 37; Luke 12: 50; Mark 14: 33, 34; John 11: 33, 38.

sinful, in his readiness to spend time on individual conversations—a significant trait which reveals his valuation of his own time and energy, compared with the need of even one other soul. He was continually speaking of himself, because it was in himself that salvation lay: but he asked no personal fêting, and sharply rejected effusive compliments.[1] When, in the house of Simon he was treated with less than politeness he passed it by until another was involved.[2] He was never humiliated—only proud hearts can be—and he could not be personally provoked or wounded in dignity. A traitor betrayed him with a kiss, a few folk called him mad, a servant slapped his face, soldiers played the fool mocking him, the crowd reviled his agonies, yet his sorrow over them all was never quenched. His spirit throughout was precisely that which in the Upper Room found perfect expression as he, their Lord and Master, washed the feet of the twelve who had just quarrelled about precedence. "He that is greatest among you shall be your servant"[3]—that expresses exactly both his judgement and his example. He was untainted with any form of self-adulation or self-importance, though how that meek humility could be combined with authority and Saviourhood almost passes comprehension.

Purity means in the third place, freedom from *pretence*. Long afterwards John could name him "him that is true"[4] and this is the brief summary of a profound and lasting impression left by the years spent with Jesus. There is about every glimpse of Jesus in the Gospels a simplicity, a naturalness, a sincerity that is the stamp of utter truthfulness. He did not pose for others' judgement, nor pretend what is only partly true: the candour which marked his message of challenge marked also his own character. There were no mock heroics. He admitted that the time of the end was not his to know[5] and the places of honour in the kingdom were not his to give.[6] In a world especially sensitive to the claims of rank and wealth he commended the giving of a poor widow[7] as "more than they all" and told Nicodemus he must be born again.[8]

His bearing and his words were always frank, his motives true,

[1] John 3: 2, 3; Mark 10: 18; cf. Matt. 23: 5-12.
[2] Luke 7: 44-6.
[3] Matt. 23: 11; 20: 27; Mark 10: 43, 44.
[4] 1 John 5: 20.
[5] Mark 13: 32.
[6] Matt. 20: 23.
[7] Luke 21: 1-4; Mark 12: 41-4.
[8] John 3: 3.

his heart transparent, his purpose single, his condemnation of hypocrisy scorching, *and men knew it.* For one crowning testimony to the truthfulness of Christ came from the mouth of his enemies, flattering and insincere, no doubt, but more true than they intended: "Master, we know that thou art true, and teachest the way of God in truth, neither carest thou for any man: for thou regardest not the person of men."[1]

Trying to describe the matchless purity of Jesus is very like trying to picture the sky or explain the lily. We marvel at the picture of Jesus walking over the waters of Galilee, unmenaced by the hungry waves: but at least equally marvellous, could we but see it aright, is the story of his walking serenely through the sin and corruption of our world with unstained garment and unsoiled feet. Israel's crossing of the Red Sea dryshod is nothing to Christ's passing through this world in the crystal purity of an unsullied soul. And yet it is not by comparison with his age or with other men that we estimate aright the miracle of his sinlessness, but rather by the depth and reality of his knowledge and experience of God. For by his own teaching it is the *pure in heart* who see God[2]—and that lifts his purity far beyond our poor probing and describing. Nevertheless, here once more his likeness is our ideal, his purity our goal.

IV. The Love of Jesus

If in our seeking to summarise the outstanding features of the impression Jesus makes upon ourselves, words have seemed to fail us as we strive to represent his strength, his tenderness, his purity, how much more true this is, quite literally, when we turn to the remaining feature, his love. At once we want to suggest a new word for it, a term more adequate to describe that total moral attitude of Jesus towards others which was the fundamental and inclusive law of his teaching and has become the distinctive moral tenet of Christianity.

Of all Bible words, the word "love" has probably suffered most in the mishandling and debasing of language that marks our time. We use the word to express our attitude to almost anything that awakens in us a reaction that is not hostile—we "love" film-stars, spring, ice-cream, Bach, our children, God, plums, the seaside, philosophy, loyal friends, our life's partner, watching television and

[1] Matt. 22: 16.   [2] Matt. 5: 8.

a host of other indiscriminate things. When we use the word in some context suggesting the relation of man to society, or the principles of good behaviour, the image the word conjures up is almost invariably that of inoffensive mildness careful to avoid up-setting anyone, having neither strong principles nor clear purpose—other than keeping out of trouble. And *that* is a caricature of Christian love !

If we use instead the word "goodwill" we shall to some extent avoid the twin pitfalls of emotionalism and sentimentalism that apparently beset all attempts to define the Christian law of love. It is sometimes suggested that "love" closes its eyes to all the uglier facts of life, the brutality, the sensuality, the avarice, hatred, stupidity and selfishness of men; that "love" treats all men as angels, and in reply to the objection that such an attitude is futile, appeals to "faith". What we have seen of the strength and purity of Jesus should suffice to prove that his love could never mean merely a disposition to turn a blind eye, for peace' sake, upon all sin and evil, or to treat men as though error, vice and enmity were figments and fancies. Whatever his love means it must be consistent with that searching, discriminating judgement, that fearless, uncom-promising exposure of wrong, that we see so often in Jesus. He at any rate was no emotional idealist, drowning his moral judgement in a sea of tears: his love was always strong, often stern, sometimes angry. And the hint of *strength of* will in the term "goodwill" suggests that.

Similarly the word helps a little to avoid the impression of vague-ness that clings sometimes to talk about universal love. It is fre-quently represented as a large-hearted enthusiasm for humanity, a magnanimous sentiment in favour of everyone in general, dilating largely on the various cures for mankind's many ills, but rarely seen in action. Our Lord said little, if anything, about loving the world, or mankind, in the mass, but much about loving your neigh-bour. In his thought love is essentially active, practical and definite, not merely warm sentiment but good *done*. To emphasise this it is worthwhile to list the examples which occur in the Gospels of his kind of love seen in action. They include gentleness, thoughtfulness, kindness, defence of others, sympathetic thought and feeling, a cup of water given, compassion, warning of trials ahead, giving, lend-ing, doing good, non-retaliation, forgiveness, the washing of others' feet, patience with opposition and with slowness, encouragement, visitation of the sick and imprisoned, provision for the hungry, the thirsty and the naked.[1] No such list could possibly be complete, but it serves to illustrate that love, in Jesus' thought, is not just "feeling good", it is doing good for someone, in specific and practical ways.

In the third place, the term "goodwill" is more true to the original New Testament thought of love, in that it avoids the implication always present in the shorter word that some *liking* of the one loved, some recognition of his inherent lovableness, lies at the root of the attitude. This is not always the case, and in moral "love" is not essential. Love as the recognition of beauty, worth or loyalty is a splendid thing, of course, and all love aims at that. But the Christian conception is of love for the unlovable, the worthless, the unlovely, the enemy. It has, consequently, little to do with liking, or attraction: it is essentially the will set deliberately upon another's good, irrespective alike of feelings or merit. This is harder, and more realistic, than the more usual meaning of love, and obviously it is more a moral quality, demanding persistent cultivation. That is not to say that feeling is excluded: good done with a cold heart is not the Christian ideal, and the practice of Christ's law of goodwill does in itself lead in a remarkable way to our liking all sorts of people whom once we thought we could never understand. But the basic thought is of the *will* to do men good, at all times, in all circumstances, in all ways: that is love.

This loving goodwill of Christ is the very bond of his perfectness: it gives nerve to his strength, depth to his tenderness, beauty to his purity. It is an attitude so invariable, so universal, so persistent, so effortless as to be "second-nature". It is impossible to recount examples without retelling the whole, for every word, act, reaction, submission is motived by the will to others' good; that is the unvarying quality of his life, the fountain of his ministry.

There are, however, two excellences of his love which might help to make vivid its meaning and depth. One is its universality, the other, its costliness.

The universal range of the Christian law of love is its chief distinction in the history of thought about the good life. Loyalty towards the family, and the tribe, are ancient virtues. Loving regard

[1] E.g. Mark 5: 34 (cf. 2 Cor. 10:11); 6: 37; 10: 49; Luke 5: 30, 31; 6: 2, 3; 23: 27–31; John 11: 35; Matt. 10: 42; 9: 36; 14: 14; Mark 1: 41; Luke 22: 31; Mark 14: 18; Luke 6: 30, 33, 36; and 27–9; Matt. 5: 38–42; 43–8; John 13: 14; 18: 33–7; Luke 24: 25; 12: 32; Matt. 25: 31–46.

for the fellow-Israelite is demanded in the Jewish code.[1] But the crucial issue was raised when a young lawyer asked Jesus, "But who *is* my neighbour?"[2] The whole meaning and significance of "Love thy neighbour" turns upon that definition.

In one sense our Lord's answer lies in his whole life. "His love was like water, seeking ever the lower levels" as one has said: but this is exaggeration if it be meant to imply he was any different in his attitude to the wealthy and powerful. It is true that his goodwill seems lavished upon the least deserving and the most needy: upon children, for whom often men had only impatience; upon women, usually regarded as waste of the wise man's efforts; upon the poor "people of the land",[3] seemingly superfluous and unimportant; upon the sinful, outcast and despised, whom the religious usually ignored. At the same time the wife of Herod's steward is among his friends, Nicodemus and Joseph of Arimathea are within his circle, Simon the Pharisee finds an invitation accepted[4] and John the disciple, and probably the home at Bethany, were not poor.

On the whole, however, nothing is more typical of Jesus than the picture of him sitting upon the well-head in Samaria talking with a woman as to whom there is abundant reason why he should have avoided all contact with her. Between them rose the natural barrier of sex, so much exaggerated in those days that the rabbi would pass his own wife and daughter in the street. There rose too the social barrier, for she was not of the best circles, but of ill-repute and evil associations. To these was added the national barrier—she was a Samaritan, with whom the Jews "have no dealings", and the racial barrier, for she was not of the elect race; and behind and overshadowing all else, the religious barrier—"Ye say that in Jerusalem is the place where men ought to worship".[5] Nor should we take entirely for granted the way in which Jesus ignored the immeasurable moral distance that separated her from him: that we are not astonished is itself due to the impression he has made upon our thinking. But neither barriers nor distance matter to Jesus.

Here then as in a miniature snapshot we see the scope of Christ's goodwill—the refusal to acknowledge any of the frontiers that normally divide men from each other, whether they be drawn by custom, prejudice, morality or religion. This is the essence of his

[1] Lev. 19: 18.
[2] Luke 10: 29.
[3] Cf. John 7: 49.
[4] Luke 8: 3; John 19: 38, 39; Luke 7: 36; 14: 1.
[5] John 4: 20.

reply to the lawyer's penetrating question "Who is my neighbour?"
The parable of the Good Samaritan with which Jesus answered it is
curiously oblique. To the question "Whom must I love?" a simple
story illustrating help given to anyone found injured on the roadside might have sufficed for answer—"Whoever needs me is my
neighbour". The parable as given does include this point: the
person helped is completely anonymous, he is met by chance, a
foundling, a nobody, having no possible claim upon either of the
passers-by. So Jesus declared that love of one's neighbour is not
the mere recognition of merit, kinship or claim, but the willing response to need, wherever and whenever encountered.

But into this simple story Jesus deliberately introduced the man
of alien race, nationality and religion. What is a Samaritan doing
on that Judean road? And why did Jesus apparently "drag in"
the controversial issue of racial and religious antagonism? It
could only be to emphasise explicitly that love refuses to recognise
the barriers that divide men—including those which the lawyer
would doubtless be quick to defend. To sharpen the point still
further, Jesus introduced also the wholly unnecessary figures of the
Priest and the Levite, and by contrasting them with the Samaritan
makes the story centre not on the one who needed help ("Whom
must I love?") but on the one who gave it. Had the Samaritan
been the one injured, *receiving* help from a kindly passer-by, the
lawyer would have been well answered. But Jesus makes his meaning unforgettable by focusing attention on the hated heretic and
stranger who though despised by the leaders of Jewry yet shames
their failure to obey their own law by his kindly care of one in need.

Jesus says, in effect, that the question of the lawyer is a *wrong*
question: we should ask, not "Whom am I required to love?" but
"Whom am I prepared to love?"[1] I *am* neighbour to all I chance to
meet upon the roadside of life; the question is whether I am willing
to act the neighbour, in deeds of trouble-taking goodwill. Whosoever needs me is my neighbour: into that definition and its unlimited responsibilities differences of rank, wealth, race, morality,
or religion, in Jesus' eyes, simply do not enter.

Most of us probably do not find the old barriers of race or religion quite so formidable, though even yet it is sometimes hard to
persuade Christians that justice and truth, not to say kindness, are
due to those who differ from us in political or religious creed. On its

[1] Luke 10: 36.

other side, however, this call to *universal* goodwill affects us all. When, sitting at the feet of Jesus, we have learned the lesson of goodwill, and go out into this somewhat ruthless and competitive world to try to obey, our tentative experiments in Christian love often break down at the obstacles we meet. The tender shoots of active love wither in the chilly reception they face; our love seeks but does not find a returning affection; our goodwill, which normally grows by gratitude, often meets instead suspicion, scorn or exploitation. Our approaches awaken little response, our apologies for wrong done, our attempts at making amends, are sceptically received, our efforts are misunderstood, or unappreciated—and how very often our love, such as it was, dies in our hearts. We conclude that the Christian way "will not work".

Until we look again at Jesus. Did he see success? Was his love answered by love? Did his service awaken gratitude, his goodwill gain recognition? He lived for a generation that was blind to his worth, unresponsive to his labour, deaf to his appeals, hardened against his love. So too he died for a world that rejected him, scorned, mocked, spat upon him, a world to which he owed no gratitude because it gave him no appreciation. Yet his goodwill never faltered. He loved his enemies—and we have not really got over our astonishment yet. *His love acknowledged no barriers,* even those erected by unresponsiveness in those he loved. His goodwill had the heroic quality of being undiscourageable: we are not sure that he did say, but certainly he might have said "Do good . . . never despairing".[1]

Thus in teaching and example the universal range of the love of Jesus is underlined. The other excellence that calls for attention is its costliness. We need not rehearse the stories that illustrate the toll of his ministry upon his own spirit. Night was turned into day, if Nicodemus came; hunger and weariness were forgotten if a woman needed helping; the sorrows and sufferings of the multitude bore upon his heart and tested his strength, and the endlessly patient ministry of goodwill threatened to exhaust him—but never did. He did nothing indifferently, gave nothing cheaply. Nor should we ever forget that the final sacrifice of the cross, when he loved his own *unto the end*—to the utmost—was far more than physical agony and pain, even the pain of death. The injustice, ingratitude, betrayal, denial, loneliness, horror, and sense of coming retribution, all

[1] Luke 6: 35 R.V. margin.

weighed as heavily upon his soul as the crown of thorns upon his brow. His cup was full, and he drained it.

The goodwill to which he calls us is likewise costly. For it is never easy to forgive the wrong done to us or ours: it requires self-discipline and self-denial to forego the luxury of bearing the grudge. It is not easy to withhold retaliation when the opportunity is offered; it costs much in pride to turn the other cheek, and it costs much too to give, do good, lend, in secret as he demands, foregoing the reward of praise. And if the need arise, he bids us love at cost of our own comfort, safety and ambition—"to sell out, give, deny ourselves, and follow".[1] In all such matters, he declared, the standard of our goodwill shall be our attitude to ourselves: what is good for us, is good also for our neighbour; what we demand of life he also has the right to demand; what we refuse, he must not be afflicted with—we shall love him *as we love ourselves*.[2] That certainly is going to cost us something !

If one formidable difficulty about our attempts to obey was the chilly reception our goodwill sometimes met, the other great difficulty is our natural, almost inevitable preoccupation with ourselves. Perhaps the most significant distinction between people is that which divides the helpers from the helped: those who can and do offer assistance, encouragement and counsel to others, from those who expect to receive these things to help them along. At first, by the simple processes of growing up, we all belong to the receiving-class; it is a great day in a man's spiritual history when he passes, in his own thinking, into the giving-class. But if our lot be hard, our circumstances difficult; even more if we have never passed through the intermediate stage where we have learned to rely less on others and more on ourselves; or if we have simply never learned the law of Christ, to bear one another's burdens,[3] then we remain absorbed in our own affairs, preoccupied with our own problems, struggles, uncertainties and fears with no attention to spare for others' needs.

Could we but see it, we should find considerable relief from our own troubles and needs if we could divert our concern outwards from ourselves and take care for those about us. This certainly is the method of the Master. What a world of troubles he might have carried upon his own heart to the exclusion of all concern for others ! Yet "anchored in God, he transferred the centre of life's gravity to

[1] Mark 10: 21.   [2] Luke 10: 27.   [3] Gal. 6: 2.

others". While his own heart was heaviest he grieved for the disciples soon to be scattered as sheep without a shepherd;[1] riding to his own death he wept for the doomed city;[2] in the garden of agony he came repeatedly to warn and prepare the three disciples.[3] At his own arrest he took pity on the injured servant of the High Priest and dismissed his own disciples from their danger.[4] Standing before his accusers he knew what was happening to Peter and turned to look upon him;[5] and in the supreme anguish of the crucifixion he thought of his mother's breaking heart, comforted a fellow-sufferer, and prayed for his executioners.[6] In all these examples he was merely being himself—ever and in all circumstances preoccupied not with his own cares but with the souls about him.

It is in this sense that the love he bids us emulate is a costly love: it costs us our selfishness, our self-pity, our inward-turning absorption with the problems which life heaps upon ourselves. It may also cost us material goods and physical pain: but these will occasion no difficulty if we have learned to supplant the natural love of self by the Christian love of others, doing ever to others as we would that they should do to us.[7]

Here then in barest outline is the love of Jesus: strong, active, undiscourageable goodwill, universal and costly, love that will not be stopped from loving, love unlimited. To speak of our imitating it might seem a hopelessly impracticable ideal but for two things: one is that we are all, in the fullest degree, unpayably indebted to just that love for our own salvation and hope. We are commanded to love *as we have been loved*,[8] and as a motive that is enough. The other is that this same love "is shed abroad in our hearts by the Holy Ghost which is given unto us"[9]—and that is our sufficient resource.

The attentive reader will not have failed to notice that in selecting these four qualities of character as the outstanding features of the portrait of Jesus, we have silently drawn attention to the fact that

[1] Mark 14: 27.
[2] Luke 19: 41–4.
[3] Mark 14: 33–42; Luke 22: 40, 45.
[4] Luke 22: 50, 51; John 18: 8.
[5] Luke 22: 61.
[6] John 19: 26, 27; Luke 23: 43 and 34.
[7] Matt. 7: 12.
[8] John 15: 12.
[9] Rom. 5: 5.

his moral perfection lies in the unique balance of *opposite* virtues. It is the presence in one soul of seemingly contradictory qualities that gives his character its completeness: it is their perfect harmony that lends to his whole life that poise which is the perfection of strength. Strength of mind and of will are so rarely wedded to gentleness; gentleness and sympathy do not always succeed in preserving the highest standards of righteousness and purity; and again righteousness and purity so rarely keep their tolerance and goodwill, especially towards the unrighteous and the impure. It seems enough if we could excel in one virtue or the other: Jesus reveals the summit of each in one symmetrical character. This is part of the meaning of that great phrase of Paul about "the measure of the stature of the fullness of Christ".[1] And in this respect once more the ideal of Christlikeness towers high over our attainment, rebuking our complacency, and dwarfing our too low aspiring with the portrait of a Master "perfect in all perfections".

[1] Eph. 4: 13.

CHAPTER 12

RULING THOUGHTS

As WE turn from the external impressions which Jesus left upon his contemporaries, and the main intrinsic qualities of his character, to consider some of the ideas that ruled his mind, we are likely to meet with an objection. It is commonly assumed that a man's character and his opinions are two quite separate departments of his life, that his beliefs are no necessary part of the man's moral portrait. If we criticise an individual's conduct or attitudes we are sometimes reminded that "He is a charming fellow, gentlemanly, cultured—such a good sort !" As a corrective of our too sharp judgements, this may be useful: but too often it is regarded as an answer to the criticism—as though attractive qualities and admirable manners somehow excused indefensible opinions and corrupting ideas. Life would be a great deal simpler, and youthful temptations a great deal easier to resist, if the vicious and dishonourable always bore an obvious trademark of uncouth and coarse boorishness ! The truth is that very "nice" people may propagate vicious opinions; that admirable social qualities may accompany appalling prejudices and attitudes. Even the genuinely honest and kindly disposed may be very foolish and harmful; and devilry itself appear angelic.[1]

Character then is the precipitate of creed, in the sense that "as a man thinketh in his heart, so is he", and evil is wrought quite as often by wrong-headed thought as by want of thought or want of heart. It is therefore no digression to include in a portrait of Jesus an outline of the great ideas that dominated his thinking. True imitation of Christ will include "the transformation of the mind",[2] which shall enable us to bring every thought into captivity to Christ;[3] it will mean that we come to share his way of looking at things, our thinking being ruled by the principles, outlook, conceptions and convictions that ruled his. As we saw, this is indeed a major part of the meaning of "having the mind of Christ".

[1] 2 Cor. 11: 14.   [2] Rom. 12: 2.   [3] 2 Cor. 10: 5.

"Great ideas belong in families": to hold any one great truth is to be led by implication to a number of others. It is not easy to isolate the formative ideas of any profound thinker and say *these* are the crucial ones. But as a beginning we may name four salient ruling thoughts that shaped the outlook of Jesus: his thought of God, his thought of people, his assumption concerning immortality and his great concept of service.

I. HIS THOUGHT OF GOD

The all-important idea in any man's mind is his idea of God. *Whether* he thinks of God, and if so *what* he thinks of God, will determine everything else in his thought and conduct. The man to whose thinking the fact of God is fundamental lives in a different world, upon different resources, and for different ends, from those of the man who leaves God out. As the light of the sun lends colour to every blade of grass, so the idea of God in the background of the mind irradiates every recess of the soul and tinges every detail of life. Here is one respect in which the daily development in Christlikeness must affect the thinking of most modern people in a very radical way.

For most of us God is an afterthought. We *end* with God, we bring him in to bless our plans, solve our difficulties, conclude our argument, answer our questions, and finally to ease our deathbeds—and we may do all this with complete sincerity. But Jesus *began* with God. He set out on every journey *from* God; his arguments assumed God at the beginning; the whole circle of his life finds its centre in his relationship to God. Nature, from the impartiality of the sun and rain to the provision for the birds and the innocence of the child[1] spoke to him rememberable things about God, and he was ever sensitive to the approach of God to him, through the Scriptures, through prayer, or in the unfolding events of his own life. This point is deeply significant. Where other men by debating God, by seeking to deduce his existence from the world, have never got beyond a "life of faith diversified by doubt", Jesus knew God as the living possession of his soul. Other men are seekers after truth: he can say "Learn of me . . . the only-begotten Son, which is in the bosom of the Father, he hath declared him . . . No man can know the Father save the Son, and he to whom the Son will

[1] Matt. 5: 45; 6: 26; 18: 10.

reveal him".[1] And the key to that central, crucial and controlling certainty about God was his own unbroken, unstruggling, unfathomable experience of the Father.

But at least equally important as certainty about God, is clarity. For wrong thought about God is as disastrous sometimes as no thought at all. To erroneous conceptions of God may be traced most of the dreadful blots upon religious history—human sacrifice, the burning of heretics and witches, the damnation of the unbaptised infant, religious crusades and persecutions and all the rest. Not to have realised that much of the purpose of the Old Testament is to record the long slow discipline by which Israel was weaned from false or inadequate thoughts of God, in preparation for the perfect revelation in Christ, is to have missed most of what the Bible is all about. That final word of Jesus about God can be simply stated but its implications are practically infinite. Older conceptions of God as Creator, Judge, Refuge and Lord are embraced and enriched in the twofold thought of God as Head of the spiritual family and Sovereign of the spiritual realm—God the Kingly Father.

Both sides of this thought are equally important, but the idea of God's Fatherhood has become the more familiar to most people. It is as a Father that God cares for us,[2] as a Father he hears our prayer,[3] as a Father he knows our need,[4] as a Father he shows us the perfection of impartial love.[5] He only who doeth the will of the Father is accepted in the kingdom;[6] in the Father's unchanging love is the hope of our welcome home after prodigal wandering;[7] in the Father's house we rest at the last;[8] while all our hope for this world is the "Father's good pleasure" to give us the kingdom.[9] Jesus himself *reasoned* in terms of the Fatherhood of God and its implication that he will give good things to those who ask him.[10] He *laboured* in the fellowship of the Father, seeking not his own will "but the will of him that sent me . . . the Father".[11]

[1] Matt. 11: 29; John 1: 18; Matt. 11: 27.
[2] Matt. 6: 26, 32.
[3] Matt. 6: 6, 9.
[4] Matt. 6: 8; 7: 11.
[5] Matt. 5: 48.
[6] Matt. 7: 21.
[7] Luke 15: 22.
[8] John 14: 2, 3.
[9] Luke 12: 32.
[10] Matt. 7: 9–11; Luke 11: 11–13. So: John Watson: "The Mind of the Master."
[11] John 6: 38–9.

L

He *rested* in the wisdom of the Father—"Even so, Father, for so it seemed good in thy sight";[1] and he *suffered* in the faith of the Father, saying "I lay down my life . . . this commandment have I received from my Father".[2] All his life he was about his Father's business, and into his Father's hands, at death, he commended his spirit.[3]

It is perhaps important to remember that the typical father of a Jewish household was not the easy-going, keep-equal-with-the-children, indulgent parent that modern fathers are exhorted to be, but the ruler of the home, and the source of its order, discipline and piety. The name "father" evoked as much of reverence as of trust, and never mere familiarity. Thus, in the model prayer Jesus bade us approach God as our Father *which art in heaven*, whose name is to be hallowed, and whose will is, above all our desiring, to be done. Even more vividly was this admixture of reverence and trust expressed in our Lord's own prayer on the eve of Calvary: for his own address to God was as Father (four times), Holy Father (once) and Righteous Father (once).[4]

Yet familiar as this part of Christ's thought of God is, it is not that most frequently upon Christ's lips. Even more often did he speak of God as King, and of the kingdom, or realm of God's rule. We have already noted the place of the kingdom hope in the gospels and epistles, and the meaning of that hope in terms of our obedience to the will of the King. Here we are concerned with the other side of that truth, the conception of God as Ruler, whose will is our law, whose aim is our perfection, whose call is to absolute obedience and the strenuous seeking after righteousness,[5] who directs the times and seasons to his own purposes[6] and who in the end will weigh the souls of men with unerring judgement and truth.[7]

We must be careful not to think of Fatherhood and Kingship as opposite qualities in God: "It is the *Father's* good pleasure to give us the *kingdom*," and it is in "my Father's kingdom" that Jesus has promised to drink with his disciples the wine of divine victory.[8] Modern Christianity would have been saved something of its moral weakness and sentimentality if this dual conception of God had been better understood—if Fatherhood had been seen as something more royal than modern fatherhood usually is, and if Kingship were

---

[1] Luke 10: 21.
[2] John 10: 17, 18.
[3] Luke 2: 49; 23: 46.
[4] John 17.

[5] Matt. 6: 33.
[6] Acts 1: 7.
[7] Matt. 25: 31f.
[8] Luke 12: 32; Matt. 26: 29.

understood more in the light of the ancient thought that the King is Father of his people. Most certainly we shall approach the mind of Christ in this respect only if we bring our thought of God into line with his teaching about the Kingly-Fatherhood.

And of course it is not only a matter of thinking, since thinking governs attitude. It is in our Lord's living relationship with God that the value of his thought is revealed. He lived by an unwavering trust in his Father which lent poise and serenity to his spirit in all circumstances. Darkness, tempest, solitude, enmity, the clear certainty of death, all left him unafraid; he showed not the least anxiety about his own needs, or the outcome of his work. On the night on which he was betrayed he spoke calmly of reunion in the Father's kingdom, and on the cross in the moment of utter darkness it was still "My God, *my* God . . ." His faith never faltered.

With it went an unhesitating obedience. "My meat is to do the will of him that sent me,"[1] he said, and he lived under the free compulsion of an inner necessity that found expression repeatedly in "I must"—go to Jerusalem, pass through Samaria, work the works of God, suffer and rise again.[2] "I delight to do thy will, O God"[3] was his confession, and it is true that obedience was never with him mere acceptance or resignation, but a glad plunging into what was appointed for him. Yet he *learned* obedience:[4] it was not automatic, inevitable, effortless, as the wilderness and the Garden make clear.[5] But his implicit trust made obedience a delight, and "love turned duty into impulse".

Which underlines the third characteristic of Jesus' attitude towards God—he did *love* God, not simply in the sense that he obeyed, but he was in love with God. The very heart of Christ's piety was his loving joy in God, the joy that asks nothing as reward from God, that seeks nothing further, beyond God, but counts itself infinitely rich in just possessing him. His exultant "I thank thee, Father . . ."[6] and his descriptions of the preciousness of finding life in God's realm[7] are glimpses of the inner delight in the Father which made of his religious life a wholly new thing. These three, then—unwavering trust, unhesitating obedience and unreserved joy—combine

[1] John 4: 34.
[2] Mark 8: 31; Luke 9: 51; John 4: 4; 9: 4, 11; 10: 32-4.
[3] Ps. 40: 8.
[4] Heb. 5: 8.
[5] Matt. 4: 1f; 26: 36f.
[6] Luke 10: 21.
[7] Matt. 13: 44-6.

to make up the personal experience of God which issued from his thought of what God was like. Here once again is part of what it means to have the mind of Jesus.

II. HIS THOUGHT OF MAN

It is no longer necessary, as a few years ago it would have been necessary, to argue the practical importance of what we think about people, in governing our attitude towards them. This may fairly be said to be one of the rediscoveries of our generation. In the concentration camps of Nazism, in Fascism and Communism, and in the ordinary sceptical materialism of the average unbeliever of our age, we have learned how plainly man's inhumanity to man is the consequence of man's inadequate or contemptuous conception of man. The general pattern of social life, the accepted political theory, the standard of living of the "masses", the basic aims of education, the care of the child, the sick and the infirm, the hatred of slavery and respect for marriage, the horror of all that is bestial and violent in human conduct, and the impulse to world missions among all races—all these are vitally affected by the view of man's nature, dignity and importance that we hold. To think truly about our fellows is the first step towards acting rightly with regard to them.

Whenever we think carefully about Christian standards of behaviour, we discover that the *code* rests upon the *creed*, and will not "make sense" without it. The Christian law of love rests ultimately upon our theological convictions, not only about God and the cross of Jesus, but about the human soul. We must therefore ask what idea of Man ruled the thinking of Jesus.

Part of the answer is given in three surprising comparisons. Once Jesus compared man with the rest of God's creation, the sparrows, lilies, grass for which God unquestionably cares, and asked— "Are ye not much better than they?" The meaning of "better" was left in no doubt by a pointed reference to the cheapness of sparrows in the marketplace.[1] Once, too, Jesus compared man's worth with the most sacred of all the institutions of the Jews, the holy sabbath, and declared "The sabbath was made for man, not man for the sabbath". This again is in a context which makes it plain that in his eyes man's hunger, or need of healing, are more important than the prescriptions for sabbath observance.[2] Once

[1] Matt. 10: 29–31; 6: 26; Luke 12: 24. [2] Mark 2: 27; cf. 2: 23 to 3: 5.

more Jesus compared the human soul with all that the world offers or contains besides, and challengingly enquired, "What shall it *profit* a man if he shall gain the whole world, and lose his own soul ? Or what shall a man give in exchange for his soul ?"[1]

The implication is clear: man is a spirit, alone in a universe of *things*, of more value than other creatures, more important than laws, customs and institutions, however venerable, and his soul outweighs the world. Man has dignity and value unequalled under the sun. So Jesus taught, and so he acted—thinking no individual too insignificant for him to talk to and to serve, no crowd too fickle or shallow for him to teach and feed, and the whole world not too sinful for him to love and to die for. That view of the *untold value* of the human soul is enough in itself to create new standards of personal relationship in political, industrial and private life. It condemns every situation and system in which the dignity, freedom and worth of the individual soul is disregarded; it points the way to a social concern in which each shall be valued as "one for whom Christ died".[2]

This value depends not on the individual's talents, wealth, rank or race, but solely upon his inherent dignity as God's creature, as actually or potentially a child of the divine family. This implies that, on the deepest level, men are of *equal* value, but we must be careful to understand the equality which the Master assumes, neither exaggerating it nor minimising it. Men are not equal intellectually— the one instance where Jesus referred to brains is the parable of the bright steward, where he praises the foresight and cleverness of an unscrupulous rascal ![3] Nor are they equal in natural gifts— the gold is distributed "according to their several ability".[4] Certainly men are not equal morally, and there is no blurring of moral differences in the Gospels. On all such levels men are diverse and of very varying value to society.

But their spiritual needs, rights and privileges are equal; all have equal claim upon our charity, our service, our sympathy, our respect for them as greater than all *things*. Beneath all distinctions of race, possessions, birth, education, talent and even character lies the common ground, that all are creatures of the one God, spiritual beings, accountable to him, and valuable to him for what they have it in them, by his grace, to become.

[1] Matt. 16: 26.
[2] Rom. 14: 15.
[3] Luke 16: 1–8.
[4] Matt. 25: 15.

This underlies our Lord's refusal to acknowledge the barriers that divide men, his interpretation of the word "neighbour", the inwardness of all his judgements, his insistence upon universal goodwill. The lamb, silly, torn and bleeding, yet *belongs* to the fold and is valuable for the shepherd; the missing and thus unusable coin still carries beneath the grime the image and superscription of the king; the rebellious youth in the far country, though lost and accounted "dead" is still child of the father's heart, grieved over and waited for. Jesus came to seek and to save that which was lost[1] and it is not for us to make distinctions where he made none. Natural divisions of race and sex, artificial differences of class, wealth or culture, give way before this conception of equality which unites Jew and Greek, male and female, bond and free, barbarian, Scythian—as all one in Christ Jesus.[2]

Man's value lies, then, not in any super-added quality or acquirement he might posses, but in the innate dignity of the spiritual nature. Man is valuable, and equal, because he is *spiritual*. While it is good to be able to say of a man that he is intelligent, nice to say he is accomplished and clever, best of all to say that he is good, yet none of these is greater than just to say he is a man—an immortal spirit. He is made and meant for sonship, fashioned for fellowship with the eternal. Jesus saw men as sheep having no shepherd[3] and grieved for their deep need. He understood that the hunger in man's heart is infinite and craves infinity for food. "Man's unhappiness comes from his greatness": he has an infinite within him that he cannot hide. Whenever prodigal man comes to himself he feels the need within him to strike for home and the Father. "Man shall not live by bread alone"[4] is Christ's own confirmation of an ancient comment upon human nature. If the greatest thing in the world is man, the greatest thing in man is his spiritual personality: the poorest, most stupid, most ignorant, most sinful is capable of salvation, has capacity for God, is precious in the sight of the Lord.

So Jesus despaired of no man, befriended all. He found men interesting, heard their stories of themselves, recognised them not as rivals but as needy, saw them with God's eyes as the crown of creation. And in a stern word which we rarely take at its full value and seriousness, Jesus solemnly warned against that contempt of people which so often accompanies cynicism and self-interest.

---

[1] Luke 15 and 19: 10.
[2] Gal. 3: 28; Col. 3: 11.
[3] Matt. 9: 36.
[4] Matt. 4: 4; Deut. 8: 3.

"You have heard that it was said to the men of old, 'You shall not kill; and whoever kills shall be liable to judgement'. But I say to you that every one who is angry with his brother shall be liable to judgement; whoever insults his brother shall be liable to the council, and whoever says 'You fool!' shall be liable to the hell of fire."[1] Difficulties of translation in this passage do not obscure the meaning, or the solemnity of the caution against treating any soul God made, with derision or contempt. Here is something stronger than pity, sympathy or sentiment to control our attitude, inspire our evangelism, govern our dealings with each other, and shape our society. To think with his mind about men would do more than perhaps anything else to transform our modern world.

III. His Thought of Life

It is our modern habit to view our lives against the background either of the vastness and power of the natural world, as explored by the material sciences—which makes us afraid; or against the background of history, our presumed origins and long slow march through the centuries—which makes some of us proud and some very humble, according to whether we fully appreciate the past! The characteristic note of the view of Jesus, in this respect, is that he ever sees human life against the background of eternity, as having illimitable horizons, possessing the perspective of life everlasting. The effect of that viewpoint is to give to life here and now an immeasurable significance.

The study of astronomy, like the journeying abroad of the village lad, is apt to set all familiar commonplace things in a totally new perspective and scale of values: even so does the view of God and of man which Jesus imparts affect the whole circle of life. And especially by setting each individual experience within the context of eternity, so that life takes on a limitless meaning as well as a glorious hope. Once more, in the thought of Jesus barriers go down: by faith life reaches upwards into the spiritual world above it, by love life reaches outward into the world of spiritual personalities around it, by hope life reaches forwards into the spiritual realm ahead of it; faith, hope and love become the dimensions of life—in Christ's view of it. And each serves to emphasise that eternal background against which each individual life plays out its part.

[1] Matt. 5: 21–2 R.S.V.

This is the key to our Lord's judgement upon worldliness. It is foolish to store up goods and build larger and ever larger barns oblivious of that final accounting when the *soul* shall be required to give answer for its success or failure.[1] It is profitless to gain this world and lose one's soul precisely because the soul must face eternity when this world has passed from sight.[2] It is shortsighted, and stupid, to set one's heart upon treasure that is liable to the decay of rust, the depredation of insects (a special menace in the Middle East!) and the thieving of burglars—to all the insecurity of material things in a temporal scene: for the heart will live on when its treasure is lost for ever. Better by far lay up treasure in heaven, in the eternal sphere where it will await the soul.[3] Life is more than meat, and consisteth not in the abundance of the things a man possesseth;[4] and to live as though this world were all—and to set one's heart upon it— is to invite disillusionment and final bankruptcy. For man's life belongs among the eternal things.

The same key explains the supreme importance accorded in Christ's thought to all issues of character. He made the moral questions of faith, repentance and obedience the all-important questions of life. He pressed his demands and underlined his warnings, he emphasised the seriousness of spiritual laws, responsibilities, interests and struggles, always with the clear implication that human welfare or ruin, life or destruction, depend upon man's response. There is weeping and gnashing of teeth, a judgement-throne, and banishment to "outer darkness", a possibility of the loss of the soul in hell,[5] all depending upon the reaction of men to the will of God revealed in himself.

In all this side of his thought Jesus is very far removed from the typical modern attitude that morals are a private concern of the individual only, happiness in this life being the supreme criterion of all questions. To Jesus the certainty of immortality made moral issues the only issues that matter, and for the same reason he urged repeatedly the worthwhile value of all struggle, persecution, sacrifice. By this world's standards and the results in this scene, they do best who eat, drink and are merry: but the strait gate is worth passing through because it leads to life, persecution is to be endured because

[1] Luke 12: 13–21.
[2] Matt. 16: 26 *and* 27.
[3] Matt. 6: 19–21.
[4] Luke 12: 23; 15.
[5] Matt. 8: 12; 22: 13; 24: 51; 25: 30, 31; Luke 13: 28; Mark 9: 44, 46, 47, 48.

"great is your reward in heaven", sacrifice of houses, lands, friends and affection will all prove profitable because they will be restored an hundredfold with "in the world to come, life everlasting".[1]

The reference to life's endless perspective is constant, and it is not a strengthened but a weakened moral sense that affects to manage without this thought of reward. In Christ's thought, it is not the enjoyment offered to those who do well, that is the inducement to struggle and sacrifice, but rather the final and eternal *vindication* of what men struggled and sacrificed for—the ultimate assurance that it was all worthwhile. So Jesus views the soul's priorities. In life many things may be valued and sought after, but all drops away at last and the soul stands naked before eternity, save only for the harvest of truth, beauty and goodness it has garnered from earth's experience, as capital with which to enter upon the life to come.

And because, in the light of eternity, worldliness is inevitably foolish, and struggle infinitely worthwhile, so it follows that decision for or against the Gospel is irresistibly urgent, and crucial. There is a time of harvest, a putting in of the sickle, a sorting of the contents of the dragnet, a closing of the door when the Bridegroom has passed within. There is a reference forward to consequences "in that day" and a solemn foreshadowing of "depart from me".[2] The result is to make life's decisions supremely significant, since they too have eternal dimensions, and to lend to earth's experience an immense importance.

And as he taught, so again did he live: not only with the memory of the glory enjoyed with the Father before the world was[3] and with the constant sense of a timeless imperative laid upon him,[4] but also with an eternal prospect set before him, a joy for sake of which it was worthwhile to endure the cross.[5] His life, above all, had this eternal context to lend significance to all its details.

It is a strange inversion of the truth that in our time makes light of the Christian hope of immortality on the ground that such hope "is no earthly use" and empties this life of importance. The very opposite is the case. Limit life's horizon to the grave and you cut the nerve of all endeavour, make nonsense of all sacrifice, mock at man's loftiest aspiration, depress life to a meaningless tale

[1] Matt. 7: 13, 14; 5: 10–12; 19: 27–9; Mark 10: 28–30.
[2] Matt. 13: 30; Mark 4: 29; Matt. 13: 47–50; 25: 10; 7: 22; 7: 23.
[3] John 17: 5.
[4] John 6: 38.
[5] Heb. 12: 2.

destined to end at last in silence and bewilderment. To see life with Jesus' eyes, is to see its eternal issues adding weight and glory to each common day, its everlasting hope making each dawn a promise and each eve a foreshadowing of man's perfect rest. But to see life so, and hold that idea of life steadily before one's mind, will demand of many of us—worldlings at heart—an effort and a grace beyond the ordinary.

IV. His Thought of Service

Of all the thoughts which ruled the mind of Jesus probably the most familiar to modern people is that of service. It has indeed become almost a definition of Christianity—a woefully inadequate one, as we have seen—to do good turns, help lame dogs, and be good neighbours. As an account of what Jesus came to accomplish this is, of course, ridiculous; insofar as it implies that men are saved by being kind to others it is misleading and dangerous. But exaggeration and distortion must not lead us to ignore the truth that here struggles for expression, and it is undoubtedly true that one of the dominating ideas of Jesus, and one of the new conceptions he gave to the world, was his thought of "serving one another".

By service is meant all the positive applications of the supreme law of love; negatively that law forbids all forms of retaliation for wrongs suffered, positively it includes every possible variety of good which one soul may do for another—the ministry of healing and relief of pain (which is Jesus' immediate thought when questioned about love of one's neighbour),[1] the relief of the poor, entertainment of the homeless, visiting of the sick and captive,[2] comforting of the sorrowful, befriending the outcast, reconciling those at enmity, forbearing to judge, exercising mercy,[3] and all the other countless reactions of kind hearts to multifarious human need. But—far less familiar to most of us, and far less popular—it includes also the service of others in things of the spirit: letting one's light shine, telling the good news, giving as freely as we have received, bearing witness to our own discovery in Christ, bringing forth fruit.[4] Some, it is true, see in this the only form of service required of them—

[1] Luke 10: 29, 30.
[2] Matt. 25: 35, 36.
[3] Luke 7: 13; Matt. 9: 10–13; Luke 15: 1f; Matt. 5: 23, 24; Matt. 7: 1–5; Luke 6: 36.
[4] Matt. 5: 16; 10: 7, 8; Luke 24: 48; John 15: 2, 8, 27.

and are strangely blind to the Master's injunctions; but many, many others think they have done all that is necessary if a charitable shilling has been given to a worthy cause.

We ought to need no other proof of the importance of the idea of service in the thought of Jesus, than the fact that he who made love the paramount law of religion then proceeded to define that love in terms of service. There are, however, other unmistakable proofs. We have set before us his own example of a life devoted to "serving the footsteps of his fellows" and the inspired summary of that life "He went about doing good".[1] We have too his own epoch-making reinterpretation of the whole idea of Messiahship in the light of Isaiah 53—and the picture of the Servant of the Lord and of men which becomes the New Testament clue to the meaning of his Saviourhood.[2] We have the clear warning in the parables of the Rich Man and Lazarus, and of the Sheep and the Goats, that the divine judgement will rest at last upon men's response to others' need.[3] And we have too our Lord's own declaration as to what constitutes excellence and decides pre-eminence in the Kingdom of God—"Whosoever shall be great . . . shall be the servant of all . . . I am among you as one that serveth".[4]

In the light of all this there is no need to say more of the place which the idea of service occupied in the mind of Christ: but there is need to reproach ourselves that we have so often failed to give to that idea the same place in our own conception of his will for us.

Service of others can, of course, be of varying quality: it can be condescending, or cold-hearted; it can even sometimes be little better than veiled self-interest. Clearly and acutely Jesus insisted that service shall be done "hoping for nothing again".[5] "If ye love them which love you, what reward have ye? do not even the publicans the same? If ye salute your brethren only, what do ye more than others?"[6] "When thou makest a dinner or a supper, call not thy friends, nor thy brethren, neither thy kinsmen, nor thy rich neighbours; lest they also bid thee again and a recompense be made thee. But when thou makest a feast, call the poor, the maimed, the lame, the blind: and thou shalt be blessed; for they cannot

[1] Acts 10: 38.
[2] Isa. 61: 1; Luke 4: 18; Isa. 52: 13—53: 12; Mark 10: 45, compare Isa. 53: 11; Matt. 8: 17; Acts 8: 32–5; 1 Pet. 2: 21–5 etc.; Acts 4: 27–30 R.S.V.
[3] Luke 16: 19f; Matt. 25: 31f.
[4] Matt. 20: 26, 27; 23: 11; Mark 10: 43, 44; Luke 22: 27.
[5] Luke 6: 35, according to one reading.
[6] Matt. 5: 46, 47; Luke 6: 32, 33, 34.

recompense thee: for thou shalt be recompensed at the resurrection of the just."[1] It would be foolish to understand this as forbidding all friendly hospitality among kinsfolk and acquaintances (such as Jesus himself enjoyed with the twelve); but such hospitality is an exchange of pleasant functions for mutual enjoyment—it does not rank as service, nor (as some strict Jews may have imagined) as the almsgiving required in connection with certain feasts: to be *service* it must be wholly disinterested.

It must be secret too. Few things our Lord said are sharper than his word against ostentatious piety, and especially paraded almsgiving. To do good only if due publicity be accorded to the deed ruins the action by corrupting its motive. It can also be cruelly humiliating to those so "helped". So Jesus said: "Take heed that ye do not your alms before men, to be seen of them: otherwise ye have no reward of your Father which is in heaven. Therefore, when thou doest alms, do not sound a trumpet before thee, as the hypocrites do in the synagogues and in the streets, that they may have glory of men. Verily I say unto you, They have their reward. But when thou doest alms, let not thy left hand know what thy right hand doeth: that thine alms may be in secret: and thy Father which seeth in secret himself shall reward thee openly." Hide it from others, *and from yourself*; no rule could be plainer, yet oftentimes it is ignored, and our giving and our service are made unacceptable in consequence.[2]

"The Son of Man came, not that others might serve him but that he might serve them, and give his life a ransom for many".[3] No service of ours can be worthy of his, unless like his it is done at personal cost. The gift without the giver is bare: if nothing of ourselves goes out to others in the help we render, then what we do is likely to be idle. Dispensing the coin we shall not miss, the garment we no longer want—these are not wrong, of course, but let us not count them service in his sense of the word. Disinterested, secret and costly, such is the quality of active goodwill that alone befits those who are followers of "the holy Servant, Jesus".[4]

Although our study of these ruling thoughts of Jesus has necessarily taken us over familiar ground, it cannot be said that when this conception of God, of people, of life and of service is taken all together it adds up to an outlook commonplace and popular

[1] Luke 14: 12–14.   [3] Mark 10: 45.
[2] Matt. 6: 1–4; 5–18.   [4] Acts 4: 27 and 30 R.S.V.

in our time. Our description of the mind of Christ has been no more than an outline, an intellectual frame within which belong a host of judgements, valuations, attitudes and reactions. But it has been sufficient even so to emphasise once again how deep and far-reaching is the change implied in making Christians Christlike.

CHAPTER 13

PREVAILING ATTITUDES

WE HAVE tried up to this point to outline the portrait of Jesus by sitting down, as it were, before the story and letting it make its own impression upon us, with as little distortion as possible from our modern questions and perplexities. For the next step, while we shall try to maintain that objective attitude, we shall probably find that we are now putting our own point of view before Jesus, seeking his mind not so much on the subjects he counted important as on the difficulties that face ourselves. We are attempting in fact no longer a portrait, but an interview!

This is worthwhile so long as we are aware of what we are doing. Certainly, we cannot begin in any serious way to face our modern world in the spirit and with the mind of Jesus without being confronted with the urgent practical questions posed so sharply by the age in which—in God's providence—our lives are set. The world about us is a sinful world, containing much of suffering and of sorrow; and it is organised to a large extent on non-Christian patterns and for unspiritual ends. We cannot therefore attempt the Christlike life without being forced to ask what was the Master's attitude to evil, to suffering, and to the organised life of the world. And just because we are looking at Jesus through the haze of our own problems we need be especially careful and humble in declaring what his attitude seems to us to have been.

I. HIS ATTITUDE TO EVIL

Our first experience of the inherent power of evil, as constituting a problem for the Christian conscience, is within ourselves. But it is not long before we confront it also in the whole environment in which we are seeking to set our standards and abide by them,—in the lives of those we seek wisely and generously to help, knowing oftentimes that the need and misfortune are largely their own

fault; in dealing with evil directed against ourselves, and in people
we know to be guilty of real crime—at no point is it harder to be
Christlike than here; in the larger political and social problems that
cry aloud for a Christian concern, and that seem so often to run
back at last to someone's evil disposition, some group's self-interest
or disloyalty to duty or to truth. We meet evil, in fact, at every point
and upon every level at which we seek to assert the Master's will
and extend his reign. At every turn, in consequence, we find ourselves asking—what was his attitude to deliberate sinfulness?

At once we remember that Jesus offended many in his generation
by the meaning he attached to sin,—by his refusal to acknowledge
as sinful the things popularly condemned, and by his extension of
the concept of evil to include things hitherto excused. He refused,
for example, to attach the usual importance to failures in the matter
of washings, sabbath-observance, fasts, and other ritual formalities.[1]
By so refusing to label as sin what drew upon the irreligious the
chief condemnation of the Pharisee, Jesus revealed his totally
different scale of values and provoked the sharpest criticisms of
the strictest sect of Jews. By his apparent leniency and friendship
towards those known to be guilty of the grosser sins of passion,
greed and impiety, Jesus confirmed this refusal to blame as heavily
as others did the more obvious kinds of sin.[2]

Behind this attitude lay a twofold motive: on the one hand Jesus
knew that many who blame the sinful action, the passionate deed,
themselves indulge the hateful, impure thought, and he condemned
the look of lust as itself the moral equivalent of adultery, the thought
of hate as no whit better than the deed. So, when a group of religious
leaders brought into his presence a guilty woman, seeking his judgement upon her, he seared their consciences with the scorching words:
"He that is without sin among you, let him first cast a stone at her":
—"and they being convicted by their own consciences went out one
by one".[3] This extension of the meaning of sin to include the thought
and desire of evil was something new and unwelcome to legalistic
Judaism.[4] It spelt the end of legalism altogether, for law cannot
prescribe for the inner life, but only for actions.

On the other hand Jesus saw, and in the figure of the Elder
Brother[5] he clearly portrayed, that the sins of vindictiveness, envy,

---

[1] Mark 7: 1–23; 2: 18—3: 5.   [3] Matt. 5: 27–8; John 8: 1–11.
[2] Mark 2: 15–17; Luke 15: 2.   [4] Compare Rom. 7: 5—8: 4.
[5] Luke 15: 28–30.

bitterness and temper not only do as much harm, and cause as much misery, as sins of passion, but are equally effective in keeping men from the Father's heart. On the whole, society is still lagging behind Jesus' standards in this respect, for the gross sins of sensuality and passion still rank first in popular condemnation.

Another extension of the meaning of sin which may be traced in Christ's thought is the recognition that wrong social attitudes expressed in, for example, the trading in the Temple, or the harsh terms of moneylending, are also sinful—certain ways of making money and certain ways of spending it,[1] within the legal code but outside the law of Christ.

Once more, Jesus laid very great emphasis upon sins of neglect, upon the things left undone, the opportunities for good that were missed. The *barren* tree figured more than once in his illustrations. The man who hid his talent was rebuked—for doing nothing; the priest and the levite were condemned—for doing nothing; the goats on the left hand were sent to everlasting punishment—for *not* giving the cup, the clothes, the kindness which they might have given. So is it again with the rich man and Lazarus.[2] This, the converse of the law of love, is another wholly new insight which we owe to the Master.

Very near the top in our Lord's scale of evil he placed self-righteous pride: the attempt to hide sin, to cover and deny and distract attention from it, by a parade of religious practices—alms-giving, public prayer, and fasting[3]—performed not for their intrinsic piety, but for their credit value in the opinions of men. This, with its inevitable reflex effect of hiding sin also from oneself, under the cloak of religious self-satisfaction, earned some of Jesus' very sternest words. But not less stern are his warnings to those whose evil hearts will set about the deliberate corruption of others, and perhaps the sharpest thing Jesus ever said was to those who would make "little ones" to offend—"Better for such a man that a mill-stone be hanged about his neck and he be drowned in the depth of the sea!"—only our familiarity with these words makes us able to hear them from the lips of Jesus without astonishment.[4]

Yet the severest word of all was reserved for that "sin against

[1] Mark 11: 15–17; 12: 40; compare Luke 16: 19f; 12: 45.
[2] Luke 13: 6–9; Mark 11: 12–14; Matt. 25: 24–30; John 15: 1–6; Luke 10: 31, 32; Matt. 25: 41–6; Luke 16: 19–31.
[3] Luke 18: 9–14; Matt. 23: 14; 6: 1–18.
[4] Matt. 18: 6; Mark 9: 42; Luke 17: 1–2.

the very Spirit of truth" which can, to justify its own ways, descend to calling evil good and good evil. It can so twist and corrupt the moral judgement, by repeated refusal of the light, as to become incapable of distinguishing truth from falsehood, right from wrong —and so reach the point where in blind and embittered hostility it can call Christ Beelzebub, or accuse him of working by the devil's co-operation. For this state there can be no forgiveness—because so "morally insane" a soul can find no place of repentance.[1]

What an original list of sins Jesus presents for our judgement: sins of thought and desire that only the sinner knows, sins of jealousy and temper and vindictiveness, sins of social attitude and sins of thoughtless neglect of good that might have been, sins of hypocrisy and self-righteousness, sins of tempting others, and confusing good and evil—and not a word about drunkenness, gambling or missing church! Every way in which a man presses his self-interest against the claims of his fellows, or opposes his self-will against the claims of God, is evil in Christ's eyes: just because love of God and one's neighbour *is* the summit of the law.

In view of this thorough re-definition of the meaning of sin, we are not surprised that Christ's own diagnosis of the nature and causes of sin should be equally original. To him it appeared as a grave *sickness* of humanity, this preference for self against others and against God. Isaiah had described the pitiable condition of Israel as "full of sores, the whole body sick",[2] but he refers rather to the result of the nation's waywardness, the consequences of national evil. Jesus, challenged to justify his mingling with sinful folk, appealed to the logical implication of their invalid condition— "They that are whole have no need of the physician, but they that are sick: I came not to call the righteous, but sinners to repentance".[3] The sinners live unnatural lives, out of harmony with the divine law and love: sin (as the ministry of parabolic healings so dramatically suggests) is a blindness of the soul, a deafness to God, a lameness and paralysis, possession and death which afflicts the human spirit, maiming and destroying its highest powers and unfitting it for life's perfection.

Here lie numerous suggestions of contagion, destructiveness, fever, peril: but the effect of this conception of sin as moral sickness upon

---

[1] Mark 3: 28–30; Matt. 12: 31; Luke 12: 10, compare Heb. 12: 17.
[2] Isa. 1: 5, 6.
[3] Mark 2: 16, 17.

M

the attitude of Jesus is rather to nourish tenderness and compassion, without condoning the wrong. He is the great Physician, making no terms with the sickness, but infinitely sorry for the patient.

In our day this attitude to sin has become widespread, but in a manner rather different from that of Jesus. We speak much of the diminished responsibility which uncontrolled passion, habitual violence, drunkenness or drug-taking involve, and *excuse* the shameful, criminal deed that so frequently results on the ground that the criminal "was not fully himself" or did not know that what he did was wrong. So far as hereditary or physical factors, or some unmistakably pathological condition of the mind or brain, can affect personal responsibility, this attitude is justified, of course. But too often it is used to minimise the guilt of those whose passion, violence, drunkenness or stupor is entirely their own fault, the moral and mental harvest of many sinful sowings, the effects upon brain and mind and moral sense of repeated refusals to listen to conscience and truth. The sinful soul is sick, wretchedly sick sometimes: and compassion is demanded, and gentleness: but if we are to be faithful to Jesus we must still see that the sickness is self-imposed, and the wretchedness, as with the prodigal son, is the sinner's *fault*, not his excuse.

For sickness is only one of Christ's words for sin: the other is "folly". The man who leaves out God and spends life enlarging barns is called "Thou fool".[1] Repentance is literally a "change of mind", coming to oneself after a period beside oneself. Sin is blindness, a foolish choice, a profitless bargain;[2] and over every act of sin could be written the words of Jesus concerning those who crucified him—"They know not what they do".[3] Builders building the house of life upon sand, bridesmaids missing life's great opportunity for lack of oil—these are his pictures of sin, and Jesus called each "foolish". Sin is opposition to the law of God which is the law also of our being and the foundation of our true welfare. Such opposition to God and to our own best interests is inevitably stupid. And thus while the *sickness* of sin awakens compassion, the *stupidity* of sin must evoke at the same time a just sternness and rebuke.

And Jesus was equally clear about the *seriousness* of sin. Sickness and stupidity are serious matters: but especially is sin a dire peril and doom. Nowhere in all literature is the ruin and degradation of the life of sin more powerfully, more relentlessly described than

[1] Luke 12: 20.   [2] Matt. 16: 26.   [3] Luke 23: 34.

in the story of the prodigal son—the forfeiting of home and loving companionship, the waste leading inevitably to want, the humiliation of hiring himself to do what once he and his father hired others to do, the lowest of tasks in the care of swine, the hunger that envied the animals' fare, and the bitterness of being deserted and neglected by those who once had helped him spend his wealth; the long and humbling trudge homeward—every step having to be retraced in bitterness and fears, and even when the father silences the burning self-reproach still the brother stands by to hurl his scornful "This, thy son . . . and harlots!" The Master minced no words when the enormity of sin was his subject.

Another great saying too familiar to have its true effect upon most of us, places beyond doubt the fiery hostility of Jesus towards every possibility of evil. Speaking of lust and the barely controlled impulse to sin, he said, "If thy right eye cause thee to stumble, *pluck it out and cast it from thee*: for it is profitable for thee that one of thy members should perish, and not thy whole body be cast into hell. And if thy right hand cause thee to stumble, *cut it off and cast it from thee* . . ."[1] Extreme and dangerous advice, some say; others, more reverently (and rightly) remind us of Christ's love of hyperbole for emphasis. But while it would be blindness always to take Jesus' words *literally* it is essential always to take his meaning *seriously*; and here all our shock at the expressions he used (when we pause at all to weigh them) is due to the fact that we do not think of moral evil, of *sin*, in the solemn and grave way that he did.

In these words we note again the background of eternal consequences, the reminder of ultimate and irrevocable issues that hang upon our "stumbling" or "offending" against the divine law. It is not alone on earth that sin works its dire havoc. The consequences reach out and are ratified in eternity. The gulf that divides right from wrong is fixed between righteous and sinful hereafter[2] and the loss of heaven and of God causes weeping and gnashing of teeth. Sin divides the sheep from the fold, the coin from the hand to which it belongs, the wretched, hungry, friendless son from a father's love and home: and its seriousness lies just in the divine judgement that as man chooses, so shall his destiny be. Knowing this, and loving men as he loved men, Jesus could not but add to compassion

---

[1] Matt. 5: 29–30; 18: 8, 9; Mark 9: 43–7.
[2] Luke 16: 26; Matt. 25: 30, 46.

and sternness, the implacable hostility to sin that took him at last to Calvary.

Of that uncompromising opposition to evil, especially in high places, we can have no doubt. He exposed, and condemned at all cost, warning and persuading, instructing and appealing, that men shall turn from evil unto God. And that he would still deal faithfully with evil in public and in private life, offering strong opposition to the forces of falsehood and sin, and condemning all that would capitalise vice or trade in human weakness, or corrupt the young or foolish for the sake of profit, is abundantly certain. Yet the wonder is that he could combine that persistent hostility to sin with persistent goodwill towards the sinner. He remains the Friend of sinners[1] hating the sin, but never the sick and stupid soul that sins. It is our way either to "love" sinners so as to condone the sin, or to hate the sin in such manner as to alienate the sinner. His way is deeper: "*Neither do I condemn* thee . . . Go and *sin no more*".[2] There lies the heart of his attitude to evil.

Yet one thing more must be added to describe his attitude completely. The problem is not only how we should react to the sin and the sinner, but what we can do to handle the evil in the world without descending to its level and copying its methods and its weapons. Here we recall once more the way Jesus met the treachery of Judas, with a kiss and a word of friendship.[3] How he reacted to the cruel act of crucifixion, by praying for those who carried out the order;[4] how he reasoned with Pilate until reasoning had no further purpose,[5] and being "reviled, he reviled not again; though he suffered, he threatened not".[6] His words about praying for those who despitefully use us,[7] doing good to them that hate us, giving to those who defraud us, doing *more* than we are unfairly compelled to do, and forgiving even till seventy times seven occasions, those who wrong us and repent[8] illumine his own example, and we realise that the apostle Paul has neatly expressed the final word about the Christlike attitude to evil: "Be not overcome of evil, but *overcome evil with good*".[9]

Oftentimes the application of that principle will call for careful and sometimes ingenious thinking. But in every situation it is a

[1] Matt. 11: 19; Luke 7: 34.
[2] John 8: 11.
[3] Matt. 26: 49, 50.
[4] Luke 23: 34.
[5] John 18: 33–8; 19: 9.
[6] 1 Pet. 2: 23.
[7] Matt. 5: 44, 40, 41.
[8] Matt. 18: 21–2.
[9] Rom. 12: 21.

possible reply to wrong, and always a more hopeful one than the vicious circle in which evil done breeds evil returned unceasingly. Sometimes it is the simple *return* for evil of some good in reply;[1] sometimes it is the *forestalling* of evil with good done in time;[2] often it is the *overcoming* of evil attitudes and purposes by the refusal to imitate or reply in kind, that constitutes the victory of good. Though in the larger affairs of life applying this principle may often be difficult, because it is crossed and complicated by other duties of personal citizenship, and defence of others against violence and wrong, still its truth and validity stand clear above our confusions, often rebuking our lack of faith. For this is certainly the Christlike attitude to wrong—overcoming evil with good.

II. HIS ATTITUDE TO SUFFERING

Much of what has been said about the meaning of love and the dominant idea of service has sufficiently illustrated the Master's attitude to the suffering that confronted him on every hand, but there are two simple distinctions in this matter which need to be observed, and two modern perplexities which call to be considered.

One important distinction is that between one's own suffering and the suffering of another. The difference could hardly be more obvious, but it is sometimes overlooked in criticisms of the Christian virtue of meekness. Christianity has occasionally been blamed for preaching resignation and acceptance in face of ills that are curable and preventable, on the pretext that all is in the will of God. Our Lord's whole ministry to the sick, afflicted and bereaved is a protest against this fatalistic acceptance of suffering: in a world that largely despised the physically unfit he was first to set a new example of sympathy and service towards those who are handicapped, and on the whole the Church's record of hospitals, schools, social concern, child-welfare, prison reform, and missionary development has been faithful to his pattern. A suffering world is no text for resignation, but in Christian eyes a challenge to endeavour.

Nothing whatever is said in the Gospels about turning your brother's other cheek to the smiter, or surrendering your brother's cloak, or freedom. Nor is it fair to imagine that Jesus implied that if the good Samaritan had passed that way half an hour earlier, he would have stood aside with wine and oil in his hands waiting

[1] Matt. 5: 44.   [2] Matt. 5: 25.

for the thieves to finish their crime. Patience, non-retaliation, meek
and trustful surrender to the ills that fall upon *oneself*, and that
cannot be avoided or removed—this Christianity does counsel,
and with excellent results in serenity and refinement of soul. But
for the ills that fall upon *others*, the suffering others bear—these
demand Christian protest, enterprise, agitation, and wherever possible cure. On the whole we tend to get these two situations strangely
confused, acquiescing helplessly in others' woe, vigorously com-
plaining of our own !

The second distinction needing to be noticed is that between
pain and suffering of a more general and "natural" kind, the common
experience of mortals, and the pain and suffering necessarily involved
in the pursuit of the ideal. Whatever privation or persecution is
met in seeking to be faithful to Jesus, whatever struggle for self-
mastery, pain of self-discipline, loss of self-denial, humiliation
heaped upon the Christian by a non-Christian world, or the nagging
friction and ill-adjustment which the Christian soul must feel in a
non-Christian society—this we are called to accept, to take willingly
upon ourselves, and even to rejoice in. To seek to evade it, by
compromise or cowardice, is to prove ourselves unworthy of Jesus,[1]
for if we would follow we must first take up the cross, and as Luke
emphasises, take it up again each day.[2]

This *is* the "cross"—not the common annoyances that fret each
irritable soul, but the voluntary and accepted suffering involved
in being Christ's, and standing in with him in the world that rejected him. We may draw for ourselves what comfort we can—
and he offers us his glorious example for our inspiration, his presence
for our strengthening, his reminder that "so persecuted they the
prophets which were before you" for our encouragement, and his
promise that "great is your reward in heaven" for our hope[3]—but
comforted or not we are called to endure for his sake. Except for
very minor annoyances, this part of the Christian conflict is almost
outlived in the comfortable democracies of the West: but in some
areas of the world still, and perhaps in most before this century is
through, readiness for martyrdom may once again be required of
those who follow Christ. But of this suffering no loyal heart com-
plains.

There remains, however, a great world of human misery, of
physical and mental ill-health, of pain, disease and poverty, of fear

[1] Matt. 10: 38.   [2] Luke 9: 23.   [3] Matt. 5: 10–12.

and heartache and grief; and the follower of Christ must face it, if not in his own life then in the lives about him. It presents to modern minds two difficulties: that of explanation,—how comes it that in a world planned by a loving Father suffering looms so large?— and that of experience,—how shall the soul called upon to suffer face it in the spirit of Jesus?

As to explanation Jesus said little. One thing crystal clear is that Jesus emphatically rejected the theory current from the days of Job to his own time that all suffering is due to the sufferer's sin. When he was told of Pilate's violent revenge upon certain Galileans, and of a dreadful accident at the Tower of Siloam, the Master enquired (knowing the popular interpretation of such events) "Suppose ye that these Galileans were sinners above all the Galileans, because they suffered such things? . . . Or those eighteen upon whom the tower in Siloam fell, and slew them, think ye that they were sinners above all men that dwelt in Jerusalem?—*I tell you, Nay* . . ."[1]

Again, when the disciples asked him to comment on the debated explanations of blindness from birth (that either the parents, or the unborn child, had sinned, or else the divine foreknowledge of sin to come has punished beforehand), our Lord's emphatic answer was "Neither did this man sin, nor his parents . . ."[2] Occasionally the connection between sin and suffering is close and obvious, as when Jesus warned one man to "sin no more lest a worse thing come unto thee",[3] and in another case pronounced the word of forgiveness before proceeding to the cure.[4] We may, therefore, draw from such events moral lessons and warnings *for ourselves*—"Except ye repent, ye shall all likewise perish"[5]—and in any experience of pain ask what God is seeking to say or do in our lives. But as a general explanation, applied indiscriminately to all who suffer, the theory is forbidden. Some suffering is due to sin, some to folly, some to social inequalities, some to others' sin;[6] but about individual cases we are unqualified to decide.

It is very possible that if we could ask Jesus our question about the explanation of human suffering, he would remind us that

[1] Luke 13: 1–5.
[2] John 9: 1–3.
[3] John 5: 14.
[4] Mark 2: 1–12.
[5] Luke 13: 3–5.
[6] E.g. Luke 15: 13–16; Matt. 7: 27; Matt. 23: 34, 35.

spiritual health is more important than comfort, that the finest gold of human character is often produced in the crucible of pain and struggle, and that this world is—by Christian definition,—a spoiled, imperfect, fallen world, not at all what God planned it should be. Perhaps he would emphasise that in making man free God inevitably risked making man unhappy. But these are only possibilities—though not unsupported guesses at the mind of Jesus. This is fact: that he who bade us believe that the hairs of our head are all numbered, that God is good, and his nature love,—he was no stranger to human suffering. He knew it well—its weight and bitterness, its dreadful impartiality, its terrible intensity, its infinite variety; and he knew it intimately and personally before he died. Yet he could live in the firm faith that God is kind, and die in the serene assurance that the Father's hands were about him. That fact is worth any amount of explanation.

The difficulty of how to face suffering in the spirit of Jesus is not one that can be very usefully discussed, since the solution must lie not in words but in courage and faith. There is little doubt that Jesus has made an enormous difference to the experience of adversity. Since he lived and suffered new standards of heroism and endurance, new depths of faith and spiritual victory, have been given to the world. Many of his finest followers have found that with the example of his patience before their eyes, the comfort of his presence at their sides, the supreme hope of his promise in their hearts, they have been able to endure what might otherwise have proved impossible to bear, and to win enrichment and refinement from what would else have brought bitterness and despair. That ennobling patience, that sustaining presence, that inspiring promise make up the "mind" of Jesus in reaction to pain and sorrow—and to those who will learn he promises himself to teach the secret in the hour when it shall be needed.

III. His Attitude to the World

The third matter about which we would like to question Jesus, as we seek to face life in his likeness, is the complex and many-sided problem of our relation, as Christians, to the non-Christian world about us. On this subject, the guidance of past ages is extraordinarily confused, and the counsel of Christians of our own time hardly less so. Already in apostolic times, in the Church at Colosse and elsewhere[1], the trend towards asceticism within Judaism, and within Greek religion, had begun to influence the young Christian communities. A suspicion of marriage, of money and of meat had begun to develop, with a tendency to emphasise the duty of complete withdrawal from the affairs of the world—a "coming out from among them, to be separate", because "if any man love the world the love of the Father is not in him".[2] The mediaeval Church seems to have combined a monastic ideal of poverty, celibacy, solitude, separation, with a great deal of luxury, wealth and loose morality; and the post-reformation Church shows much the same admixture, with its Puritan tradition ever contending against the laxer standards of the rank and file.

Both tendencies persist, the "world-renouncing" which aims at total separation, fearful of spiritual contamination, concentrating upon evangelism only as the sole Christian duty towards society; and the "world-affirming" which claims to share all earth's delightful things as divinely given, seeks to influence the world in Christian ways, and aims to transform the kingdoms of this world into the kingdom of Christ. Extremes are found on both sides; many have a double standard—one for active Christian workers and a lower, easier one for "other" Christians; many too are confused and inconsistent, allowing certain kinds of pleasure and condemning other kinds, acknowledging some of the world's claims but denying others.

As we turn back to Jesus it is well to remember that in certain important respects our situation differs from that of the apostolic Church, so that we need take care in resting entirely upon the counsel given to those new communities of believers. Especially did they find their responsibilities to the outside world limited by the fact that they lived under a military dictatorship, by the realisation of their exceedingly small numbers, by the fear that young converts from paganism might easily slip back, and by their vivid expectation of the immediate return of Jesus.

In neither of these respects are we quite in their situation. Democracy lays upon each a responsibility that cannot be evaded even by refusing to vote. Christians today are at least as large in number as any other group in society. We have centuries of example and experience to steady our early enthusiasms; we know that Jesus did not return as they expected, and some mode of living in this world just had to be devised. It is not being suggested that the written

[1] Col. 2: 16; 1 Tim. 4: 1–5.   [2] 2 Cor. 6: 17; 1 John 2: 15.

precept may be set aside: but only that we should recognise the special factors which shaped the earliest thought, and turn back to the example of the Master with a free and open mind.

It may be said at once that there is nothing in the least like a monk or hermit about Jesus, nothing of contempt for the world or of hatred towards it, nor any wholesale condemnation of its joys and pursuits. He did not shun the society of men, but rejoiced in it, calling his followers to go out into the highways and by-ways in living contact with men to speak and live for him. He was interested in the clothing of kings,[1] the beauty of the Temple,[2] the playing of the children,[3] the working life of farmer, sower, fisherfolk, vinedresser, the ways of businessmen, judges, servants, tenants.[4] The world's benefits and joys he accepted naturally and freely when they came. He was often present at feasts and banquets, some of them given in his honour, and we have seen how his genial naturalness at such could be twisted into a gibe about gluttony and drunkenness.[5]

He accepted without rebuke Mary's costly anointing of his feet.[6] The beauty of landscape, flower, lake, mountain, sunrise, storm and birdlife were not lost upon him[7] and marriage, wine, feasting and family joys are all used as illustrations of the joy of God's kingdom. Marriage he could not share, being who he was, and in view of what he came to do, but the way he spoke of its divine institution[8] shows he had no thought that his disciples should avoid it. In short, to his childlike spirit all the benefits of earth were the gifts of the Father, to be enjoyed with gratitude. Paul well says "I know and am persuaded by the Lord Jesus that nothing is unclean of itself . . . but that every creature of God is good, and nothing to be refused if it be received with thanksgiving".[9] It is difficult to see how with this picture of Jesus before her the Church could ever have imagined that the monastic life was an imitation of Christ.

At the same time it is far easier to criticise the ascetic ideal of the monks than to rise above it. If the life of Jesus is far removed

[1] Matt. 11: 8.
[2] Mark 13: 1, 2.
[3] Matt. 11: 16, 17.
[4] Matt. 13: 24f, 3f, 47f; John 15: 1f; Luke 16: 1f; 18: 2f; 12: 43–8; 20: 9f.
[5] Matt. 11: 19.
[6] John 12: 3–8.
[7] Luke 19: 41; 12: 27, 28; Matt. 5: 45 etc.; Mark 2: 18–22; Matt. 25: 1f; 22: 1f.
[8] Matt. 19: 3–9.
[9] Rom. 14: 14; 1 Tim. 4: 4.

from that of the hermit or monk, it is equally far removed from the luxury, self-seeking, self-indulgence, and worldly ambition of many of his followers. His life was simple, the glittering prizes of the world held no attraction for him, and the modern conception of a happy life, getting and spending money at high pressure and ever-increasing speed, bears no relation to his call to make spiritual values supreme, and by self-discipline to deny one's own inclinations for the sake of the Kingdom.

We have no authority to condemn the material benefits of a highly organised society—and in *fact* none of us does. But we have the clear duty to strive after the ideal of the spiritual athlete, voluntarily undergoing self-imposed discipline, denying ourselves various pleasures and pursuits, keeping a firm rein upon the body and its desires, in order to press toward the mark for the prize of the high calling of God in Christ Jesus.[1] This is for the Christian the basic matter: all things are lawful, but all things are not expedient, all things do not build up the spiritual life.[2] Even things that are good must be kept in their place. Enjoyment without enslavement: detachment without condemnation—this would seem the true attitude of the Christlike soul towards the joys of the world.

And towards its responsibilities, a similar detachment is needed, but with a deep and genuine concern. The rise of democracy with its wide increase of responsibility upon all citizens, the vast growth in numbers and influence of the Christian section of society, and the lengthened perspective due to the delayed Advent—these new factors in our situation (referred to above) *must* be weighed. Beside the injunction "Love not the world" must be set the Gospel "God so loved the world . . .";[3] with the warning "Marvel not if the world hate you" must be heard the call "Go ye into all the world . . ."[4]

We must not by an attitude of superior unconcern, or a fear of spiritual contamination, so withdraw ourselves in selfish isolation from the life about us, as to defeat the purpose of our Lord's great prayer "I pray not that thou shouldest take them out of the world . . ."[5]

That we should be kept from evil, that the *world* should be taken out of *us*, is one thing: but God's purposes for mankind cannot be accomplished nor a true witness be borne to his saving and

---

[1] 1 Cor. 9: 24–7; Phil. 3: 14.   [3] 1 John 2: 15; John 3: 16.
[2] 1 Cor. 10: 23.   [4] 1 John 3: 13; Mark 16: 15.
[5] John 17: 15.

transforming grace, if we hold aloof from the needs, the problems, the fears and the responsibilities, of the world God loves. Wilberforce, Elizabeth Fry, Barnardo, Shaftesbury, Booth, Penn, Damien, Nansen and hosts of others with a concern for social conditions, and for the people who live in them, have helped men to believe, and to understand, the Gospel. They have worked (in the words of a living Christian reformer), "That there may be a little less of suffering in the world, and that God may be a little less misunderstood."

And their concern has been fed directly by the words and spirit of Jesus. Jesus did not make the social reconstruction of secular life his aim, but (i) he did lay upon his followers a profound sense of responsibility towards all suffering, poverty, sorrow and injustice. As the Old Testament prophets had done, so he also rebuked severely the greed and hard-heartedness of those who felt no concern for the poor, the weak, and the ill-used; and added to that rebuke his call for love and service.

(ii) He did too lay emphasis upon the effect of social conditions upon spiritual life, noting how hardly they that have riches shall enter into the kingdom of heaven[1] and how covetousness and envy in those that have none can also spoil the soul,[2] and anxiety destroy spiritual peace.[3] Evangelists may find as did Moses that men listen not "for anguish and for cruel bondage"[4] and then evangelism may need to prepare its own way by seeking simple social justice.

(iii) Jesus, moreover, preached "the gospel of the kingdom of God"[5] in which the Father's will should be done *on earth* even as it is done already in heaven.[6] The foundations of that kingdom are in the surrendered heart: but its power and its law reach out to the whole circumference of each life. This is, in Jesus' eyes, God's world, and in it God's people are to establish God's rule, until the earth shall be filled with the knowledge of God as the waters cover the sea.

(iv) Jesus insisted firmly upon the duty of disciples to the world about them. There is that which they must render even unto Caesar. Their duty is variously defined, but the crucial words are salt, light, leaven. As the salt of the earth the Christian community works for the moral *preservation* of society against all that makes

---

[1] Mark 10: 23-5.
[2] Luke 12: 13-15.
[3] Matt. 6: 31-3.
[4] Ex. 6: 9.
[5] Mark 1: 14.
[6] Matt. 6: 10.

for corruption and decay in the life of men; she is here to purify and preserve—however unwelcome her protests and cleansing influence may be. As the light of the world, the disciple band brings to bear upon the darkened minds of men the intellectual *illumination* of a living faith, by testimony, teaching and witness. As the leaven within the lump, the souls in which the kingdom already is established wield an increasing influence of social *inspiration* by the ferment of suggestion, activity and leadership "leavening the whole lump".[1] These familiar injunctions must not be evaded if we are to face our world in the spirit of the Master: and together they constitute a wide range of duties to the world in which we are set.

(v) Jesus did give us the assurance that it is the Father's good pleasure to give us the kingdom,[2] and that he shall reign.[3] The Spirit has been given to convict the world of sin, righteousness and judgement: and the world, *with Christ in it*, is moving towards the ultimate goal that God has set. We are called to serve that kingdom, and to claim the world for Christ.

In one important respect the two parts of this truth about the Christlike attitude to the world belong closely together: we shall fail miserably in our duty towards the world if we become careless in our indulgence in the ways of the world. To serve the cause of Christ in the common life of men we must be at least distinguishable from that common life. Neither witness, influence nor leadership is possible to those immersed in the world's life and absorbed in the world's delights. "The Christian is called to live in the world, but inwardly above it, ever seeking with his soul the country that lies beyond it"—in the world, for it is there among the common things and the common people that he is called to live the Christian life; yet inwardly above the world, needing neither its support, its approval, nor its pleasures; and ever seeking the higher world that lies beyond it, his affection set on things above, where Christ sitteth on the right hand of God.[4]

We have in this chapter moved rather more freely than in previous chapters in the realm of inference and opinion, considering more the implications of things Jesus said and did in the light of our own need, than seeking to get back into that far-off world of the first century and to see him. Caution was offered in our opening paragraphs about this change of viewpoint, and the hesitation it should

[1] Matt. 5: 13–16; 13: 33.
[2] Luke 12: 32.
[3] Matt. 24: 30; 25: 31, etc.
[4] Col. 3: 1, 2.

involve. But it should also be remarked that unless the Christlike ideal is capable of giving such moving and growing guidance to succeeding generations, as new situations and possibilities confront new times, it can be of but limited value to the Christian heart of today and tomorrow.

In New Testament understanding of it, Christlikeness is an ideal of thought and character which while clear, and definite, and even rigorous, yet can be applied to the developing life of the world and the different needs of Christians in all races and times. For, as we have tried to emphasise, it is *not* a backward-looking imitation of the outward features of the Master's career in the first century: it is the possession of his mind and spirit and qualities and attitudes amid the pressures and demands of our own time.

CHAPTER 14

CHARACTERISTIC OUTLOOK

THERE is no discouragement which the young Christian faces that is more damaging or dangerous than that which dismisses the Christian ideal as impracticable. Outright opposition to the faith and code of Christianity is rare, and when we meet it we often feel braced and ready for argument. But when the excellence of the teaching is freely admitted, and the wistful hope that it might one day be practised is expressed, and then we are solemnly warned that this is not a world in which it will *work*—that we are unwise, or naïve, in thinking we could ever follow the example of Jesus in this age and in such an environment—then we feel undermined by our friends, and wonder if they are not perhaps right after all. We are advised to "come down to earth"; we are assured that we could not apply true Christianity to actual life nowadays, we are urged to learn to give as good as we get and be prepared for life in the real world. Faith, we are told, is wishful thinking; and Christian ideals a blueprint for heaven, not a practical programme for life on earth. Christlikeness is impossible until we reach the perfect world.

It would be an effective answer to say that Christian faith and ideals would there, presumably, be unnecessary. Or to say that such a world must be forever beyond us unless someone tries to move towards it by applying its principles to *this* world. "Christianity is fine, but impracticable" is a cry of despair. But there is another answer: it is to ask what kind of world Jesus thought this was. Was he misled about the weaknesses of human nature, the downdrag of environment, the trends of society, the forces opposed to truth and right, the ways of the world? Was Jesus the victim of his own wishful thinking and unreal sentimentalism about life and people?

The true reply is rather startling. Look carefully at some of the people he observed about him and described with unflattering accuracy. There is the unfeeling glutton, "rolling in wealth" but ignoring the beggar at his door; the churlish neighbour, irritably impatient of the simple request of a friend for bread; the avaricious farmer with no thought for anything above his crops and his barns; the foolish, rebellious youth, resenting restraints and impoverishing his father to run away from home. There is the ruthless money-lender mortgaging the homes of widows until he owns half the village; the inconsistent debtor, forgiven himself but unforgiving to those in his own power; the unsuccessful, jealous farmer, bitterly envious of a neighbour's prosperity, and sowing tares among his growing wheat for spite. There is the evil-minded blackguard with whom no children can be trusted; the unsociable, quarrelsome acquaintances who refuse an invitation to a wedding and give the infuriating, trivial excuses that are obviously untrue—what a miserable village community that crowd would make![1] Let Jesus describe for us the life of working people as he had seen it: the slave-driving boss who offers no thanks and demands his supper before his employees may rest or eat; the domineering foreman, starving and beating the servants in his charge; the untrustworthy employees carousing when the master's back is turned; the rascally steward embezzling accounts to cover previous thieving; the lazy servant hiding his lord's money to avoid responsibility or labour[2]—he saw the work-a-day world with clear eyes! Nor did the leaders of the people escape Jesus' accurate appraisal: the ostentatious Pharisee parading his piety; the flattery-loving Scribe, delighting in titles; the heartless priest, ignoring the needy; the indifferent levite, passing by on the other side; the fortune-hunting monopolists cornering the sacrifices[3]—so shallow and worthless did much that passed for religion appear to the Master. Political figures too he saw for what they were—not only the oppressive Roman press-gang demanding free service from the peasants, but the conscienceless Judge, caring for neither God or man until nagged into action by a defenceless widow (and on the other side, the cunning litigant using the processes of law to defraud and steal); the crafty unprincipled king—that fox, Herod; the tyrant rulers of the Gentiles (a dangerous word this) who are given titles of "the Great", the "Benevolent", "Majesty", just in proportion as they lord it over their subjects

[1] Luke 16: 19; 11: 5–8; 12: 16–20; 15: 11f; Matt. 23: 14; 18: 23–35; 13: 24–8; 18: 6; Luke 14: 16–20.
[2] Luke 17: 7–10; Matt. 24: 45–51; Luke 12: 42–8; 16: 1–8; Matt. 25: 25.
[3] Matt. 6: 1–18; 23: 5–7; Luke 10: 31, 32; Mark 11: 15–17.

and "take it out of" their peoples.[1] And finally the disciples themselves he knew for what they were, with their weaknesses and failings open to his eyes: the boastful but utterly unreliable Peter; the bargain-hunting crowd, following for a feed; the children of light who are so easily outwitted in brains and craftiness by the children of darkness; the loud profession of "Lord, Lord" on the part of people who have no intention to obey his words; and the willing, earnest few who would keep vigil with him but whose "flesh is weak".[2]

Here are thirty characters Jesus knew—all unattractive, some repellent, but all observed with unsentimental clarity: thirty unlovely "types" such as we all know. Nor do they stand alone as indications of the open-eyed judgement of Jesus about life and people. To them we must add certain remarks that he made on more general subjects, and situations he described without varnishing the truth. How many preachers have found a wry comfort in the frank warning of Jesus that about a quarter of the people who listen to preaching will show any real fruit from all your teaching![3] How honest he is about the mixed results of the Gospel dragnet, and the "catches" that are not worth keeping, but must be thrown back! How candid he is too about the real reason for the Mosaic laws about divorce: in an age which venerated Moses as infallible, he declared that the divorce provision was Moses' own concession to man's obstinacy, not the divine intention or ideal—and what a view of man that implies![4] Few things have ever been said about the human heart, even by modern psychology at its most depressing, more disparaging and humiliating than this: "From within, out of the heart of man, proceed evil thoughts, adulteries, fornications, murders, thefts, covetousness, wickedness, deceit, lasciviousness, an evil eye, blasphemy, pride, foolishness—all these evil things come from within, and defile the man."[5] Study his sayings carefully and it is soon obvious that there was not much about human nature, its shallowness, self-advertisement, love of praise, evasiveness, indolence, imagined wrongs, hypocrisies, lusts, violence of temper, stubbornness, lack of perspective, partiality, warped judgements

---

[1] Matt. 5: 41; Luke 18: 2f; Matt. 5: 40; Luke 13: 32; 22: 25; Mark 10: 42.
[2] Matt. 26: 33–5; Luke 22: 31–3; John 13: 38; 6: 26; Luke 16: 8; Matt. 7: 21–3; Matt. 26: 41, 42.
[3] Mark 4: 3–8.
[4] Matt. 13: 47, 48; 19: 3–8.
[5] Mark 7: 21–3.

N

and cold self-interest that he did not know. "He knew what was in man"—and he did say "Beware of men".[1]

The storm and wind beat upon the house of wise and foolish alike, a tower falls, an enraged ruler takes terrible vengeance, on innocent and guilty impartially;[2] wealth hardens the heart against the rule of God, sin blinds the eyes of the soul, ruins the young, warps the judgement.[3] The world is not safer for the godly than for the sinner, and faithfulness will lead to a Calvary for each disciple.[4] So Jesus saw things. And how in face of all this utter *realism* about life and people it can be said that Jesus and his message are unfitted for the real world, a blend of wishful thinking and pious sentimentalism that knows nothing of the facts, passes explanation. Whatever may be true of some of his followers, Jesus was above all else a realist. If what we have just considered were all he ever said, the world would be justified in dismissing his outlook as jaundiced pessimism breeding anti-social bitterness. But to dismiss his outlook as unrealistic, impracticable idealism, is pure nonsense. It was in this world, for this world, and with unerring knowledge of this world, that Jesus lived and taught: and in this world he calls us to follow and serve him.

This is a characteristic of the outlook of Jesus which only a careful study of the story would force upon us, so accustomed are we to the assumption that Jesus looked on life and men with eyes that saw only good. But it is a trait in the "mind of Christ" which would make us all immensely stronger and more effectual in our witnessing, if we too could learn to blink no facts and misrepresent no situations to our own illusory comforting, and could share his realistic appraisal of men and affairs as well as his faith. For given such courageous truthfulness, the shocks and disappointments that shake our faith *lose their power to hurt*; and to believe in God in spite of what we know is far better than to persuade ourselves that things are other than they are.

But two other characteristics of the outlook of Jesus demand attention if the account is to be true: one is the consequence of his realism, the other its corrective, or at least its counterpart.

It follows from the candid understanding Jesus reveals of the real state of human nature and society, that to follow him and do his

[1] John 2: 25; Matt. 10: 17.
[2] Luke 13: 1–5.
[3] Mark 10: 23–7; Matt. 6: 22, 23; Luke 15: 11f; John 8: 42, 47.
[4] Matt. 10: 16f; 16: 24.

will, must involve considerable conflict, sacrifice and peril. It follows in fact from Christ's realism that the Christian ideal is a code for heroes. And heroism is unpopular. The Jewish conception of morality sought a system of rules, a negative and legal guide to the good life in which all possible situations might be foreseen and the appropriate action or attitude prescribed. This was rigorously and often sincerely followed, but the exceptions and casuistical distinctions often made the code an ingenious accommodation to the interests of the devotee. The Greek (and modern) preference was for a life careful to avoid all extremes, a standard of the mean or average, excelling in its ability to compromise and avoid unpleasantness, and find the middle way of agreement, ease and peace. Neither would make of morality a matter for great initiative, effort or sacrifice, though it must be admitted that both Jewish and Greek moralists were a great deal more in earnest than the modern attitude which makes all moral issues questions of personal taste and opinion.

The Christian challenge therefore came, then as now, somewhat austerely into the world of more limited and more comfortable demands. It proclaimed the *absolute* imperative of the sovereign will of God, the call to take up the cross, to deny oneself, to be faithful if need be unto death, to lose this life for the sake of the next. It called for a moral heroism that matched the height of its ideal on the one hand and the darkness of its vision of sin on the other: for a pilgrimage of blood and toil and tears and sweat.

And this was no mere acceptance of the inevitable. From the first Jesus made the terms plain. When Pharisees questioned the omission of the fasts by the disciples, he declared that men could not fast at a feast—while the divine bridegroom is with them; but the days are coming when the bridegroom will be wrested from them, and then they shall fast, and appropriately, for they will be sorrow-laden men.[1] From those who offer to follow him, he demands a frank acceptance of a situation in which they might well find themselves homeless, and a final and irrevocable decision with no regrets for life left behind.[2]

In the same way he asks for a love superior to all human ties, taking priority over love for wife or parents or child;[3] "Think not that I am come to send peace on earth: I came not to send peace, but a sword. For I am come to set a man at variance against his father, and the daughter against her mother, and the daughter-in-

[1] Mark 2: 18-20. [2] Luke 9: 57-62. [3] Matt. 10: 34-8.

law against her mother-in-law. And a man's foes shall be they of his own household. He that loveth father or mother more than me is not worthy of me: he that loveth son or daughter more than me is not worthy of me. And he that taketh not his cross, and followeth after me, is not worthy of me."

"Behold I send you forth as sheep amidst wolves . . . ye shall be hated of all men for my name's sake . . . Blessed are ye when men shall persecute you, cast out your name as evil, say all manner of evil against you falsely for my sake . . ."[1] This is a call to undergo social ostracism, to set oneself against the temper and trend of one's world, and pay the price for that temerity. And Jesus, of all men, well knew the consequences. Striving to prepare the disciples for the life that awaited them he recalls to them that once they had gone forth into the towns and villages of Galilee "in faith", and had lacked nothing. Now, however, on the eve of the crucifixion, things have changed, and they must take purse and scrip, and "he that hath no sword, let him sell his garment and buy one". Apparently the literally-minded disciples find it impossible to understand all he means, or to accept his view of the future. One assures him, "Lord here are two swords"—and Jesus gives it up: "All right, that's enough about it!"[2]

Behind all these sayings, which if we were not so used to them would shock us into denial, there lies a conception of Christianity that is unfamiliar and unpopular, even yet. Can we ever hope to make such a message, such a challenge, attractive to the crowds we long to see accept the Gospel? Christianity is a creed for heroes, a programme for martyrs, a challenge for the spiritual élite. It is also a way out for those who feel earnestly and desperately the reality of sin, for behind the challenge is the good news of the available mercy of God for our failures and the power of the Spirit for our weakness. Even so it is only "He that endureth to the end shall be saved".[3]

The situation so clearly seen, the demand set so high—what of the future? The result might so easily have been despair, and Christians have fairly earned sometimes the reputation of pessimists. Yet Jesus showed no shadow of doubt that ultimate victory will be his. "The Son of man shall come . . . sit upon the throne of his

---

[1] Matt. 10: 16, 22; 5: 10–12; Luke 6: 22, 23.
[2] Luke 22: 35–8.
[3] Matt. 10: 22; 24: 13; Mark 13: 13.

glory . . . with the holy angels. . . ."[1] The leaven will leaven the whole lump, the seed grow until the harvest. Secretly, silently the progress of the kingdom continues, until from the very tiniest of all seeds shall grow a shrub in whose branches birds may roost. He will draw all men unto him, none shall be cast out, and the saving invitation is for "whosoever".[2] Even in the shadow of the cross our Lord's confident expectation of triumph remains: "My peace I leave with you . . . that my joy may remain in you . . . I will drink it new with you in my Father's kingdom . . . in my Father's house I prepare a place for you . . ."[3]

To the same confidence he calls the disciples. *The confident optimism of answered prayer* may be theirs as they go forth into Caesar's world as witnesses—"for whatsoever ye shall ask in my name, it shall be done". And with that, *the basic optimism* of faith in the power of God—"for with God all things are possible". And always *the assured optimism that springs from the knowledge that we are not alone*—"When they bring you into the synagogues, and unto magistrates, and powers, take ye no thought how or what thing ye shall answer, or what ye shall say: for the Holy Ghost shall teach you in the same hour what ye ought to say . . . Ye shall receive power, when the Holy Ghost is come upon you . . . He shall convict the world . . ."[4] It is this undismayed optimism that is the true counterpart to the realism of Jesus, and that makes his whole outlook so unintelligible to the man of no faith—to all who see only the facts of life, and see not God.

With this attempt to describe the fundamental outlook of Jesus we close our outline-portrait of the Master of men. Of its inadequacy, its imperfections, its incompleteness, there is no need to speak. When we have earnestly tried to look at Jesus through the eyes of his contemporaries, when we have listed the outstanding qualities of his character and the ruling thoughts of his mind; when to this sketch we have tried to add a description of his prevailing attitudes to great questions that perplex us, and then tried to probe beneath the words and deeds to the fundamental points of view, we are still poignantly aware that we have missed the secret, that the glory of the Master has escaped the mass of words.

[1] Matt. 16: 27; 25: 31; 19: 28; Mark 8: 38.
[2] Matt. 13: 30–3; John 12: 32; 6: 37; 3: 15, 16.
[3] John 14: 27; 15: 11; Matt. 26: 29; John 14: 2–3.
[4] John 16: 23; 15: 7, 16; 14: 13; Mark 10: 27; Matt. 19: 26; Luke 12: 11, 12.

Certainly the common people saw in him a Prophet in whom authority and graciousness intermingled. Suppliants found him inexhaustible. His enemies testified that he was sociable, natural and friendly, but with an air of something supernatural about him, and withal dangerous and courageous. His friends remembered most his searching, cleansing holiness. His character revealed astonishing strength of mind and purpose, expressed in courage, anger, policy and action. Yet a wonderful tenderness guided and controlled that strength as he dealt with suffering and sinful alike. His purity from passion, pride and all untruth dwarfs our description, and yet his loving goodwill overflowed all barriers and frontiers and reached out especially to the sinful. And though composed of seemingly opposite qualities, that perfect character maintained a poise and proportion that are the hallmark of perfection.

His mind was ruled by the assurance that God is the Kingly-Father, in whom he found delight and serenity, and by a conception of the value of men which placed first that spiritual nature in which all are equal. Life was, in consequence, set ever against the background of eternity, and the supreme duty of loving service governed the whole teaching on man's duty and opportunity.

Such qualities and thoughts found clear expression in his defence and service of the suffering, and in his sympathetic though strong attitude towards evil; while towards the joys and responsibilities of the world he exhibited a personal detachment, mingled with enjoyment of the one, and concern for the other. Behind all lay what in others we might call a temperament, or cast of mind, but which in his case we prefer to call an outlook, which combined the most clear-eyed realism with moral heroism, and undoubting optimism that centred in God.

But even when we thus strive to gather the threads together we know that the radiance and beauty still evade us. He is greater than all that we can say of him, stronger, nobler, purer, lovelier than we can ever tell. Others we may analyse, "explain", describe, excuse—

> But Thee, but Thee, O Sovereign Seer of time,
> But Thee, O poets' Poet, Wisdom's tongue,
> But Thee, O man's best Man, O love's best Love,
> O perfect Life in perfect labour writ,
> O all men's Comrade, Servant, King or Priest—
> What *if* or *yet*, what mole, what flaw, what lapse,
> What least defect or shadow of defect,
> What rumour tattled by an enemy,

Of inference loose, what lack of grace
Even in torture's grasp, or sleep's, or death's,
Oh what amiss may I forgive in Thee
Jesus, good Paragon, Thou Crystal Christ !
(SIDNEY LANIER)

Inevitably the portrait fails. Nevertheless, if our attempting sends us back to the Gospels with a keener desire to see Jesus, and perhaps with the outline of a method, we shall not have studied in vain. We shall "follow on to know the Lord" in his word and through his presence, and with that image in our hearts, and our will learning daily surrender to his control, there shall be formed in us the mind of Christ. Thus as the days and years pass we shall grow like him, till we see him as he is, and find ourselves changed—"into the same image".

CONCLUSION

15. *Evangelical Ethics*

CHAPTER 15

EVANGELICAL ETHICS

EVANGELICAL Christianity—by which is meant that Christian tradition which lays great stress upon the authority of the Scriptures, the experience of conversion, the primacy of personal faith in a living Saviour, the need for evangelism—has many excellent qualities compared with the more "institutional" or "high Church" tradition. It has less taste for speculative or critical theology, but it is not on the whole intellectually inferior. It kindles and nourishes a profound zeal for the work of Christ, and a fervour of devotion unsurpassed in any other form of Christian faith. Evangelicals are usually keenly alive to responsibilities for evangelism and foreign missions, are oft-times exceedingly generous in their support of Christ's work, and frequently they show careful concern for high standards of behaviour and consecration. In spite of all this, it may often be observed that evangelicalism is weakest in the realm of ethics—in the understanding and exposition of those new moral principles which are implicit in the conversion-experience and essential to any faithful following of Jesus.

So much stress being laid upon conversion, it is natural that the necessity for working out in daily life and relationships the new ideals so eagerly embraced should be somewhat obscured. Conversion itself is understood sometimes in terms so largely emotional—the thrill of decision, the relief of acceptance, the joy of assurance—that the deep changes wrought by the surrender to Christ as Saviour and Lord are overlooked. The spiritual experiences beloved of the young Christian may lack all practical and moral content or effect, and the "evangelical experience" may come to be quite purposeless and barren, an inward state desired for its own sake only, or perhaps desired in order to be communicated to others by fervent witness.

Symptoms of this weakness are not hard to seek. Distressing instances occur of earnest and active Christians, sound in doctrine, fearless in profession, falling prey to some obvious and overwhelming temptation which ruins all their Christian career. The moral break-down is bad enough: the casual and irresponsible way in which, on such occasions, a distinction is drawn between Christian standing in Christ and Christian obedience—so that acceptance of the Gospel intellectually, and surrender to the Lord's control practically seem separate things—is worse still.

Similarly indicative of misunderstanding is the suspicion that sometimes attaches in evangelical circles to any emphasis upon Christian ethics and moral standards, lest the freeness of God's saving grace be in any way overshadowed by human merit. This fear may be understood, but the suspicion is a sign that the meaning of salvation is being too narrowly interpreted. "By grace are ye saved, through faith; and that not of yourselves: it is the gift of God: not of works, lest any man should boast. For we are his workmanship, created in Christ Jesus unto good works, which God hath before ordained that we should walk in them."[1] That classic statement is the final answer to all such doubts: we are not saved by good works of our own, but we are saved with a view to them.

And indeed "saved" means "rescued" not only from the consequences and the power of sin, but *from sin itself*—the sin being taken out of us. It is the prerogative of grace to accept us as sinners —but never to accept our sinfulness: to forgive in order to transform, to pardon in order to cleanse.

In other words, to mention a third symptom of the ethical weakness of evangelicalism, "salvation" and "sanctification" are not the completely separate and distinct aspects of spiritual life that theologians and expositors, with their love for "headings", seem to imply. Paul wrote the letter to the Romans very largely to dispel such an idea, and to insist that no man can claim to be saved by faith and still continue in sin.[2] For *by that faith which saves him* he has already taken his place with Christ upon the cross, and died to sin—the crucial point of his sanctification is already achieved in the repentant trust which makes him Christ's. By missing this deep unity of the Christian experience evangelical teachers have often seemed to offer two gifts of Christ, salvation and sanctification, of which the believer *must* take one, the first, and *ought*, if he is properly grateful, to accept also the other! The stress laid in some quarters upon the second and deeper blessing to be obtained by sanctified

[1] Eph. 2: 8–10.   [2] Rom. 6: 1f.

living, is itself a confession of something missing in the understanding of conversion: and that something missing is a vivid sense
of what the convert is converted *to*, and what his new Master and
Lord intends to make of him.

Such considerations have lain behind our study of the New
Testament ideal. The answer to this weakness of the evangelical
faith is not to turn to some other form of teaching, but to unfold
the deep ethical implications of apostolic Christianity itself. This
we have sought to do, stressing the moral transformation which
the Gospel achieves, while preserving also the essential keynotes
of evangelicalism, *the centrality of Christ, the inwardness of spiritual
experience*, and *the supremacy of Scripture*.

The Christian ethic is Christ-centred. The living Christ of personal
faith is known only through the written records of his words and
deeds. The revelation of his will to each believer comes not merely
by the inward motion of the Spirit but by the avenue of the Gospel
stories. Thus we have looked back to him, but always to see the
permanent and unchanging truth beneath the temporary forms and
dress of the first century. For Christ *is* Christianity, and we do not
seek our way by probing within our own changing moods and
inclinations, nor by uncritical acceptance of the standards of
our Church or circle of Christian friends—but from him. We
are to *see him*, and our goal is, to be changed "into the same
image".

*The Christian ethic, moreover, rests upon the inward experience
of the soul* in its relation to the living Lord. We are changed from
within, not from without: not by the practice of a code but by the
submission to a process of spiritual re-creation and development.
We have seen different sides of that process: *the onward growing*
towards Christlikeness by the inherent power of the new life, nourished and unhindered; *the outward fashioning* by divine chastening
and providence, setting the pattern of our circumstances as may best
achieve the goal; *the upward striving* as we cultivate the mind of
Christ in spiritual understanding and moral imitation; *the inward
moulding* by the Lord the Spirit, the Spirit of Jesus, as we seek ever
to behold his glory, and be changed in beholding. There is nothing
"unspiritual" or external about our theme. It springs from the heart
of our hidden life with Christ, and draws us ever nearer to him
in faith, surrender and obedience.

And, whatever may be thought of these reflections, this at least is beyond question: *the Christian ethic* as we have expounded it in these pages *is scriptural*. Doubtless there are many points where the interpretation or illustration of passages may be debatable; but that the main theme is New Testament teaching cannot be denied. It may rest upon four great passages whose plain meaning cannot be evaded:

We know that all things work together for good to them that love God, to them who are the called according to his purpose. For whom he did foreknow, he also did predestinate to be conformed to the image of his son, that he might be the firstborn among many brethren.

He gave some, apostles; some, prophets; and some, evangelists; and some, pastors and teachers; for the perfecting of the saints, for the work of the ministry, for the edifying of the body of Christ: till we all come in the unity of the faith, and of the knowledge of the Son of God, unto a perfect man, unto the measure of the stature of the fullness of Christ.

But we all, with open face beholding as in a glass the glory of the Lord, are changed into the same image from glory to glory, even as by the Spirit of the Lord.

Beloved, now are we the sons of God, and it doth not yet appear what we shall be: but we know that when he shall appear we shall be like him; for we shall see him as he is. And every man that hath this hope in him purifieth himself, even as he is pure.[1]

Here is ample warrant for claiming that the divine programme is made clear, the process described, the purpose defined, the promise assured—that we shall be conformed to the image of his Son, changed into the same image, from glory to glory, even as by the Spirit of the Lord.

What then shall be our response? In view of so great purposes treasured in the heart of God for us we cannot surely remain complacently satisfied with the level of Christian experience and character we have already known, content to tell of one great experience of conversion or blessing, and think that is all God means to do with us. Nor can we remain "complacently dissatisfied", content to say the ideal is high, and we cannot attain unto it. Christians have no right to *rest* in the apostle's confession "not as though I had already attained, either were already perfect";[2] by all the mercies of God we are bound to add with Paul "But I follow after, if that I may apprehend that for which also I am apprehended . . . this

---

[1] Rom. 8: 28, 29; Eph. 4: 11–13; 2 Cor. 3: 18; 1 John 3: 2, 3.
[2] Phil. 3: 12; and 13–14.

one thing I do, forgetting those things which are behind, and reaching forward unto those things which are before, I press toward the mark for the prize of the high calling of God in Christ Jesus". With Paul we must learn to travail again "till Christ be formed in us".[1]

[1] Gal. 4: 19.